WRITING MAJORS

WRITING MAJORS

Eighteen Program Profiles

Edited by
GREG GIBERSON
JIM NUGENT
LORI OSTERGAARD

UTAH STATE UNIVERSITY PRESS
Logan

© 2015 by the University Press of Colorado

Published by Utah State University Press
An imprint of University Press of Colorado
5589 Arapahoe Avenue, Suite 206C
Boulder, Colorado 80303

 The University Press of Colorado is a proud member of
The Association of American University Presses.

The University Press of Colorado is a cooperative publishing enterprise supported, in part, by Adams State University, Colorado State University, Fort Lewis College, Metropolitan State University of Denver, Regis University, University of Colorado, University of Northern Colorado, Utah State University, and Western State Colorado University.

The paper used in this publication meets the minimum requirements of the American National Standard for Information Sciences—Permanence of Paper for Printed Library Materials. ANSI Z39.48–1992

ISBN: 978-0-87421-971-5 (paperback)
ISBN: 978-0-87421-972-2 (ebook)

Library of Congress Cataloging-in-Publication Data
    Writing majors: eighteen program profiles / Edited by Greg A. Giberson, Jim Nugent, Lori Ostergaard.
        pages cm
    Includes index.
    ISBN 978-0-87421-971-5 (pbk.) — ISBN 978-0-87421-972-2 (ebook)
1. English language—Rhetoric—Study and teaching (Higher)—United States.
2. Report writing—Study and teaching (Higher)—United States. 3. Academic writing—Study and teaching—United States. 4. Creative writing (Higher education)—United States. 5. Writing centers—United States. 6. English philology—Study and teaching (Higher)—United States. I. Giberson, Greg, editor of compilation.
    PE1405.U6W755 2010
    808'.042071173—dc23
                        2014003784

Cover photograph © Zanderxo Photography, Seattle, WA

CONTENTS

FOREWORD

Sandra Jamieson

This is a significant collection of essays, both in the narratives that provide a historical archive of sorts and in the descriptions of programs, courses, and institutional politics. Building from theoretical examination of the rapidly growing writing major, it offers concrete examples of the range and variety of majors at a cross-section of colleges and universities, and I predict that it will quickly become an essential resource for the field of writing studies. The chapters add to three equally important strands of the conversation about the writing major, what current majors look like, how they developed their current shape, and how—and where—new majors might evolve. By tracing the development of independent programs and majors, the evolution of long-standing majors, and the tensions and benefits of locating the major within an English department, the collection highlights the alternatives available to writing studies faculty and emphasizes the importance of context and local conditions on this major. Most important, it provides a snapshot of where the field of writing studies is today and suggests where it is going and what it might become.

To fully understand the significance of this collection and the programs discussed herein, we need to place the writing major and the study of the writing major into historical context. As Nugent observes in his introduction to this collection, the rapid growth of this major and the equally rapid development and evolution of existing programs have obscured the history of that growth. Likewise, the coherence and the history of many of the majors described herein could make us forget the fact that this major is still in its infancy. In 2000, when Shamoon, Howard, Schwegler, and I published the edited collection *Coming of Age*, we subtitled it *The Advanced Undergraduate Writing Curriculum*, and although some of the advanced courses described were part of writing majors, we presented them as discrete courses (Shamoon et al. 2000). The overwhelming majority were offered as part of traditional English majors by faculty whose primary responsibility was teaching first-year

DOI: 10.7330/9780874219722.c000

writing. We noted the existence of independent writing programs, and we had the temerity to propose a shape for new writing majors, but that shape was based on the range of courses we reviewed and disciplinary best practices rather than on a study of any existing majors or concentrations. There is a reason for that focus: according to a list created by Doug Day a year after our collection was published, just twenty-four institutions had writing majors and an additional thirteen had writing tracks or concentrations. Day noted, "Because the writing major seems to be as much the purview of small liberal arts colleges as of larger universities, and there are so many such institutions, and because programs change relatively quickly, the list of writing majors available at a given time will always be difficult to track" (Day 2001). Both his observation about tracking and his reflection on the relative speed of development proved to be accurate, and the number of majors continues to grow. In 2002, I updated that list, adding ten more majors, and by 2005, when the CCCC Executive Committee created the Committee on the Major in Composition and Rhetoric, the number had almost doubled (Jamieson 2006). In April 2006, Gina Genova expanded my list and made it available as a downloadable document via the website of Susan McLeod, the first chair of the committee. That list provided information on forty-five majors; just one year later, when I became chair of the committee, the list made available via the CCCC website included fifty majors and an additional fifty-one tracks and concentrations, nine of which are discussed in this collection (Genova and McLeod 2006). Some majors were accidentally omitted from these lists and the committee's rather narrow definition of the writing major reduces it further; however, as the committee works on the most recent update, the list of majors stands at more than three times that number. Phenomenal growth in just over a decade. This collection provides important insight into how those early writing majors have evolved and how the more recently developed majors came to be what they are.

In 2010, when the word "composition" disappeared from the name of the last major on the CCCC list, the committee's name was changed to the Committee on the Major in Writing and Rhetoric. This marked, the committee argues, a moment of transition when a collection of "English" or professional courses became a recognized *writing* major. Part of the committee's ongoing charge is to track the emerging writing major and describe its developing structure. To that end we have been building a database of information about existing majors, and this collection provides a glimpse of how useful such comparative data will be. By providing a summary list of institutional data offered for each program, this collection will be of immediate use to institutions currently developing a major. Data such as enrollment numbers in the context of institution size and number of faculty, for example, help make the case for new programs and demonstrate the impact of those that already exist, especially those discussed in this collection. Data and narratives together reveal a major that has come of age.

As interest in the major has increased, so have scholarly texts on the subject. Until now, the most important of those have been the essay "The Undergraduate Writing Major: What Is It? What Should It Be?" (Balzhiser and McLeod 2010) and the essays in *What We Are Becoming: Developments in Undergraduate Writing Majors* (Giberson and Moriarty 2010). Janice Lauer accurately identified that collection as making "a vital contribution to the field" and serving as "an indispensable resource for building undergraduate majors" (Lauer 2010, vii). This new collection, also edited by Giberson with Jim Nugent and Lori Ostergaard, compliments the first and, if possible, makes an even more vital contribution to the field as an essential resource and a thought-provoking stimulus for the discussion and development of programs. Several of the authors of chapters in the collection serve on the Committee on the Major in Writing and Rhetoric, and together these essays vastly expand the work of the CCCC in this area. These essays are a must-read for anyone considering establishing their own major or revising an existing major, but they are equally central to an understanding of the evolving field of writing studies. This collection both traces the development of existing models and will help to shape the future of the writing major.

References

Balzhiser, Deborah, and Susan H. McLeod. February 2010. "The Undergraduate Writing Major: What Is It? What Should It Be?" *College Composition and Communication* 61(3): 415–33.

Day, Doug. Oct. 29, 2001. "Starter List of Writing Majors." http://www.cc.utah.edu/~dd4/writing_majors.html/. Accessed October 1, 2002.

Genova, Gina, and Susan McLeod. April 2006. "Writing Majors at a Glance." http://www.writing.ucsb.edu/faculty/mcleod/index.html/. Accessed September 3, 2006.

Giberson, Greg A., and Thomas A. Moriarty, eds. 2010. *What We Are Becoming: Developments in Undergraduate Writing Majors.* Logan: Utah State University Press.

Jamieson, Sandra. March 12, 2006. "Writing Majors, Minors, Tracks, and Concentrations." http://www.depts.drew.edu/composition/majors.html/.

Lauer, Janice M. 2010. "Foreword." In *What We Are Becoming: Developments in Undergraduate Writing Majors,* edited by Greg A. Giberson and Thomas A. Moriarty, vii. Logan: Utah State University Press.

Shamoon, Linda K., Rebecca Moore Howard, Sandra Jamieson, and Robert A. Schwegler, eds. 2000. *Coming of Age: The Advanced Undergraduate Writing Curriculum.* Portsmouth, NH: Heinemann-Boynton/Cook.

WRITING MAJORS
INTRODUCTION

Jim Nugent

In the absence of historical reflection, it's easy to presume that our curricula, our programs, our department configurations, and even our disciplines have always been the way they are today. Conservatives, in particular, like to depict higher education as an unchanging monolith and a creaky institution that is unable to adapt to new developments on the economic, political, and global scenes. They suggest opening higher education up to the free market, encouraging private ownership and profit, and "making higher education accountable" through quantifiable metrics. However, historical reflection shows us that the millennia-old enterprise of academia is surprisingly adroit and has consistently evolved in the face of shifting societal needs.

Higher education in the United States has proven its versatility and adaptability in remarkable ways over past centuries. American higher education has created entirely new forms of scientific, agricultural, and technical institutions to meet the needs of an industrializing nation. It has overhauled its curricula, shedding the medieval trivium and Renaissance quadrivium in favor of a German model of electives. It has embraced the academic major and minor as curricular structures to meet new demand for specialized graduates. It has undertaken numerous bureaucratic, technological, social, and pedagogical transformations in the face of ever-changing student populations. It has evolved to be more equitable, more accessible, and more diverse.

And yet, it is quite easy to look at the modern university and think that things have always been this way. It's easy to forget that undergraduate majors and minors as we know them today have been prevalent for scarcely over a century (Adams 1993, 8–10). It is easy to forget that American universities and colleges once served only a fraction of the students they do today, and that baccalaureate degree attainment has grown fivefold over the past seven decades (US Census Bureau 2012, 1).

Over time, new disciplines have sprouted into being (biochemistry, computer science, and women's studies) while older disciplines have withered (agriculture, the classics, library science, and home economics) (Basterdo 2011, 420). Even one small but seemingly immutable feature of higher education—the syllabus—only took its contemporary form around the turn of the twentieth century (Snyder 2010). The most cursory historical reflection shows us there is remarkably little about higher education that has remained unchanged through the years.

The present collection seeks to document one particular piece of the unceasingly dynamic landscape of American higher education: the undergraduate writing major. Such majors are, at this historical moment, experiencing tremendous growth in their numbers and evolution in their character. Christian Weisser and Laurie Grobman term the first ten years of the twenty-first century the "decade of the writing major" and note that "no other curricular movement within writing studies has proliferated at so rapid a pace" (Weisser and Grobman 2012, 39). As Greg A. Giberson and Thomas A. Moriarty observe, "The growth of undergraduate majors in writing and rhetoric is unmistakable. They are appearing at big research universities, small liberal arts colleges, and every kind of campus in between, from independent writing programs to those housed in traditional English departments" (Giberson and Moriarty 2010, 2). The field of writing, they note, is currently "moving toward a ubiquitous major" (2). Put simply, the writing major is one of the most exciting scenes in the evolving American university.

This volume has gathered firsthand stories of growth, origin, and transformation from eighteen writing programs in order to document this exciting moment of change. In doing so, this volume serves at least two goals. First and foremost, this collection is intended to serve as a practical sourcebook for those who are building, revising, or administering their own writing major programs. This project originated in part from the Conference on College Composition and Communication (CCCC) 2010 annual convention. There, contributors to the collection *What We Are Becoming: Developments in Undergraduate Writing Majors* (Giberson and Moriarty 2010) participated in a roundtable discussion about the growth and future of undergraduate writing majors. As the floor opened for discussion, almost every question posed by the standing-room-only group of participants was some variation of "How do we do this?" This collection is designed to provide a variety of perspectives on—and answers to—this vital, practical question. It is designed to respond to the clearly evident demand from the field for administrative insight, benchmark information, and inspiration for new curricular configurations for writing major programs. Toward these ends, each of the eighteen profiles in this volume includes a detailed program review and rationale, an implementation narrative, and a reflection and prospection about the program.

Second, this collection is intended to serve as a historical archive of a particular instance of growth and transformation in American higher education—it offers a contemporary history of the writing major movement, written by its immediate participants. Recognizing this collection's archival function, we resist the urge to broadly narrativize or overgeneralize from the accounts presented within. As Kelly Ritter argues, historians should fight against the pressure to push "on historical texts, artifacts, and objects to get us to a satisfying 'plot'" and instead understand "archival spaces as sites of communal representation" (Ritter 2012, 464). As she notes, "The archival history of composition studies, at backward glance, often makes little narrative sense" (461), so we will try to refrain from fashioning overly tidy, sweeping stories of cause and effect from our contemporary vantage point. Instead, this collection will allow the eighteen voices to speak from their individual contexts as "sites of communal representation."

As a result of this approach, we have found that the profiles in this volume frequently have as much to do with bureaucratic, practical, and institutional matters as our ideals and ideologies—they carry what James E. Porter et al. (2000) describe as a "material punch" (612). We believe this focus on the local and material is of critical importance. As Richard E. Miller (1998) notes, "sustainable educational ventures have always worked *within* local, material constraints," but we have frequently "papered over their involvement in such bureaucratic matters with rhetoric that declares education's emancipatory powers" (9, emphasis in original). He reminds us that "To pursue educational reform is to work in an impure space, where intractable material conditions always threaten to expose rhetorics of change as delusional or deliberately deceptive; it is also to insist that bureaucracies don't simply impede change: they are the social instruments that make change possible" (9).

With this in mind, the present collection seeks not just to document eighteen stories of writing major programs in various stages of formation, preservation, and reform, but also to reveal the contingencies of their local and material constitution. We believe this volume can speak as much to the "how to" of building writing major programs as it does the larger "what," "why," and "how" of institutional growth and change.

This book is divided into two parts. Part I contains profiles from writing major programs that are housed within independent or combined department configurations, while Part II contains profiles from programs housed in traditional English departments. We should note that this organizational scheme is not intended to be rigidly taxonomic; we believe that the profiles contained here are most usefully interpreted by considering their respective institutional locations along with information about those institutions' local and material contexts. For this reason, we have included a table at the beginning of each chapter that describes the institution type, its size, the nature of its student population, the number of writing specialists on its faculty, etc. Each profile is also followed by a brief curricular summary that provides an "at a glance" view of the writing major program requirements.

Even while resisting the impulse to overgeneralize or over-narrativize the profiles presented here, a number of themes become apparent throughout the collection:

• *Almost uniformly, these writing major programs situate themselves somewhere between the binary extremes of liberal arts education and vocational training, analysis and production, and theory and practice.* Even though there is a tremendous diversity in these programs and the intellectual justification they provide for their work, almost all of them aim to furnish students with a combination of marketable skills and the insights of a traditional liberal education. The discipline of rhetoric has always confounded such binaries, of course, but the common approach of these programs may reflect the kairotic opportunity the discipline now faces to differentiate itself against other liberal arts disciplines; it may also reflect how writing majors are marketed in an economically tenuous time.

• *Program building is local work.* Since the blueprints for a standardized writing major program cannot simply be pulled off a shelf, all programs are necessarily shaped by the local resources available to them at the time of their creation. A pervasive theme in the implementation sections of these profiles is that program creators found ways to take advantage of immediate infrastructure, courses that were already "on the books," and the expertise of existing faculty to launch their majors. Several profiles attribute a share of their program's success to the fact that their curricula emerged from and complement their respective institutional cultures—presumably as opposed to being an outwardly-imposed, discipline-mandated design.

• *Within the local contexts of program building, defining who you are is sometimes as much about defining who you are not.* The politics of maintaining academic turf become quite evident at the onset of a major program, both within departments and across campus. In some of these profiles, the realities of turf politics meant forging strategic alliances with existing programs and shaping the major to occupy the gaps between other disciplines. In other profiles, turf politics meant fostering new distinctions between programs and creating entirely new curricular spaces and claims to institutional resources. Naming plays an important role in the politics of self-definition—not only the names of the programs themselves, but also the names of individual courses and even course classifications.

• *Technology is vital.* Almost all of the programs profiled here recognize the changing nature of writing in the twenty-first century and have made at least some room in their curricula for digital, multimodal, and new media composition. This reflects developments in the field and the desire of program builders to keep their curricula fresh. However, there is an additional kairotic dimension in that the creation of a new program frequently presents an opportunity to request and develop new technology resources.

• *Programs must be assessed and continually revised.* For many of the writing majors profiled here, program assessment was carefully considered and planned before the major was established. Further, many programs were revised surprisingly soon after they were established. These revisions tended to be not so much about advancements in the field as they were about shifting political realities at each local institution. Programs that were established using whatever political means available at the time quickly found that with new majors, more faculty, and greater resources came new political agency and the ability to do more than just passively respond to institutional happenstance. Neither the vision nor the reality of these major programs has remained static since their establishment.

• *The first-year course can be instrumental to program building.* Several of the chapters in this volume describe the strategic importance of the first-year composition (FYC) course as a source for cross-institutional ethos, as a required course in their major, or even just as a platform for program recruitment. Several profiles also draw attention to the fact that the first-year course serves very different institutional and disciplinary needs than a writing major program, and that pedagogies suited to students in an introductory course must be adapted to the needs of students within the major.

• *The challenges presented by recruitment and growth are not trivial.* One of the most immediate measures of a program's success is the number of majors it serves, and several of these profiles speak to the institutional "strength in numbers" that can accompany a popular major. Drawing in new students and persuading them of the value of a writing major is not always easy. Still, excessive growth can present its own challenges and leave programs struggling to staff courses and provide a quality student experience.

• *In establishing a new writing major, failure sometimes precedes success.* At many institutions, the process of inaugurating a program requires tremendous rhetorical legwork and engagement with many stakeholders across many lines of institutional division and hierarchy. This process can present several openings for territorial squabbles, procedural logjams, "personality issues," and institutional politics to block the progress of hopeful program builders. As such, early failure is not uncommon—nor, obviously, is it always fatal.

It is apparent from these profiles that there are many ways for writing major programs to be cultivated. They can germinate, take root, and grow in a wide variety of local soils. Some form unique hybrids with existing programs, while others form lasting new strains on their own. If there is one takeaway from these profiles, it is likely this: the story of the writing major is, at this moment, multiple, fragmented, and unfinished. As a practical sourcebook and contemporary history, this collection is not meant to reduce a complex national movement to a simple, unified narrative or serve as a strict "how to" guide that can provide guaranteed success in every institutional context. Rather, we hope the stories presented in this collection illustrate how this important moment of growth for writing major programs has its origins in many diverse, local contexts.

Acknowledgments

The editors wish to acknowledge a debt to *Composition Forum* for presenting the innovative series of writing program profiles that inspired this collection, and for allowing the adaption of the article "Unifying Program Goals: Developing and Implementing a Writing and Rhetoric Major at Oakland University" (Ostergaard and Giberson 2010) for this volume. We also urge readers to pursue *Ecologies of Writing Programs: Profiles of Writing Programs in Context*, edited by Christian Weisser, Michelle Ballif, Anis Bawarshi, and Mary Jo Reiff. The volume is forthcoming from Parlor Press's Writing Program Administration series (Susan H. McLeod and Margot Soven, series editors).

References

Adams, Katherine H. 1993. *A History of Professional Writing Instruction in America: Years of Acceptance, Growth, and Doubt.* Dallas: Southern Methodist University Press.

Basterdo, Michael N. 2011. "Curriculum in Higher Education: The Organizational Dynamics of Academic Reform." In *American Higher Education in the Twenty-First Century.* 3rd Edition, ed. Philip. G. Altbach, Robert. O. Berdahl, and Patricia J. Gumport, 409–32. Baltimore: Johns Hopkins University Press.

Giberson, Greg A., and Thomas A. Moriarty. 2010. *What We Are Becoming: Developments in Undergraduate Writing Majors.* Logan: Utah State University Press.

Miller, Richard E. 1998. *As If Learning Mattered: Reforming Higher Education.* Ithaca: Cornell University Press.

Ostergaard, Lori, and Greg A. Giberson. 2010. "Unifying Program Goals: Developing and Implementing A Writing and Rhetoric Major at Oakland University." *Composition Forum* 22.

Porter, James E., Patricia Sullivan, Stuart Blythe, Jeffrey T. Grabill, and Libby Miles. 2000. "Institutional Critique: A Rhetorical Methodology for Change." *College Composition and Communication* 51 (4): 610–42. http://dx.doi.org/10.2307/358914.

Ritter, Kelly. 2012. "Archival Research in Composition Studies: Re-Imagining the Historian's Role" *Rhetoric Review* 31 (4): 461–478.

Snyder, Jeffrey A. 2010. *Brief History of the Syllabus with Examples.* Cambridge, MA: Derek Bok Center for Teaching and Learning, Harvard University.

US Census Bureau. 2012. *Educational Attainment in the United States: 2009. Population Characteristics. Current Population Reports.* Washington, DC: US Census Bureau.

Weisser, Christian, and Laurie Grobman. 2012. "Undergraduate Writing Majors and the Rhetoric of Professionalism." *Composition Studies* 40 (1): 39–59.

PART I

Writing Departments

1

DEPAUL UNIVERSITY'S MAJOR IN WRITING, RHETORIC, AND DISCOURSE

Darsie Bowden

INTRODUCTION

The Department of Writing, Rhetoric, and Discourse (WRD) separated from DePaul's English department on July 1, 2007. WRD assumed immediate oversight of the first-year writing program and the minor in professional writing, which, at the time, had twenty-six declared students. In the course of the next year, we established a master's in WRD, annexed an existing master's in new media studies (an interdisciplinary degree already directed by a WRD faculty member and staffed primarily by WRD faculty), and created a TESOL (Teachers of English to Speakers of Other Languages) certificate program. Finally, in March of 2010, we submitted a proposal for a BA in WRD, which was approved in the summer of 2010.

The journey to a free-standing department with its own major was predictably tumultuous. Change is difficult in the conservative culture of education, and DePaul—the largest Catholic university in the US, with an enrollment of 25,398, including 7,983 graduate students (mostly master's students)—is not immune to the power of the status quo. The scarcity of resources due to the economic downturn of the past three years has served to exacerbate tensions and competitiveness between departments and programs. In addition to struggles for resources, some of the drama in our separation stemmed from local conditions, including existing institutional structures, areas of expertise, alliances, and personalities. The split also put into stark relief assumptions about writing—how it is defined, how it is perceived, and who *owns* it in terms of disciplinary jurisdiction.

DOI: 10.7330/9780874219722.c001

Department Name:	Writing, Rhetoric, and Discourse
Institution Type:	Private, Catholic, Doctoral/Research University (DRU)
Institution Size:	25,000 students
Residential or Commuter:	87% commuter
Student Body Description:	Diverse student body; high percentage first in their family to go to college; high school GPA average 3.55; 33% come from out of state
Year Major Began:	2010
Official Name of Degree:	Bachelor of Arts in Writing, Rhetoric, and Discourse
Number of Majors:	In year one: 8 In year three: 40 In year five: N/A Current: 40
Number of Full-Time R/C Faculty:	13

OVERVIEW AND PROGRAM RATIONALE

In the negotiations surrounding the physical and curricular separation from English, one of the most heated conversations concerned the naming of the new department. English department representatives, a majority of whom were creative writing faculty (poetry, fiction, and "creative nonfiction"), were insistent that the new unit NOT include *writing* in its name, unless it was "writing studies." While at first only a problem as we worked to divvy up the courses from an existing (and successful) master's degree *in writing* (both units wanted to retain "writing"), the naming issue would later fuel debates about the undergraduate major as well. The creative writers who identified strongly with literature—both professionally and personally—not only wanted to remain with English, but also wanted to retain primary status as the "writers" of the DePaul community. As such, they also felt they should be entitled to keep first-year writing in the English department. Thus, the question of who could control *writing* became both disciplinary and symbolic—should it be English with its long, illustrious history and investment in literature and "creative" writing or the new department, nested in the field of composition and rhetoric, with its even longer history and intellectual and practical investments in language and rhetoric? There is no convenient (or perfect) answer.

To add to the jurisdictional confusion, the university writing center, which had been supervised and managed by English department faculty since the mid 1970s, had become a unit of Academic Affairs in the previous year. Shortly afterward, Academic Affairs hired a staff director rather a faculty director, who, as it happened, had a graduate degree in literature, exacerbating jurisdictional issues and distancing *writing* even further from the control of those with disciplinary expertise in writing center theory and pedagogy.

Ultimately, compromises were made and departmental naming and course jurisdictions were sorted out, resulting in gains and losses for all parties. Because the development of the major came on the heels of the creation of a new department, we had already begun to tackle the kinds of issues that would shape our major proposal. The following section deals with the development of the major, describing our goals and the subsequent choices and their motivations.

DEVELOPING AND IMPLEMENTING A MAJOR

Developing a new major (and department) from scratch was, at first, a heady experience. This was a department we could build from the ground up, and we all felt we wanted to create something that would make a significant contribution to both the university and our field. That giddy idealism faded as we began to recognize and then engage in the hard work of setting up a major that would satisfy numerous constituencies—faculty, students, and other units in the institution as a whole—each who had a variety of assumptions about the role of writing in the university and how to teach and study it.

First, we wanted to try to make use of the expertise each faculty member brought to the major. Initially, we considered the disciplinary interests and specializations of each of the tenure-track faculty. The most senior faculty had expertise in rhetoric, composition theory, and pedagogy, including writing centers, writing program administration, and new media. One advanced assistant professor was a linguist with interests in global Englishes and writing for non-native speakers; another specialized in civic and political rhetoric (both were later tenured). These were rounded out by faculty whose interests and expertise included professional and technical writing, new media studies, and Mexican and Latin American rhetoric. All nine tenure-track faculty had strong backgrounds in composition and rhetoric. We soon moved to invite adjunct faculty into the deliberations as well. We had an extraordinary (in both size and quality) group of adjunct faculty, most of whom had considerable training in the teaching of writing and/or experience in the workplace.

The name *Writing, Rhetoric, and Discourse* emerged out of the discussions to capitalize on our expertise, as did the structure of the major. We developed *writing* courses that would offer practical experience and instruction (professional and technical writing, style, editing, revision, internships, and special topics such as grant writing and legal writing), as well as *rhetoric* and *discourse* courses that would blend practice, theory, and history (rhetorical analysis, genre analysis, digital rhetoric and culture, alternative rhetorics, and intellectual property). Our professional interests in service learning—work we were already doing with our classes (literacy, ESL, professional and technical writing, and social justice)—would be highlighted as a prominent feature of the major, particularly important at DePaul, where institutional connection with the local Chicago community has been fundamental to the university's mission since its founding in 1898.

The process of approval required that we work to define ourselves in opposition to other units, especially English, which retained the creative writing courses. Drawing from prominent discussions in composition and rhetoric, we articulated key differences in various approaches to studying texts. While literary studies focuses primarily on the interpretation of literary text, writing studies is inextricably grounded in production of *non-literary* text, such as writing in professional, legal, non-profit, corporate, civic, academic, digital, religious, and personal contexts. In addition to these basic differences (which can, of course, be seen as complementary), literature scholars and writing studies scholars work within separate disciplinary domains, drawing on distinct epistemological paradigms and modes of inquiry and participating in distinct professional and scholarly communities. As writing studies has matured and professionalized as a discipline, these differences have increased and become a source of tension in many English departments (Department of Writing, Rhetoric, and Discourse 2010).

Further, our developing major was unlike other majors at the university who had interests in writing, rhetoric, and media (communication, education, and computer science). Using the following language, we explained how we situated our major within and among other fields of study, taking care to define what we meant by *writing*.

WRD is grounded in the theory and practice of symbolic expression, from its broadest cultural manifestations to its most particular instances of production. We understand that the 2,500-year-old discipline of rhetoric functions as a productive and analytic art—a system for creating and interpreting the social and cultural knowledge that sustains, shapes, and alters the way people interact personally, professionally, and publically. We define *writing* as a particular mode and instance of rhetorical production, or language-in-use, a concrete manifestation of social and cultural orientation (Department of Writing, Rhetoric, and Discourse 2010).

During the process of developing our major, the university was in the midst of a five-year strategic plan, called *Vision Twenty12* (DePaul University 2012). One of the key goals of the plan was the enhancement of academic quality in the following areas: educating students for a globalized world, extending the classroom to include the city of Chicago, providing opportunities for students to learn ethical practice, and becoming the dominant provider within certain markets. We took advantage of these goals, foregrounding them in both our proposal and our proposed (and eventual) curricula. Additionally, with no other independent writing departments in the Chicago area, we could make the case for becoming the dominant local provider of undergraduate education in writing studies.

In a time of scarce resources, we took care to attend to the university's budgetary concerns. The health of our minor in professional and technical writing enabled us to use existing courses in the minor as an initial foundation or jumping-off point for the major. These courses included professional writing, grammar and style for writers, technical writing, introduction to reasoned discourse, composition and style, rhetoric, and writing and social engagement. Taking advantage of what was already on the books enabled us to start signing on majors immediately without creating new courses. In addition, we could adapt many of our graduate offerings to be appropriate for undergraduate students. We had sufficient faculty to cover courses, and we would not have to add courses until our major began to grow.

Finally, we wanted to nest the vocational within the context of the humanities in order to situate ourselves squarely in the liberal arts and sciences. We made the case that a WRD major could serve students in the workplace by teaching them how to be professional and technical writers, while at the same time providing students with a well-established cornerstone in liberal arts education through the advanced study of rhetorical theory and history, literary practices in contemporary culture, language and style, and writing pedagogy. In other words, we could provide majors with a rhetorical education that would enable students "to engage the ethical implications of language use, an engagement that [would] allow them to act as ethically and socially committed people both in their local communities and in society more broadly" (Department of Writing, Rhetoric, and Discourse 2010).

We established a set of five core courses that all tenure-track (and many adjunct) faculty would be expected to teach, and which every student in our major would take:

- WRD 203: Style for Writers
- WRD 205: History of Literacies and Writing
- WRD 209: Genre and Discourse
- WRD 301: Writing in Workplace Contexts
- WRD 306: Rhetorical Traditions

Students would then be required to take at least one course from the writing category, at least one course from the rhetoric and discourse category, and a service learning course (already a liberal studies requirement), up to a total of fourteen courses. Electives were open. We were careful to avoid front-loading the program with requirements and instead worked on creating a major with considerable flexibility. Consequently, students could shape a writing major according to their goals and interests and could easily double major (with, for example, commerce, political science, education, computing, and digital cinema).

CHALLENGES

One of the most difficult challenges was in marketing. How could we attract incoming students whose high school background situates writing almost exclusively within English or language arts—with a primary focus on literature—and where even "writing" courses are often conflated with literary study? The name we selected did not help much in this area. In addition to the confusion about who teaches writing ("What? This is not an English class?"), the mention of *rhetoric* often drew blank stares from students and other university faculty, and the term *discourse* seemed even more mystifying.

To meet these challenges, and in a concerted effort to compete with more established majors at the university, we worked quickly to form recognizable programs that would appeal to writing demands in the new century. We created an internship program to make use of the rich opportunities in the Chicago area—in business, publishing, and workplace writing. We embarked on a vigorous internal marketing campaign, developing innovative program structures like the combined BA/MA. We collaborated with the English department and the School of Education on a five-year secondary education degree, in which we were responsible for designing the parts of the curricula that had to do with writing and rhetoric. Building on our MA in new media studies, we worked to emphasize digital literacies in many of our course offerings. We partnered with the writing centers to promote national efforts to increase the visibility of writing through the National Day on Writing (now an annual celebration). And we secured a multi-year grant from the Department of Education and Chicago Public Schools to help low-income high schools develop successful AP English language and composition programs.

Our first-year composition (FYC) program continues to be advantageous to our major. Although we are resisting the impulse to situate FYC as a gateway course to the undergraduate writing major (as in Downs and Wardle's (2007) compelling argument), the FYC program is highly visible within the university. Almost all incoming students, including transfer students, take at least one course in the FYC sequence (called Composition and Rhetoric) and most take two. FYC also presents an annual spring student writing showcase that features the best writing from freshmen at DePaul. Many of these students, some of them understanding for the first time their power as writers, tend to gravitate to either the major or minor. FYC has also taken the lead in developing a robust digital portfolio system that is quickly spreading to other units, especially within our liberal studies programs.

REFLECTIONS

The creation of the undergraduate major in WRD illustrates how important local conditions are to the nature of our program—the particulars of our existing departments and programs, the nature of our university culture, the large urban environment, the faculty with their specific professional and scholarly interests, and the various administration structures all contributed to the shape of our major. At the national level, the proliferation of independent writing units with majors in a variety of configurations provided us with plenty of examples to use when making arguments and designing curricula.

One of the key reasons for the creation of our own unit was to be able to move in directions that were not possible while connected with the English department. Despite the challenges in establishing the unit itself, we did indeed find ourselves no longer constrained by powerful departmental forces that privileged literary writing and literary theory above all else as the nucleus of studies in writing. Instead, we could rely on the epistemologies that emerge from our own field of composition and rhetoric. Our approaches to teaching writing, for example, were often a source of friction between us and our English department colleagues: we didn't spend as much time on skills and drills and grammar instruction. More important to us was the freedom to move forward with some of the pedagogies that had currency in the field and to which many in English were resistant: online courses, digital writing, digital portfolios, outcomes-based assessment, directed self-placement, and the value of reflection.

Among the WRD faculty members pleased with the separation were our contingent faculty. Resituating responsibility for teaching writing (at all levels) to those with dedicated training and interest in writing pedagogy resulted in a huge morale boost for adjunct faculty in our department. Contingent faculty representatives now have voting rights in the department and serve on departmental committees; in other words, they have a say in the work of the department. Tenure-track and contingent faculty work more closely together on teaching projects and, in some cases, on research and assessment. Once limited to teaching FYC and business writing classes for the College of Commerce, contingent faculty are now called upon to teach other courses in the major, depending upon their qualifications and inclination. All tenure-track and non-tenure-track faculty work (research, scholarship, and creative publications) is prominently displayed in departmental locations (onsite and online).

Radically improved quality control in the hiring, supervision, training, and evaluation of contingent faculty has the potential for positively impacting the quality of instruction. We now have a comprehensive review system for contingent faculty that is transparent and both formative and summative. Among the results was the successful program-wide adaptation of digital portfolios, thanks in part to a dedicated group of instructors who meet monthly to trouble-shoot, develop assignments and assessments, and keep up with the digital portfolio literature. The department now incorporates multimodal assignments and activities in the wide variety of courses we offer. Although there is still much to do to grant contingent faculty the rights and privileges to which they are entitled, the creation of the major has greatly enhanced community building within the department.

Of course, not everything has worked out as we had hoped. We assumed that the FYC program, our professional and technical writing courses, *and* the writing center (as a locus for writing in and across the curriculum initiatives) could finally be coordinated and supervised by one administrative structure that relied on disciplinary expertise in writing. We argued that the improved efficiency and creation of structural links would result in the enhanced delivery of high quality writing instruction to DePaul students at all levels. This coordination was not to be. The writing centers and their role in helping faculty with writing instruction across the curriculum remains outside our purview for reasons that may have little to do with our unit or with English.

LOOKING FORWARD

Recently, our department underwent an academic program review. This was fortuitous; it gave us both the opportunity and exigence to reflect on our program after it had been in operation for a year and to plan for the future. As part of this process, we developed a program profile and a self-study, and the university invited two external reviewers to come to campus and undertake a study of our unit. The result was a memorandum of understanding between the department and university administration, which laid out what worked well to support student learning and the university, what could be improved and how, and where university resources were necessary for the continued health and growth of the department and the major.

After receiving these recommendations, we were able to hire more faculty and staff. We are working to provide more opportunities for faculty–student collaboration on research and professional projects, and we are making plans to apply for undergraduate research grants and develop a research methods class. Currently—given the success of our TESOL program—we are working with our English Language Institute to provide writing support (including special classes) for students who are not native speakers of English. Finally, because of the large percentage of adjunct faculty in WRD, the review put a renewed focus on the sorry status of adjunct faculty working conditions in the university and added momentum to the push for better working conditions for our contingent faculty—something that the university deans' council and the university's faculty council already have on various agendas.

In his afterword to *A Field of Dreams: Independent Writing Programs and the Future of Composition Studies*, Larry Burton makes the following observation:

> To the best of my knowledge, none of the independent departments represented in *A Field of Dreams* makes this claim to superiority [that independent writing programs produce better writers]. Perhaps they should. Perhaps the time has come to ask where students should go to reach their potential as writers, and while we are asking the question of "where" students should go, we should also ask questions about our definition of good writing and good writers. (O'Neill, Crow, and Burton 2002, 299–300)

While I hesitate to make the claim for superiority as well, I do have every confidence that DePaul's writing students (and I suspect this is true of most undergraduate majors in writing) are better writers because they are better informed about writing and its relationship to the world—to culture, power, politics, society, history, and, more importantly, to themselves. Their experiences as writers have depth and breadth, and I would argue that the departments that offer these majors —whether they are within English or communication or whether they are independent—can and do contribute to what Burton calls a "new mentality" that can make a positive difference in students' lives and ours (300).

Curricular Summary: The Major in Writing, Rhetoric, and Discourse at DePaul University

The Department of Writing, Rhetoric, and Discourse (WRD), one of the largest departments at DePaul, is dedicated to studying the history and theory of literate activity, as well as to helping students excel as writers in a wide range of academic, professional, and public settings. WRD is home to DePaul's FYC program; in addition, the department offers the minor in professional writing and the major in WRD. At the graduate level, the master of arts in WRD addresses writing in professional and technical contexts, the preparation of postsecondary teacher-scholars in writing, and the study of language for writers. The combined BA/MA in WRD allows undergraduates to begin taking graduate courses in their senior year. The department's master of arts in new media studies prepares graduates to function as productive and responsible individuals in social contexts created by new media through both critical interpretation and situated practical activity.

The act of writing in general and each student's writing in particular are of central concern in all WRD courses. Theories of language, rhetoric (how to make effective choices as writers), and discourse (the way writing structures human activity) develop students' understanding of how the individual act of writing is grounded in broader contexts of institution and culture.

MAJOR REQUIREMENTS (56 CREDIT HOURS)

Core courses:

- WRD 203: Style for Writers
- WRD 205: History of Literacies and Writing
- WRD 209: Genre and Discourse
- WRD 301: Writing in Workplace Contexts
- WRD 306: Rhetorical Traditions
- WRD 390: Rhetoric and Public Writing (senior capstone seminar)

Writing (one course):

- WRD 204: Technical Writing
- WRD 206: Introduction to Professional Writing
- WRD 240: Argumentative Writing
- WRD 300: Composition and Style
- WRD 320: Topics in Professional Writing
- WRD 323: Editing
- WRD 340: Writing and Revising
- WRD 376: Fieldwork in Arts Writing (experiential learning course or "EL")
- WRD 377: Writing and Social Engagement (EL)
- WRD 395: Writing Center Theory and Pedagogy (EL)
- WRD 396: Writing Fellows Theory and Practice (EL)
- WRD 398: Internship (EL)

Rhetoric and Discourse (one course):

- WRD 208: Introduction to Reasoned Discourse
- WRD 260: Rhetorical Analysis
- WRD 261: Digital Culture
- WRD 360: Topics in Rhetoric
- WRD 361: Topics in Alternative Rhetorics
- WRD 362: Semiotics
- WRD 363: Visual Rhetoric
- WRD 368: Global Englishes
- WRD 378: Teaching and Tutoring ESL in Chicago (EL/Junior Year Experiential Learning [JYEL])

Additional requirement:

All students are required to take an experiential learning course. Elective courses may be drawn from either of the elective categories above or from the following:

- WRD 398: Internship
- WRD 399: Independent Study

References

Department of Writing, Rhetoric, and Discourse, DePaul University. 2010. *Proposal for the WRD Undergraduate Major.* Unpublished.

DePaul University. 2012. *Vision Twenty12.* Website no longer available.

Downs, Douglas, and Elizabeth Wardle. 2007. "Teaching about Writing, Righting Misconceptions: (Re)Envisioning 'First-Year Composition' as 'Introduction to Writing Studies.'" *College Composition and Communication* 58:552–85.

O'Neill, Peggy, Angela Crow, and Larry W. Burton, eds. 2002. *A Field of Dreams: Independent Writing Programs and the Future of Composition Studies.* Logan: Utah State University Press.

2

RESHAPING THE BA IN PROFESSIONAL AND TECHNICAL WRITING AT THE UNIVERSITY OF ARKANSAS AT LITTLE ROCK

Barbara L'Eplattenier and George H. Jensen

INTRODUCTION

The bachelor of arts in professional and technical writing (PTW) is housed in the Department of Rhetoric and Writing at the University of Arkansas at Little Rock (UALR). Not surprisingly, the curriculum of the PTW major is related to the character of UALR and the history of the department.

UALR is a metropolitan university located in central Arkansas that offers fifty-three baccalaureate degrees, forty-four graduate degrees, two law degrees, and eight doctorates. UALR began as a community college—thus, it has a history of serving nontraditional students. The institution also takes its identity as a metropolitan university seriously. Faculty members often serve on community committees that focus on solving problems in central Arkansas. The university's most successful programs tend to focus on preparing students for jobs that will benefit the community in direct and practical ways.

The Department of Rhetoric and Writing was created in 1993, when it split from the Department of English. Although many versions of the split are still recounted regularly on campus, most agree that the catalyst was a disagreement over voting rights for "instructors," or the university's full-time, non-tenure-track faculty. Six instructors had been hired in 1992 to teach four sections per semester of first-year composition. In 1993, the English department chair came up for reelection. These instructors felt they should be able to vote in the chair election. The literature faculty largely agreed that they did not, in their reading of the bylaws, have voting rights. After a number of acrimonious faculty meetings and failed attempts to mediate between the two camps, the provost made the decision to create a new department.

DOI: 10.7330/9780874219722.c002

Department Name:	Rhetoric and Writing
Institution Type:	Public, Doctoral Research University (DRU)
Institution Size:	13,000 students
Residential or Commuter:	Commuter
Student Body Description:	Almost all students work; diverse in terms of ethnicity, socio-economics, age, etc.; high percentage of transfer students; high percentage first in their family to go to college; majority are women
Year Major Began:	1993
Official Name of Degree:	Bachelor of Arts in Professional and Technical Writing
Number of Majors:	In year one: N/A In year three: N/A In year five: N/A Current: 58
Number of Full-Time R/C Faculty:	19

The FYC program and an already existing master of arts in professional and technical writing went with the new department. (Interestingly, the undergraduate PTW major did not yet exist, so it was, to some extent, a back formation from the MA.) The literature BA, the English secondary education minor, the creative writing major and minor (focusing on fiction and poetry), and the linguistics minor remained in the Department of English. Expository writing (later renamed nonfiction) went with the new department because it was part of the master's in PTW, and it was, maybe more importantly, not considered "creative." (One faculty member in English recently referred to the Department of Rhetoric and Writing as the "Department of Noncreative Writing.") We should also mention that UALR had, at the time, a Department of Journalism, which has since morphed into the School of Mass Communications.

PROGRAM OVERVIEW AND RATIONALE

This brief history of the department's creation explains certain curricular parameters, and the curriculum of the PTW major is a testament to learning to work within those restrictions. While the department (once independent from English) had the freedom to develop courses and a curriculum for the PTW major, certain kinds of courses were the territory of other departments and, therefore, off-limits. To respect the territory of English, the department could not develop courses in literature (although we do teach nonfiction texts as models for writing), English education (though we do teach a topics course that covers writing for children and adolescents), creative writing (though we do teach courses in nonfiction, which we teach as creative nonfiction), or linguistics (though we do teach courses in editing). To respect the territory of what would eventually become the School of Mass Communications, the department could not develop courses in journalism (though we often teach oral histories in nonfiction courses) or video (though we ask students to do video projects in a topics course on new media). Thus, the curriculum of our major could be considered a long exercise in rhetorical mediation.

During their first semester in the major, students take RHET 3200: Introduction to Professional and Technical Writing—the gateway course to the major. The purpose of the course is to provide students with information about the curriculum, faculty, and potential careers so they will be more successful in the program and more mindful about preparing for a career. In the course, we stress the importance of building skills, especially knowledge of important software, beyond those directly taught in the curriculum. One of our main messages, which almost becomes a mantra, is that more demands are being placed on writers and students need to supplement coursework to be prepared for the workplace.

A number of guest speakers—all successful professional writers or editors, and many of them program alumni—provide a broad spectrum of advice about building a career, which students seems to find beneficial. The course was designed for students in the major, but, surprisingly, a number of non-majors take the course, registering on their interpretation of the title without reading the catalog description. Toward the end of the course, a number of these non-majors declare as PTW majors; thus, the course has had the unexpected benefit of recruiting new majors.

Four required 3000-level (junior-level) courses provide an introduction to the key areas of the major (editing, persuasion, nonfiction, and technical writing) and serve as prerequisites for the 4000-level (senior-level) required courses and electives: RHET 3301: Editing for Usage, Style, and Clarity; RHET 3315: Persuasive Writing; RHET 3317: Nonfiction; and RHET 3326: Technical Writing.

RHET 3301: Editing for Usage, Style, and Clarity is not a grammar course. It does provide a review of grammar and mechanics as needed, but the course focuses on editing techniques and procedures used by professional editors, such as proofreading marks, the creation and use of style sheets, and multi-pass editing. It is the prerequisite for the advanced editing courses that serve as electives. RHET 4322: Advanced Editing extends the techniques learned in 3301. RHET 4304: Technical

Style and Editing covers issues related to the editing of technical documents, such as handling mathematical equations. RHET 4321: Editing for Publication provides supervised, guided experience of the entire editing process, from acquisition editing through developmental editing and line editing. Students work with actual authors who have submitted essays to *Quills and Pixels*, the department's nonfiction publication. A course in production editing has been offered as a topics course and will soon be proposed as a standard catalog course. Enrolled students take the edited submissions to *Quills and Pixels* and prepare them for the printer, learning about layout and design in the process.

RHET 3315: Persuasive Writing covers the technique and practice of argumentative writing. It serves as the prerequisite for advanced courses on persuasion that serve as electives. RHET 4315: Advanced Persuasion provides a more theoretical investigation of persuasion, and RHET 4325: Legal Writing, Reasoning, and Argumentation is often taken by prelaw students.

RHET 3317: Nonfiction has come to be called "creative nonfiction." While the focus is on writing true stories, students learn how to craft a nonfiction narrative by adopting many techniques that might be employed in the writing of fiction. It serves as the prerequisite for advanced courses in nonfiction. RHET 4317: Advanced Nonfiction includes a survey of the range of the genre, including the personal essay, memoir, graphic memoir, and oral history. RHET 4318: Writing Auto/biography provides an opportunity for students to write about themselves and others and to critique each other's projects in peer groups. Travel writing has been taught as a topics course (RHET 4347: Topics in Nonfiction) and will be developed into a standard catalog course. We also have plans to develop nonfiction courses in ghost writing and writing for publication.

RHET 3326: Technical Writing provides an introduction to the kind of writing done by and for engineers. Projects typically include writing instructions for a manufacturing process or procedural manual. This course serves as the prerequisite for advanced courses in technical writing and communication. RHET 4306: Writing for Business and Government covers the research and practice of writing within bureaucratic institutions. RHET 4307: Writing Software Documentation covers the creation of help menus that are embedded within software programs. This course is always taught in a computer classroom, and students learn to become proficient with RoboHelp. RHET 4371: Writing for the Web provides both an introduction to website design and practice in writing texts that are suitable for web publication. RHET 4375:

Grant Writing provides an introduction to the process of writing a grant. During the course, students write a grant for a nonprofit agency and then submit it. About fifteen percent of the grants submitted through the course are funded.

In addition to the four required 3000-level courses, students are required to take three courses at the 4000-level. It should be noted, however, that most of the electives students take are also at the 4000-level.

RHET 4305: Document Design is always taught in a computer classroom. During the course, students learn to use important authoring and design software. Document Design covers a wide array of design issues, such as matching colors both in print and online, matching type fonts, use of white space, placement of charts and graphs, and so on. Students are encouraged to take this course as soon as they are seniors so all of their documents look professional by the course's conclusion. In our survey of comparable programs, we found nine examples of similar courses.

RHET 4301: Theories of Rhetoric and Writing provides an introduction to rhetorical theory (major rhetoricians include Aristotle, Cicero, Toulman, and Burke), and students learn to apply the theory by practicing rhetorical analyses.

RHET 4190: Colloquium in Rhetoric and Writing is a capstone class. Students compile a professional portfolio of their work in the major, which they can later use to apply for jobs or graduate programs. In our survey of comparable programs, we found no examples of a similar course.

IMPLEMENTATION NARRATIVE

The version of the PTW major emerged in a moment of crisis, literally in the days, not months, following the split from the Department of English. As the technical writers and compositionists packed their desktop computers onto their office chairs and rolled their way across campus to the space that would house the new Department of Rhetoric and Writing, they took with them the FYC program and an already established master's in professional and technical writing. However, for the vulnerable department to thrive, the faculty believed they also needed an undergraduate major. Faced with an Arkansas Department of Higher Education mandated freeze on new programs, a quickly formed alliance with the Department of Journalism allowed the rhetoric and writing department to obtain approval for a BA in professional and technical writing with two tracks. The Department of Journalism administered track one, which understandably presented a twenty-eight semester-hour curriculum more focused on journalism with three courses in rhetoric. The Department of Rhetoric and Writing administered track two, a thirty semester-hour curriculum that included one journalism course and the option for a second twelve hours of upper-level RHET electives, which may include three hours of Journalism.

These two tracks continued with only minor revisions until the fall of 2007, when a number of factors called for a thorough revision of the major. First and foremost, students were often confused by a major with two tracks that was administered by two separate departments from two separate colleges. For example, it was not unusual for a student in track two to apply for graduation in track one. Additionally, the Department of Journalism had morphed into the School of Mass Communications and revised its curriculum to reflect developments in new media. Following a convergence model, the School of Mass Communications developed a curriculum with a fifteen-hour core, which included a course in web design, and three areas of emphasis: journalism, media production, and strategic communication. Perhaps because of their focus on the new curriculum, the number of active majors in the first track option of PTW had dropped to single digits. Finally, from years of assessment data, the Department of Rhetoric and Writing realized that a thorough overhaul of the second track was needed—students often did not see the need for the single JOUR 2350: Techniques of Writing for the Mass Media course, while noting that electives such as Document Design or Writing for the Web were much more useful for their professional development.

In the fall of 2007, when *not* in a moment of crisis, the faculty of the Department of Rhetoric and Writing began to explore reshaping the BA in professional and technical writing to merge the two tracks into one degree. This occurred through programmatic assessment, consultations with the School of Mass Communications, and a departmental retreat. The process began with informal discussions of issues raised by graduating seniors during exit interviews. A number of our seniors felt that the required course in journalism was a distraction. As the department had developed new elective courses (Editing for Publication, Writing Software Documentation, Technical Style and Editing, Writing for the Web, Grant Writing, etc.), largely in response to developments in the field, students felt a need to expand their knowledge of professional writing techniques and practices by taking these courses. They felt that a single course in journalism would not make them more attractive in the job market as would a course in Writing Software Documentation, for example. Students argued that anyone who wanted to be a journalist should major or minor in it. Graduating seniors often remarked that they felt Document Design, in particular, should be a required course. Similarly, faculty had consistently noticed differences in students' portfolios based on the coursework they had done. Those who had taken Document Design, for example, tended to compile a more cohesive and professional (especially in appearance) portfolio than those students who hadn't taken the course. Anecdotes and discussions about the current job market from locally employed alumni also supported students' feelings about the types of coursework needed in the program. Students seldom saw Techniques of Writing for Mass Media as a useful course.

Largely as an acknowledgment of the increasing complexity of professional writing, the faculty felt that the thirty-hour major was too limited to adequately prepare students for careers as professional writers. The English major on campus was then a thirty-six-hour degree, and the recently revised major in mass communications was a forty-two-hour degree. Thus, a consensus began to emerge that we needed to add an additional three hours of electives, as well as shift the required courses.

During exit interviews, graduating seniors expressed dissatisfaction with RHET 3316: Writing for the Workplace, an entry level course in business writing. The department had, a number of years ago, also developed RHET 3326: Technical Writing. Of the two courses, which had overlapping content, Writing for the Workplace—required by a number of majors outside the department—had evolved into a service course. As a result, instruction tended to move at a slower pace and projects were a bit more generic. Rather early in our discussions, the consensus emerged that Technical Writing would be the stronger course for our majors and that Writing for the Workplace should be considered a service course, not an elective option for majors. A key point in this discussion was the realization that students could get a degree in professional and technical writing without ever having taken a course entitled Technical Writing. Recognizing that technical writers require different information about technical writing than say computer scientists or engineers, some faculty also suggested that there be a majors-only section. Due to institutional and scheduling constraints, this option was not pursued.

A few years earlier, the department had developed RHET 4390: Colloquium, a three-hour capstone course. In the course, students developed a portfolio, which they could use for their job search or application to graduate school and the department could use for assessment. In general, the course helped students transition to either the job market or graduate school. During exit interviews, a number of seniors said they would have preferred to have much of the information earlier on in their studies. If they knew about job opportunities, for example, they could then take the courses that would make them more marketable. As the faculty continued to discuss this issue, they began to see the need for both a gateway and capstone course. We decided to make the gateway course (RHET 3200) a two-hour requirement and the capstone course (now RHET 4190) a one-hour requirement to prevent the total hours requirement in the major from ballooning.

Finally, the advisors in the department were concerned that some students were using internships to fill their entire elective requirements. While the faculty felt that internships were important (in fact, opportunities for internships had expanded in recent years), they also strongly believed that students needed classroom experience to prepare for their careers. Thus, we agreed, as a general principle, that the number of hours a student could devote to internships needed to be limited.

Because the BA in professional and technical writing was administered by two academic units, any revision of the major would require coordination with the School of Mass Communications. After a general consensus was reached among rhetoric and writing faculty, a meeting was scheduled with communications. The chair of the Department of Rhetoric and Writing and a faculty member specializing in technical writing met with the director of the School of Mass Communications and a faculty member specializing in journalism. After some discussion of the problems with the two tracks, the group examined how the revision of the second track might accommodate students who preferred the curriculum of track one. (Because the number of track one majors at the time was rather low, both units felt it made more sense to fold track one into track two.) Both units agreed that the tracks could be merged by allowing students in the professional and technical writing major—which would now be administered entirely in the Department of Rhetoric and Writing—to take up to six hours of electives from offerings in the School of Mass Communications.

About two weeks before our departmental retreat, the chair circulated a draft of the revised curriculum's catalog description. While the content of the draft emerged from years of assessment reports and six months of faculty discussions, it still provoked some heated debates on the departmental listserv.

Agreeing upon the final wording of any document is a tedious process. Much of this work was accomplished at a day-long departmental retreat off-campus. During the course of the day, supplied with ample food and beverages, we were able to reach consensus on final wording for the catalog and approve it. The appendix summarizes the changes approved.

REFLECTION AND PROSPECTION

Since the implementation of the new curriculum in the fall of 2008, the department has continued to assess the program through portfolios and exit interviews. In spring 2012, the program underwent an extensive program review, as required by the Arkansas Department of Higher Education. Data, curriculum vitae, and course syllabi were compiled into a 500-plus page report, which was externally reviewed by Duane Roen and Doug Hesse. The reflections that follow are a summary of both our internal assessment and the program review.

Both students and faculty have been particularly pleased with the introductory/gateway class. It seems to help students settle into the major/department as well as create a good mindset for beginning coursework in the major. Originally designed to help students reflect metacognitively on their learning, the colloquium/capstone class seems to have found its identity in the last year or so. The instructor of this course now meets informally with students to workshop their portfolios and solve problems with their job/graduate school applications. One minor unexpected issue is that the two-hour gateway course sometimes causes problems fashioning a full course load, as required for financial aid. In coming year, we plan to convert this to a three-hour course.

The switch from requiring RHET 3316: Writing for the Workplace to RHET 3326: Technical Writing seems to have been an improvement for our majors. The addition of RHET 4305: Document Design as a required course has universally been viewed as a positive change.

Departmentally, we have seen improvement in both the final portfolios and the students' preparation for the workforce. In addition, we have seen the workforce respond to our curriculum. Often, jobs that focus on communication or writing now describe qualifications as "a degree in English, communication, or rhetoric"; ten years ago, rhetoric was not included in such job ads. Similarly, we often see "knowledge of RoboHelp" in job advertisements. Until we started teaching RoboHelp in our Writing Software Documentation class, this criteria didn't exist in job advertisements.

The program includes a number of topics courses: Topics in Nonfiction (some recent topics include production editing, writing and healing, survey of nonfiction, travel writing, and writing about families, children, and adolescents) and Topics in Technical Communication (some recent topics include science writing, game theory, and new media theory). These topics courses have provided a means of exploring new offerings. The faculty enjoy developing new topics courses, and students often prefer them over standard offerings from the catalog. When we developed these topics courses, we expected that a topic would only be offered once or twice. Once the course content had been developed and student demand clearly demonstrated, the topic would be developed into a standard course. Not surprisingly, overworked faculty are sometimes reluctant to complete the forms for approving the topic as a course. One of the major problems with teaching the content through a topics course is that, in our university's system, the topic is not listed on a student's transcript. Thus, students cannot easily demonstrate that they have had a course in science writing because that phrase does not appear on their transcript.

As with many departments across the country, rhetoric and writing will experience 30 to 40 percent retirement rates in the next five years. At least one of these retirees will be in the area of creative nonfiction. We would like to recruit a writer (perhaps with an MFA rather than a PhD, which would be new for our department) who has extensive experience in publishing and working as a freelance writer. In 2009, the department developed a curriculum for the MA program in editing. This new nonfiction faculty member would assist in developing additional courses in editing and publishing. We would also like for this faculty member to incorporate more discussion of working as a freelance writer into existing nonfiction courses as well as develop new nonfiction courses, perhaps in travel writing and food writing.

Certainly, one of the major shifts in our curriculum over the last ten years has been toward multimodal authoring and new media. For most of our hires in the next five years, we will focus on recruiting faculty who are skilled in new media. The department is in the process of creating a usability lab. Employers are beginning to see usability testing as increasingly important. Once the usability lab is in place, we will develop a course in usability testing.

The university is presently revising its general education requirements, which will prompt some changes to majors. The committee proposal for the new general education program, which was presented to the Faculty Senate in May 2012, includes a wide range of recommendations (the elimination of the requirement for a minor, a requirement for a writing-in-the-disciplines course, a research course, a values course, an ethics course, and so on). These recommendations would be difficult to legislate and even more difficult for advisors to monitor. As means of respecting the importance of the committee proposal, while at the same time simplifying it, a motion emerged to (1) eliminate the requirement for a minor and (2) fold the other requirements into the major, including forty-five hours of upper-level credit—twelve hours of which would come from outside the major—a communications-in-the-discipline course, and a research methods course. The idea behind the motion was to build all upper-level general education requirements into the major. Then students and advisors could focus on the requirements of the major. Once students meet the requirements for the major, they will also meet all requirements for graduation beyond the core (the first- and second-year requirements).

With the elimination of the requirement for a minor, while maintaining the need for exposure to other disciplines (i.e., the new requirement that majors include twelve hours of upper-level credit outside the program), students will have more space in the curriculum to explore interests or build competencies for the workplace. The Faculty Senate has had preliminary discussions about developing certifications (some universities are calling these badges) that would be more focused on workplace skills than a minor and less extensive that an official "certificate." In order to earn a certification, students would take three or four courses related to a particular skill area from a menu drawn from within and outside the major. The certification could be noted on a supplemental page to the transcript, along with extracurricular activities (this supplement to the transcript is called a Student Extra-Curricular Activity Transcript, or SEAT, at some institutions). Our department has discussed developing certifications in website design, editing, and document design.

CONCLUSION

The BA in professional and technical writing has been successful in both attracting majors and placing them in jobs. We have been particularly encouraged by how many of our majors take jobs as technical writers or grant writers before moving on to new jobs, with better salaries and more opportunities for professional growth, during the first few years after graduation. We are equally encouraged by how many companies or institutions in the area recruit our majors. One local company hires four to six of our majors a year. This success is largely due to the perception that our majors have developed the skills needed to perform on the job.

Curricular Summary: The Professional and Technical Writing
Major at the University of Arkansas–Little Rock

The department offers first-year composition, a variety of specialized courses to help improve writing skills, a major in professional and technical writing, and a master's degree in professional and technical writing. The department also maintains the university writing center, where all students who wish to work on specific writing needs are welcome.

MAJOR REQUIREMENTS

Core requirements (44 credit hours):

- RHET 3220: Introduction to Professional and Technical Writing (gateway course)
- RHET 3301: Editing for Usage, Style, and Clarity
- RHET 3315: Persuasive Writing
- RHET 3326: Technical Writing
- RHET 3317: Nonfiction
- RHET 4305: Document Design
- RHET 4301: Theories of Rhetoric and Writing
- RHET 4190: Colloquium in Rhetoric and Writing (capstone course)

Electives (15 credit hours):

Electives may not include RHET 3316: Writing for the Workplace or more than six hours total in the following: internships, independent writing projects, and/or upper-level MCOM courses. We recommend students take RHET 3300: Introduction to Research. Through advising, we help students map out a program that will help them met their career goals.

Editing concentration:

- RHET 3301: Editing for Usage, Style, and Clarity (required)
- RHET 4304: Technical Style and Editing
- RHET 4321: Editing for Publication
- RHET 4322: Advanced Editing
- RHET 4191, 4192: Internship

Persuasive concentration:

- RHET 3316: Persuasive Writing (required)
- RHET 4315: Advanced Persuasive Writing
- RHET 4325: Legal Writing, Reasoning, and Argument
- RHET 4345: Topics in Persuasive Writing (may be repeated)
- RHET 4191, 4192: Internship

Nonfiction concentration:

- RHET 3317: Nonfiction (required)
- RHET 4317: Advanced Nonfiction Writing
- RHET 4318: Auto/Biography
- RHET 4347: Topics in Nonfiction Writing (may be repeated)
- RHET 4191, 4192: Internship

Technical writing concentration:

- RHET 3326: Technical Writing (required)
- RHET 4306: Writing for Business and Government
- RHET 4307: Writing Software Documentation
- RHET 4371: Writing on the Web
- RHET 4375: Grant Writing
- RHET 4346: Topics in Technical Communication (may be repeated)
- RHET 4191, 4192: Internship

Appendix

Table 2.1 Summary of Changes to Professional and Technical Writing Major

30 total hours	36 total hours	Six hours added to create gateway and capstone course and to add additional hours to electives, which will accommodate former track one majors.
PTW major divided into track one (School of Mass Communication) and track two (Department of Rhetoric and Writing).	No tracks, major administered and advised in the Department of Rhetoric and Writing.	Tracks eliminated, but accommodations for the former track one majors are embedded in the curriculum.
	Add to catalog "PTW majors are encouraged to take MCOM 2330: Mass Media and Society as part of their social sciences requirement in the core."	Added to accommodate former track one majors.
RHET 3316: Writing for Workplace	RHET 3326: Technical Writing	The content of RHET 3326 is more appropriate for PTW majors than the content of RHET 3316.
JOUR 2350: Beginning Reporting	RHET 4305: Document Design	Students can take the MCOM 2350 course as part of their electives. Exit interviews with graduating seniors and meetings with prospective employers indicate that RHET 4305 is crucial to PTW majors.

continued on next page

Table 2.1—*continued*

Current Curriculum	Proposed Curriculum	Rationale for Change
	RHET 3200: Introduction to Professional and Technical Writing	Added as a required course to serve as an introduction to the major, portfolio assessment, internships, and career opportunities. Course will also introduce key technology skills.
	RHET 4190: Colloquium in Rhetoric and Writing	Added as a required course to complete portfolio process and transition students into careers or graduate studies.
Twelve hours of upper-level RHET electives, may include three hours of JOUR courses.	Fifteen hours of upper-level RHET electives (not RHET 3316), not more than six hours total in the following: internships, independent writing projects, and/or upper-level MCOM courses.	Three hours of electives added and the option of taking MCOM courses increased to six hours to accommodate former track one majors. Restrictions added to prevent students from taking both RHET 3316 and 3326, which are similar courses, and to prevent students from taking too many hours in internships and independent writing projects.

3

THE UNIVERSITY OF RHODE ISLAND'S MAJOR IN WRITING AND RHETORIC

Libby Miles, Kim Hensley Owens, and Michael Pennell

INTRODUCTION

The writing and rhetoric major at the University of Rhode Island (URI), a medium-sized public research university, is housed in the Department of Writing and Rhetoric. Our history is bumpy and windy: what began as an innovative standalone program in the early 1970s folded into a program within the Department of English in 1979, but in 2003 again separated into a stand-alone program, which was granted full departmental status in 2010. Our major was approved in 2007, and has since provided intellectual vitality and pedagogical variety for our department.

Since initiating the major, we have attempted to learn from it—from our students and from each other. This, of course, is easier said than done. What works beautifully on paper doesn't always work with actual human beings. What follows is our attempt to make sense of what we have done, and what we are continuing to learn.

OVERVIEW AND PROGRAM RATIONALE

Our major emphasizes rhetorical concepts and theories, offering a wide range of classroom and co-curricular opportunities with an emphasis on varied practice over time, on process plus production, and on repeated reflection/revision cycles. We stress heterogeneity and rhetoric with real audiences. We highly value repeated practice over time, wildly varied, with increasing sophistication and complications. For example, what students learn and practice as "rhetoric" in a 100-level course (a simplified version of the rhetorical triangle) may be questioned and complicated in WRT 201: Writing Argumentative and Persuasive Texts, where they learn about Aristotle's "available means." They often leave that class with

DOI: 10.7330/9780874219722.c003

Department Name:	Writing and Rhetoric
Institution Type:	Public, High Research Activity University (RU/H)
Institution Size:	16,300 students
Residential or Commuter:	44% residential
Student Body Description:	Most students work part-time, though some work full-time; lack of diversity in terms of ethnicity and age (71% white); high percentage of writing and rhetoric double majors
Year Major Began:	2007
Official Name of Degree:	Bachelor of Arts in Writing and Rhetoric
Number of Majors:	In year one: 12 In year three: 45 In year five: 90 Current: 92
Number of Full-Time R/C Faculty:	7

an understanding of rhetoric as a tool of argument. We then explode and further complicate this understanding in WRT 360: Composing Processes and the Canons of Rhetoric, which offers up rhetoric as a means of collaborative meaning making for the social good. Our 400-level offerings, particularly the internship and field experiences, move students to practice these concepts outside the classroom, and test them against real-world situations.

The major culminates in a digital capstone e-portfolio that students design for both academic and non-academic audiences. This e-portfolio brings the elements listed above into one complicated, multimodal, and all-too-public text and presentation. A thirty-credit major, we require four classes in addition to the 400-level e-portfolio course: At the 200 level: Writing Argumentative and Persuasive Texts and Writing in Electronic Environments; at the 300 level: Composing Processes and Canons of Rhetoric; and at the 400 level: Writing and Rhetoric, a course focusing on audience, rhetorical theories, writing processes, and professional writing. Remaining classes are chosen by students, but must include two additional 300- or 400-level courses. Students are encouraged to secure an internship as part of their program of study, throughout which they are mentored by faculty and can earn up to six credits.

To maintain writing and rhetoric's (both the major and minor) commitments and responsibilities for general education on campus, many of the courses students can apply to the major are general education classes. This means that even our 300-level classes, which range from Scientific and Technical Writing to Travel Writing, don't have prerequisites and are open to any student on campus. While this open structure has its drawbacks—i.e., instructors cannot count on shared knowledge among students except in 400-level classes—it also has significant benefits. For example, the structure encourages recursivity in our courses. It also enables students to discover and declare writing and rhetoric majors comparatively late in their college careers. And while the major was designed with a four-year curriculum in mind, it accommodates well those latecomers, who have helped our numbers grow consistently in the major's initial years.

The program is both process- and production-focused—for example, the vast majority of our courses are graded on a portfolio system that privileges revision over time. At all levels students are encouraged or required to write for audiences beyond their professors, and to write in a myriad of genres, including but not limited to those common to academe. Students in WRT 235: Writing in Electronic Environments, for example, contribute material to Wikitravel, and in WRT 302: Writing Culture students move beyond understanding or even analyzing genres like a museum display, instead creating those genres themselves. All our courses encourage revision and reflection, providing students opportunities to move between theory and practice over time.

IMPLEMENTATION NARRATIVE

Surely there is an element of *kairos* in any story about building a major. We became aware of four crucially important factors for anyone engaged in programmatic curricular development: 1) reading and embracing the moment, 2) recruiting personnel, 3) imagining what students should know and be able to do, and 4) accurately and ethically assessing one's own resources and limitations. Although these four factors needn't follow in a linear progression, they did for us: first, after years of failed attempts at curricular reform, the moment was finally right; second, we needed to figure out who "we" were; third, we were able to actualize a design; and finally, unsurprisingly, we realized we needed to rein in the dreaming and work in the context of limited resources and territory issues.

Our kairotic moment blossomed from three coalescing movements on campus in the early years of the twenty-first century. First, student members of the Dean of Arts and Sciences' Advisory Committee clamored for a minor in writing. The dean listened and asked members of what was then the College Writing Program (CWP) to design a minor that might eventually grow into a major. The design of that minor was pure convenience—we took our existing advanced courses in writing, creative writing, and linguistics and declared it a minor if a student took eighteen credits of those courses. Our proposal passed through the departmental and university curricular legislative processes with ease, students responded well, and the minor quickly took off as a popular offering. More than a decade later, it still is.

Second, perhaps a year later, Rhode Island's Office of Higher Education delivered a statewide mandate for all undergraduate majors in the state's public colleges and universities to engage thoughtfully in student learning outcomes articulation and assessment. They mandated that all majors would create and publicize their student learning outcomes, that each outcome would be aligned with either new or existing courses so it would be "covered" by the curriculum, that each department would have a plan for assessing their majors' outcomes using direct measures, and that pedagogical and instructional changes would follow based on assessment results. The timeline was short, the task monumental. At first, this didn't affect us—we didn't have a major. However, the interim vice provost at the time pulled together a small group of faculty representing programs throughout the university and sent them to an Association of American Colleges and Universities (AAC&U) summer institute on general education and assessment, also known as their Greater Expectations Institute. Two members of that select team were from the Department of Writing and Rhetoric. During the AAC&U institute, we quickly got a crash course on assessment. More importantly, we started to realize the positive potential of something we had—up until that point—deliberately avoided: the spectrum of assessment. This became both a valuable lesson and a generative moment for us.

The third development, not unlike one experienced by dozens of English departments nationwide, was a gradual increase in the tension between the literature faculty and the writing faculty. Tensions had, in fact, escalated to such an extent that the dean appointed an ad hoc committee to study the relationship between the two programs. That committee ultimately recommended that the English department and the CWP split, rendering it an independent entity once again. Within a year of our renewed independence, the dean and our students encouraged us to grow our writing minor to a full-fledged major. Finally the moment was right, and those coalescing movements guided our discussions in ways both material and theoretical. Whether or not we realized it at the time, they framed our discussions.

Guiding Question 1: Who would like to be a part of this new enterprise?

Anyone engaging in this sort of programmatic reform work would do well to conduct a full self-study, following the model offered by the Council of Writing Program Administrators (2014). We found ours to be immensely generative. At the time, we invited the sole linguist to join us, hoping that he would opt- to move with writing if the two units split. For several months, the working title of our dream department was "Writing, Rhetoric, and Linguistics." Eventually, however, our linguistics colleague decided to remain in English for his final decade of teaching. (As a side note, since his retirement in 2010, the English faculty have not pursued a linguistics replacement, and may decide not to include linguistics in the future of their department, an outcome which could reopen the possibility of including linguistics in our department.)

Nationwide, where writing and English faculty have opted to separate, creative writing seems evenly split; approximately half stay with literature, while the other half go with writing. In our institution, we believe creative writing can fit well in a writing department. However, with a split like this, it is the people, rather than the specialty, which ultimately decide the outcome and make—or unmake—that elusive "fit." Of the four English faculty who identified as creative writers at the time of our split, three had been trained and hired as literature specialists, and one had been hired as a rhetoric and composition specialist. All were teaching both creative writing and their original specialties, and had published their own creative writing or were pursuing creative publications. The three hired as literature specialists identified strongly with English, and saw no benefit in joining writing instead. The rhetoric and composition specialist sincerely hoped that creative writing would be included in the new department, but it was not a viable option. Her disappointment was palpable, and not fully eased, despite the opportunity to infuse creativity throughout our curriculum and develop and teach new courses with clear opportunities for students' personal and creative expression, such as WRT 270: Writing Our Selves: Writing in the Expressivist Tradition.

Guiding Question 2: What would we like writing and rhetoric majors to know and be able to do by the time they graduate?

Simultaneously one of the most theoretical and one of the most practical, this is also the most basic question program designers can ask. But it was new to us. In designing a brand new major with few externally-imposed constraints, we were free to dream in any direction. What, then, did we wish to create? In our newly reclaimed program in the Ocean State, the world was our oyster. We began by brainstorming the "habits of mind" we thought writing and rhetoric majors might need to develop. Although this may be common parlance now, it was a very new and a very important conversation for us. The habits of mind we listed included revision, persistence, collaboration, inquiry, creativity, citizenship, and many others. In a classic student learning outcomes progression, the next step was to build specific student learning outcomes that would support the development of those habits of mind (see appendix 1 for our student learning outcomes). We consulted the WPA Outcomes Statement for First-Year Composition (2014), but diverged from it as appropriate for a full-blown major, not simply a first-year writing program.

After we developed our outcomes, we began to look at each course in the curriculum to see which outcomes had adequate practice and increasing sophistication over time, and which ones did not. We used our curriculum map to determine which new courses we would need to design, and at which level. Mapping also helped us decide which courses should be required as core courses, which ones would be highly recommended, and which ones would remain electives.

By the end, we had clearly articulated student learning outcomes, mapped the curriculum to show how it all fit together, and designed a plan for continually assessing those outcomes over time. Although these were required elements in the curricular approval process, necessary for attaining the Board of Governors' seal of approval, we found the process extraordinarily generative.

Guiding Question 3: What can we realistically and ethically offer, given existing resources, to ensure a high quality curriculum?

Here is where the discussion about creative writing resurfaced, in all its complexity. Because we could not ethically claim any expertise in creative writing, and because claiming so would raise the legitimate ire of the English department, we agreed to embrace an approach in which courses throughout our curriculum would "infuse" creativity in appropriate ways, but we agreed to avoid using that label as such. Some of our courses, such as Travel Writing, clearly lent themselves to incorporating elements of creative nonfiction, but we were bound by tacit agreement not to use that label.

What we *could* do was another matter. We knew that our faculty had a common core of theoretical and historical training in the field of rhetoric and composition, and we had identified good public citizenship as one of our "habits of mind." We also knew that we wanted our major to have a useful balance of practical learning, real-world experience, and technological proficiency, along with rhetorical theories and histories. To that end, we designed a vertical core that we knew we could provide, given the talent and facilities available to us.

All five core classes provide students with opportunities to respond to a range of rhetorical situations. The two 200-level core courses, Writing in Electronic Environments and Writing Argumentative and Persuasive Texts, were intended to establish foundations in technology, practice, theory, and rhetoric. Writing in Electronic Environments emphasizes practice with digital composing and production processes, while Writing Argumentative and Persuasive Texts focuses on practice with various argumentation theories. With that scaffolding, our 300-level core course, Composing Processes and the Canons of Rhetoric, tempers rhetorical history and theory with research on real-world writers—as students learn about theories of invention, they also interview and report on what practicing writers have to say about invention, arrangement, style, memory, and delivery. Finally, our 400-level courses are designed to extend, and perhaps even explode, what the earlier courses introduced and reinforced. By graduation, we hope that students will have had a myriad of experiences within a matrix of theory, practice, technology, and field experience, so much that they will be able to respond effectively to any new rhetorical situation.

Over time, we have more fully developed our internship practicum to allow our students to gain valuable onsite experience connected to our major. Our students have participated in internships throughout the New England region, both on- and off-campus, for non-profit and private organizations. In the final reports for the practicum, students are asked to reflect on the internship, including their expectations, surprises, and activities. These internship sites offer a unique opportunity to practice, apply, and reflect on the more theoretical aspects of the major. Inevitably, one "habit of mind" students reflect on is collaboration. By witnessing and participating in the production of a non-profit organization's annual report, an online fashion retailer's website, or a review of an educational video game, students begin to understand how collaboration exists in the production of various written texts. In addition, as faculty, we are allowed some insight into how our major relates to writing practices in the workplace. For example, our communication with internship supervisors is invaluable, as they offer an outside perspective on our students and, in turn, our major.

REFLECTION AND PROSPECTION

With each new semester, we tweak—or at least discuss tweaking—the curriculum. Such conversations provide fruitful discussions regarding how our vision for the major functions both in practice and alongside the university's current agenda. For example, a recent campus-wide shift to a four-credit curriculum provided the opportunity to reevaluate, prioritize, and hone our course requirements, even though our major is still quite new.. The shift, still in process, emphasizes increased learning opportunities, but on our campus (unlike some others) the fourth credit does not usually entail a fourth hour of seat time each week. Thus, we have had to consider how courses might be expanded with out-of-class learning opportunities. We began our shift slowly, applying particular designations to certain clusters of our courses. We began with the classes that already required extensive out-of-class research or work, such as Travel Writing and Writing and Community Service. We designated these types of courses "fieldwork-based," and created the four-credit versions by enhancing, standardizing, and quantifying the field research components already in the three-credit versions. Similarly, we designated courses that require students to work with and learn new technologies as "technology learning" courses, where the fourth credit—along with instructor guidance—supports students as they play, experiment, and begin to establish familiarity with and produce new technologies. In each case, we worked to create a definition that all faculty could agree with, and a proposal for the revised courses worked its way through curricular oversight committees.

As mentioned before, we regularly acquire new majors who are already upper-level students. At our university, like many others, students often do not graduate in four years, so we have tried to accommodate later arrivals to the major. This has included rather acrobatic prerequisite exceptions and individual program adjustments. These on-the-spot adjustments sometimes place students in the position of being able to graduate, but not always in the most advantageous position to learn and fully benefit from our major. With the university's attention focused on retention and timely graduation, we find ourselves exploring potential "bottlenecks" in our curriculum. In other words, where do students get hung up? Recently, the department decided to alternate the offering of two required upper-level courses, making a formerly spring-only class into a fall-only class, and vice versa (enrollments don't yet justify a multiple-semester offering of either). This way, students can take the prerequisite in the fall for a 400-level class now offered in the spring, enabling last-minute majors to take all three upper division core courses within their senior year. Such immediate attention to curricular need may prove more difficult as the major grows, but, for now, we adeptly manage the curriculum, addressing such problems as they arise.

We hope that changes like this will allow us to continue to be sensitive to students' and the university's needs for good time-to-graduation rates, but also provide all writing and rhetoric majors with scaffolded and sequenced learning opportunities akin to what was originally envisioned as a several-year process.

At this point, we—perhaps like many other faculty involved in writing majors across the country—find ourselves moving beyond the creation narrative and into the "looking forward" phase. With each subsequent class of majors we graduate, we find ourselves learning about what our major can be and do. For example, our major excels as a double major. We strongly encourage students to double major, and we have found both majors are enriched by such an arrangement. Rather than weaken our major, adding a second major has revealed two key benefits. First, what we do is not being done by another department. It may seem surprising that we have numerous writing and rhetoric and English double majors, but, while some may see this as problematic, these students are clear in their feedback that each of these majors does very different things—and they enthusiastically articulate each of those differences. Second, our major, and writing in general, proves vital to the work students complete in other majors and in future careers. While those versed in writing across the curriculum (WAC) would not be surprised by such a finding, many of our students are. They find themselves applying concepts and practice learned in our classes to their studies in computer science, fashion design, or anthropology. In turn, those departments learn more about us and what we do, and new collegial relations are born.

CONCLUSION

As one of the only writing and rhetoric majors in the New England region, along with our position in a small state, we are committed to increasing our connections with and within the state of Rhode Island. Whether through internships, community-based courses, or public writing opportunities, our students and our major reflect and have an impact on writing in Rhode Island. We continue to strengthen our allegiance to the land and sea grant mission, paying particular attention to how our major situates us and our students in the Ocean State. We remain in touch with many of our alumni, now finding themselves in graduate school, government agencies, and private corporations. Some of these alumni may play an active role in our major's future as we look to the development of an advisory board. Conceivably, we could then implement trends or feedback in our curriculum through course offerings, future hires, or tracks within the major.

As we look forward, we will be guided by a promise we made to ourselves: to learn from our students as they help us expand our notions of what writing is, what writing can be, and what writing can do. It turns out that doing this is much more difficult than we had thought. For example, we have not yet developed a good way to listen to our students; it appears that, as a group, we don't actually know how to do this very well. To be sure, there are a myriad of ways to gather this information: anecdotal evidence, gut sense, data collection of student learning outcomes, focus groups, exit interviews and surveys, and in-class feedback. But we haven't yet figured it out. However, we will continue to move among the spaces created by our ability to dream, our appreciation for the strengths and gifts of each member of the faculty, our understanding of the constraints that face us, and our abiding respect for the challenges of the learning in which we have asked our students to engage.

Curricular Summary: The Writing and Rhetoric Major at the University of Rhode Island

The major at the University of Rhode Island is designed for undergraduate students who seek to expand their repertoire of writing for various public and private audiences. Graduates will have a strong foundation in rhetorical theory, balanced with a wide range of situational practices common to professional writers. Coursework is balanced between in-class learning and experiential fieldwork in real-world settings. All graduates design their own digital electronic portfolios prior to graduation, demonstrating their ability to work with a range of technologies to produce and distribute their polished writing.

Writing and rhetoric majors must complete thirty credits (maximum fifty-one), including core courses. At least fifteen credits of the major must be completed from writing courses numbered 300 or above. Writing and rhetoric majors are strongly encouraged to complete a practicum experience, such as an internship (WRT 484) or field experience course (WRT 383 or 385). A maximum of three credits for each of these experiential courses may count toward the major, unless the project substantially changes.

MAJOR REQUIREMENTS (30 CREDIT HOURS)

Core courses:

- WRT 201: Writing Argumentative and Persuasive Texts
- WRT 235: Writing in Electronic Environments
- WRT 360: Composing Processes and Canons of Rhetoric
- WRT 490: Writing and Rhetoric
- WRT 495: Capstone: Electronic Portfolios

Electives:

- WRT 227: Business Communications
- WRT 240: The Essay
- WRT 270: Writing in the Expressivist Tradition
- WRT 302: Writing Culture
- WRT 303: Public Writing
- WRT 304: Writing for Community Service
- WRT 305: Travel Writing
- WRT 306: Writing Health and Disability
- WRT 313: Introduction to Video Games: Users and Contexts
- WRT 333: Scientific and Technical Writing
- WRT 353: Issues and Methods in Writing Consultancy
- WRT 385: Field Experience with Writing Rhode Island
- WRT 391: Independent Study in Writing and Rhetoric
- WRT 415: Perspectives on Reporting
- WRT 435: The Teaching of Composition
- WRT 442: Strategic Media Communication
- WRT 484: Internship in Writing and Rhetoric
- WRT 512: Studies in Rhetorical Theory

References

Council of Writing Program Administrators. 2014. Guidelines For Self-Study To Precede WPA Visit. 1st ed. *WPA: Writing Program Administration.* Accessed online Nov. 4, 2014.

"WPA Outcomes Statement for First-Year Composition." Council of Writing Program Administrators. Accessed online July 17, 2014.

4

REFORMING AND TRANSFORMING WRITING IN THE LIBERAL ARTS CONTEXT
The Writing Department at Loyola University Maryland

Peggy O'Neill and Barbara Mallonee

INTRODUCTION

The Department of Writing at Loyola University Maryland is a vibrant, full-fledged academic unit that offers two major programs of study and a minor, administers the university writing center, and supports a host of co-curricular activities, including a writing academic honor society, three literary magazines, and a student writing workshop. The vertical curriculum spans rhetoric, composition, professional writing, and creative writing and includes courses that support university-wide initiatives, such as service learning, diversity, honors, interdisciplinary minors, and special first-year programs. Faculty members regularly contribute to both the university community and their scholarly communities.

The current state of the department is rooted, in part, in its original separation from English, its approach to writing across the curriculum at Loyola, its later metamorphosis into a communication department, and its eventual separation from communication. Early on, the department cast a wide net, taking responsibility for creative writing, for professional writing, for rhetoric, and for shaping Loyola's distinctive approach to writing in the disciplines. As a result, our department and programs are distinct from most of those described in various literature (e.g., Estrem et al. 2007; Giberson and Moriarty 2010; McLeod and Balzhiser 2010; O'Neill, Crow, and Burton 2002). This difference stems from many factors, including the position of first-year writing in relation to both the writing major and the university's core curriculum, as well as the breadth of courses offered. To convey the distinction, we provide a description

DOI: 10.7330/9780874219722.c004

Department Name:	Writing
Institution Type:	Private, Jesuit, Catholic, Master's L University (awards at least 200 Master's degrees/year)
Institution Size:	6,000 students
Residential or Commuter:	Residential
Student Body Description:	The majority of undergraduate students identify as white, with less than 20% identifying with another ethnic group; most are not first-generation college students; only 18% come from Maryland, with the majority of students coming from the Mid-Atlantic and Northeast; about 60% of students participate in study abroad programs; about 84% of students graduate in six or less years
Year Major Began:	Interdisciplinary Writing (IW): 1983 Writing (W): 2006
Official Name of Degree:	Bachelor of Arts in Interdisciplinary Writing and Bachelor of Arts in Writing
Number of Majors:	In year one: 26 (IW), 2 (W) In year five: 37 (IW), 52 (W) In year three: 26 (IW), 47 (W) Current: 27 (IW), 47 (W)
Number of Full-Time Writing Faculty:	15

of our current academic programs, including our learning goals and course offerings. We offer a brief overview of the department's history. We conclude with a look at some of the transformations and issues that are currently under discussion.

PROGRAM OVERVIEW AND RATIONALE

In the Department of Writing, we focus on writing, broadly defined, from a liberal arts perspective. We aim to help students develop as writers who can, for the rest of their lives, create successful texts across a variety of contexts. The notion of a standalone writing department offering its own major is derived from the reconceptualizing of the traditional FYC course. Situated among all the other departmental introductory courses in the humanities, WR 100: Effective Writing serves both as a core course and as the foundation course for writing majors and minors. Conceiving the FYC course in this way locates it in the liberal arts tradition, not as a service or remedial course centered on academic writing. This approach was further underlined in the 1980s, when Loyola embraced writing across the curriculum (WAC). The prevailing notion was that ultimately departments are responsible for the writing of their majors and the FYC experience is just a beginning step for novice writers in many fields.

While the link of writing to the liberal arts tradition has always been clear to writing faculty, it was also confirmed by the institution through the Core Review Committee (2005), who reaffirmed the 1992 Core Curriculum Statement of Purpose: "Both long tradition and the needs of contemporary life mandate the ability to communicate effectively and elegantly as a primary goal of liberal education. Therefore, writing plays a central role in the core curriculum" (2). Loyola positions writing as more than an academic performance; rather it is a means of thinking, communicating, and entering into what Kenneth Burke (1973) describes as a "parlor" filled with others who "are engaged in a heated discussion" that "is interminable" (110).

The FYC course, Effective Writing, aims to teach students how to approach writing tasks from a rhetorical perspective, not a generic academic writing perspective, as explained in the introductory comments to the course learning aims:

> Writing is a complex activity that requires ongoing practice and guidance. It is a meaning-making activity used to make sense of the world around us and to communicate to others. It is closely connected to reading and critical thinking. Writing strategies, expectations, and criteria are context dependent; effective writing depends on the writer's ability to understand and address audience, purpose, and topic. WR100, therefore, focuses on higher order activities, not remedial or basic skills. The goal is to teach students to approach writing as a rhetorical activity, not as a set of rules or conventions. In achieving this goal, the course attends to writing as both process and product within a community of writers. (Writing Department 2011)

Our specific learning aims—drawing on the WPA Outcomes Statement (Council of Writing Program Administrators 2014), as well as our course description and self-study—delineate specific goals for the course:

> Over the course of the semester, students in Effective Writing will:
>
> - Use writing and reading for inquiry, learning, critical thinking, and communicating
> - Explore how genre shapes reading and writing as they write different types of contemporary American essays
> - Analyze and respond to different rhetorical situations by adopting appropriate voice, tone, and level of formality
> - Formulate an original thesis, focus, or controlling idea and support it by using a variety of strategies, including analyzing and the integration of ideas and information gathered through research
> - Use flexible strategies for generating ideas, drafting, revising, editing, and proofreading
> - Critique their own and others' work (balancing the advantages of working with others with the responsibility of doing their part)

- Develop an effective writing process that encourages later invention and rethinking to revise their work
- Use multiple drafts to create and complete an effective text, and
- Generate texts that conform to conventions of edited American English.

These writing major outcomes represent an attempt to self-consciously build on the Effective Writing course and Loyola's Jesuit liberal arts tradition. The curriculum, as we say on the department website, "frames the spectrum of writing from literary to professional with the aim to help students understand the demands of each genre as a rhetorical act (a form of communication)." We explain that writing is intimately connected to thinking and conclude, "Through the systematic study of the writer's art and craft, you will develop particular habits of mind, practices, and civic responsibilities that will serve you well no matter what field of study you pursue or what professional goals you seek." (Writing Department, Loyola University Maryland 2014)

Majors and minors take introductory courses in both creative writing and rhetoric, and are then able to choose advanced courses that span a wide range of genres, contexts, and themes. All seniors take a seminar course that focuses on contemporary writing and writers. Below are the current requirements for each of our academic programs:

Writing major

For the writing major, students take a total of fourteen writing courses, starting with the core composition course, WR 100: Effective Writing (or the equivalent WR 101 or HN 200), and ending with WR 400: Senior Seminar.

REQUIRED COURSES

(Three 200-level courses):
- WR 200: Art of Nonfiction (or its equivalent WR 201)
- WR 220: Art of Rhetoric (or its equivalent WR 221)
- WR 230: Art of Poetry and Fiction (or its equivalent WR 231)

FLEXIBLE CHOICES

(Nine 300- or 400-level courses): The department recommends at least three courses be taken in a particular genre or area of interest: nonfiction, fiction, poetry, professional writing, or rhetoric.

SENIOR SEMINAR
- WR 400: Senior Seminar: New Writers

Interdisciplinary writing major

In the interdisciplinary writing major, students take a total of nine writing courses, the first of which is our core course, WR 100: Effective Writing (or its equivalent). Students also take seven to nine courses in another major (the particular courses and number are determined by the other department), which means they will spend an equal amount of time in two disciplines: writing and another subject.

REQUIRED WRITING COURSES
(Three 200-level courses):
- WR 200: Art of Nonfiction (or its equivalent WR 201)
- WR 220: Art of Rhetoric (or its equivalent WR 221)
- WR 230: Art of Poetry and Fiction (or its equivalent WR 231)

FLEXIBLE CHOICES
(Four 300- or 400-level writing choices): The department recommends at least three courses be taken in a particular genre or area of interest: nonfiction, fiction, poetry, professional writing, or rhetoric.

SENIOR SEMINAR
- WR 400: Senior Seminar: New Writers

Writing minor

For the writing minor, students take a total of eight writing courses, including WR 100: Effective Writing (or its equivalent).

Required course
- WR 200: Art of Nonfiction (or its equivalent WR 201)

Flexible courses
- Five additional WR courses

Senior seminar
- WR 400: Senior Seminar: New Writers

The Loyola writing curriculum is an unusually rich offering of courses designed to turn novice writers into mature and versatile contemporary writers. When the writing major was first conceived, there were no templates in place for writing majors like there were for English and other more traditional majors. We set out to determine what combination of skills, craft, and content our upper-level courses would teach and to assemble them into a sequence for majors and minors. Looking at the FYC course as the introductory course to the discipline of writing, we developed advanced courses in rhetoric, such as Art of the Argument,

Audience and a Writer's Voice (no longer offered), and Style. Today, we have a broader array of courses, including Art of Rhetoric, Gendered Rhetoric, Rhetoric of Professional Writing, Speech Writing, and a more recent addition, Special Topics in Rhetoric and Civic Literacy.

For creative writing, we began with three tiers, from introductory creative writing to the advanced level. However, we opened up the traditional curriculum to the study of additional genres and topics such as the essay, biography and autobiography, nature writing, social and political writing, and literary reviewing. We added special topics courses, such as WR 350: Art of Prose, in which students study the life of a noted writer (e.g., E.B. White, John McPhee, and most recently Rachel Carson), reading a wide representation of the writer's texts and working in the same genres. Our current list of writing courses includes these same courses as well as Travel Writing (offered online), Writing about Science, Screen Writing, and Writing about Music and Culture. Many of these advanced nonfiction courses blend together creative writing, rhetoric, and literary journalism. We have also added Writing for the Web and revised the literary publishing course, which originally focused exclusively on literary journals and small presses, to include the digital revolution in publishing. Students can also choose to participate in a writing internship for credit, and, in spring semester of their senior year, all majors and minors take WR 400: Senior Seminar: New Writers. This course emphasizes reading as a writer with a focus on contemporary American writing across genres.

IMPLEMENTATION NARRATIVE

The forty-year history of our writing department helps in understanding our current curriculum and staffing. As with most writing departments, its development was serendipitous, dependent upon particular contexts, characters, and circumstances. The writing department's growth reflects—and has been influenced by—Loyola's own commitment to both its core values and continued transformation.

Loyola was founded in 1852 as an all-male Catholic college educating undergraduate commuter students, largely from Baltimore's Catholic community. By 2009, Loyola College had become Loyola University Maryland, a co-ed comprehensive Catholic university located just north of downtown Baltimore, with four additional sites in the metro area that are primarily associated with graduate programs and clinical fieldwork. Although Loyola evolved and adapted to changing circumstances, it has remained committed to its Jesuit Catholic tradition. The writing department, too, has remained committed to its core, while still adapting as needed to stay vibrant and viable in the twenty-first century.

As in many institutions, the writing curriculum started with an exclusive focus on the FYC course. Over the last four decades, it has transformed into its current manifestation. This transformation has passed through several distinct phases, each one leading to our current program.

In 1972, Loyola moved the responsibility for composition to a new communication arts department (housed separately from English in its own building). Within one year, Effective Writing, while at first no-credit but required, became a credit-bearing course required of all students focusing on language and inquiry. Effective Writing also served as an introductory course for communication arts majors and poets and fiction writers enrolled in a new creative writing workshop.

By 1977, communication arts disappeared, and the writing program was developed as part of an English/fine arts major. In that same year, two writing faculty secured a grant from the National Endowment for the Humanities (NEH) that brought Effective Writing, focused on essays, and the introductory creative writing course, focused on poetry and fiction, together as a two-course sequence, entitled Empirical Rhetoric. This experimental linking of composition and creative writing became the foundation for the vertical curriculum.

In 1981, Loyola won an NEH grant for a WAC project organized by the writing program. The grant-funded WAC initiative put the Effective Writing course at the center of institution-wide writing. Across a span of six years, FYC instructors partnered with faculty from fourteen different Loyola departments to team-teach semester-long courses. With the remaining departments, writing faculty consulted one-on-one with a faculty member for a semester. The FYC course laid the groundwork for the teaching of writing in the disciplines, whose faculty were trained (through workshops, lectures, the preparation of scholarly articles, and travel to national conferences, as well as the one-on-one semester-long collaborations) to take up the responsibility of preparing majors to write with distinction in their respective fields. Faculty members involved in the WAC program garnered national recognition for their work and for WAC (e.g., Fulwiler and Young 1990; Mallonee and Breihan 1985; McCarthy 1987; Walvoord 1982; Walvoord and McCarthy 1990).

The two NEH grants, both of which emphasized Effective Writing as a critical component of students' development as college writers, set the stage for growth in other areas of the writing program. Upper-level courses in creative writing and rhetoric were developed and enrollments increased. By 1983, enough courses had been created to constitute a full writing curriculum, separate from the English department's, and the institution approved the writing department's first major program, the Interdisciplinary Writing Major, with half of the courses in writing and half in another discipline. Media, a new emphasis in the writing curriculum, was also growing, with courses that included journalism, advertising, and public relations.

In 1986, the institution approved a communications major and the name of the department was broadened to reflect the wide range of writing addressed by our curriculum—the Department of Writing and Media. With the expansion of media courses, the department experienced rapid growth: thirty to forty writing majors graduated each year and about sixty graduated in media concentrations of journalism, advertising, and public relations. By 1992, the department added several media and writing faculty, including both tenured and full-time, non-tenured positions.

The rapid growth created problems, some rooted in the department and some in the institution and upper administration, which jeopardized the future of the department and the writing program. By the fall of 1998, four senior writing faculty members proposed that the Department of Writing and Media be divided into two departments. Over the next seven years, much of the energy of the department was absorbed by personal and professional conflicts. Modifications were made to try and resolve the conflicts, including conducting a self-study and changing the name to the Department of Communication with the same two majors, the interdisciplinary writing major and the communications major, now with concentrations in writing, journalism, advertising/public relations, and digital media (television and radio production). With the tremendous growth in the number of majors and the development of new areas of study in communication, tension among senior members remained high, predicated mostly (although not exclusively) on questions of faculty autonomy, governance, and curricular development. With the popularity of the communication major, which allowed students to specialize in writing while still taking many communication courses, as well as a push to expand the communication curricular and co-curricular offerings, writing was in danger of being overshadowed in the communication department. A key indicator was Effective Writing. Traditionally, all faculty, both tenured and tenure-track as well as adjunct, taught the FYC course. Untrained to teach writing, communication faculty almost exclusively taught courses for majors in their specialty. Without Effective Writing at its center, the department no longer had a shared sense of its foundation and mission. The dean eventually hired a consultant to work on conflict resolution and communication with senior faculty. Tensions among faculty, however, remained high.

In December 2004, the dean split the Department of Communication into two autonomous departments—writing and communication—splitting the personnel, the curriculum, and the resources with limited input from faculty. While a complete surprise to faculty, it was generally considered welcome news. Writing once again became a distinct, standalone department, in command of its own curriculum, hiring, and resources.

Since the split, the writing department has developed a full writing major, continued the interdisciplinary writing major, conducted a program review, developed learning aims for the major, hired a new chair through a nationwide search, and created a five-year strategic plan (Writing Department Loyola University Maryland 2011b). While writing gained independence and visibility in the division, it lost journalism (which was primarily a writing-based program) and technology—all of the computer classrooms and technology-related courses. The curriculum now ranges from traditional creative writing to a variety of nonfiction courses, including rhetoric and professional writing. All tenure-track faculty members teach the core writing course, Effective Writing, as well as upper level courses in their areas of specialty.

REFLECTION AND PROSPECTION

From the very beginning, our department was built upon our FYC course. It still is. Recently, the writing faculty revised the course description for Effective Writing to respond to the changing needs of Loyola students and the changing context in which the course is offered. Other course descriptions, too, are periodically revisited. Faculty are currently considering whether seniors should have a new course (or a redesigned senior seminar) that culminates in either a significant piece of their own writing or a portfolio—this discussion is typical of the level of serious reflection that the department has carried on since it first imagined a full vertical writing curriculum. Likewise, course offerings undergo steady review, with new courses added and others dropped as we refine our goals and respond to change. We are, for instance, currently expanding our professional writing program and fighting for more technological support to enhance the multimedia offerings. In order to effectively analyze our curriculum, we are developing methods for systematically gathering information as we work to balance our liberal arts tradition with the need to remain relevant in the twenty-first century.

We have also developed a rich co-curricular agenda, including two student-run literary magazines and a writing honor society, *Pi Epsilon Pi*, which we founded. We typically host several social events throughout the year, many of which feature student work. For thirty years we have administered a distinguished reading series, Modern Masters, funded by the university's Center for the Humanities, which brings both established and new writers to campus.

With the robust curriculum and co-curriculum, the number of writing majors and minors has continued to grow since the department split from communication. According to the university's 2010 Fact Book (Loyola University Maryland Office of Institutional Research 2010), 100 students were writing majors—62 full writing majors and 38 interdisciplinary majors—which is almost 3% of the undergraduate population (first-year students, however, do not formally declare majors). Although minors aren't included in the fact book, we typically have 35–40 students who have declared a minor in writing. These numbers make us one of the strongest majors in the humanities, on par with English and history and outpacing others, such as philosophy, art history, and modern languages. We also continue to attract excellent students—the 2011 graduating class of writing majors included four Phi Beta Kappa honorees, according to the department's Annual Report (Writing Department, Loyola University Maryland 2011a), and many graduates are pursuing advanced degrees in areas such as writing, English, law, and theology, continuing the success of former writing alumni.

Beyond our own curriculum, the writing department now supports WAC through the writing center and smaller outreach programs. Formal departmental outreach to faculty in various disciplines has been limited by staffing and budget constraints. For the institution, competing initiatives—such as service learning, Ignation pedagogy seminars, and first-year programs—have succeeded WAC in terms of attention and resources. Though WAC now flies under the radar, the university's approach is still guided by the theories and assumptions that first made writing vibrant and visible in the 1980s. Core courses emphasize writing in their disciplines, and departments prepare majors to be better writers in their fields. Writing is also found diffused across the campus in various programs—for example, in a university-wide, first-year seminar program that includes writing as one of its four key habits of mind.

The refusal to be a service department has given us time to focus on our own writing curriculum, positioning us to be like, rather than unlike, all other academic departments at Loyola. Like them, we participate in many other campus-wide initiatives, such as service learning, first-year seminars, and diversity courses, and department members still serve the university by participating in committees, task forces, and special projects.

The department continues to grow. Changes in hiring practices at the university level now emphasize more tenure-track faculty, while mandating that full-time instructors cannot be renewed for more than six years. Junior faculty members have been hired with specialties in environmental writing and professional and technical writing. A new writing center director also specializes in nineteenth-century women's rhetoric. We are in the process of hiring a full-time, tenure-track creative writing instructor to teach fiction and screenwriting. And finally, plans are in the works for hiring additional tenure-track faculty to support our commitment to a new university-wide, first-year living and learning initiative.

CONCLUSION

Thirty years after its conception, the writing department at Loyola now offers a *template*, not a *timeline*, for creating a writing department positioned for success within the framework of a twenty-first century American university. There are many reasons why writing, as both a department and an academic discipline, has flourished at Loyola. From the start, we were eager to look beyond our particular institution and at the broader landscape of undergraduate education rooted in the humanities, as well as at the history of Jesuit education. We were poised to support bold campus-wide initiatives at Loyola, for which we sought significant outside grants. We willingly partnered with a variety of departments both at the professional level—i.e., WAC and the writing center—and at the curricular level with our interdisciplinary writing major and participation in interdisciplinary minors.

Over the decades, we have discovered how to navigate the institution. We have steadily advocated for a department organization and budget consonant with our disciplinary roots, and we have worked to develop a clear mission statement and strategic plan. Though we have had our share of the infighting that all too often characterizes academia, we strive to place our commitment and efforts on the fields the faculty represent—whether creative writing, professional writing, or rhetoric and composition—and the goals of the department rather than on the desires of individuals. Maintaining these priorities has not always been easy, and we have sometimes floundered, but a healthy, vibrant department creates an atmosphere that allows individual members to flourish. Since the separation from communication, we have been better able to achieve a shared set of goals that value individual contributions without derailing the department. We value teaching, and have many exemplary teachers. We meet a high standard for scholarship, and are each active in our fields. We have offered an expanding institution leadership and steady service within an ever-evolving governance structure.

The early separation from the English department has sharpened our focus on writing and reduced opportunities for squabbling over the timeworn conflicts between literature and composition, rhetoric, or creative writing. We recognize that we share values and interests with our colleagues in English, and we comfortably co-exist with them. We know that the study of literature is important for all writers, and one of our most popular interdisciplinary writing majors has been the writing/ English split. We also have productive relationships with many other departments, such as those in education and business.

Because our department represents only writing, we can shape a compelling vision for majors and minors that is familiar at a national level and draws on the rich history of our many sub-disciplines. Three decades of control over our curriculum and personnel decisions have given us a deep understanding of our obligation to produce students who will be noted for their ability to write. We have a voice in college and university discussions. Our autonomous standing as a department positions us to further reform and transform our structures, curriculum, and standards as we move through the century that lies ahead.

Acknowledgments

We would like to acknowledge all of our colleagues in writing, both past and present, who have contributed to the development of the teaching and study of writing at Loyola. Of special note are Philip McCafferty, Xavier Trainor, and Barbara Walvoord, all who provided leadership and vision early on in our journey.

Curricular Summary: The Writing Major and the Interdisciplinary Writing Major at Loyola University Maryland

Students interested in writing can pursue either a writing major or an interdisciplinary writing major, which allows students to divide their time evenly between writing and another discipline. There is great flexibility in the program in order to allow students to meet their goals as well as the department's learning aims. Those who choose either major will enter into a community that develops expertise in a broad array of skills and genres. Furthermore, the writing department affords students many opportunities for internships, co-curricular activities, and pre-professional development. See the Writing Department section of the Loyola Undergraduate Catalog (Loyola University Maryland 2011) for detailed information about the curriculum.

MAJOR REQUIREMENTS (39 CREDIT HOURS)

The Writing Major

The writing major requires that students take a total of thirteen writing courses beyond WR 100: Effective Writing (the core curriculum writing requirement).

Core courses:

WR 200: Art of Nonfiction (or its equivalent WR 201)

WR 220: Art of Rhetoric (or its equivalent WR 221)

WR 230: Art of Poetry and Fiction (or its equivalent WR 231)

Elective courses (nine 300- or 400-level WR courses):

The department recommends that at least three courses be taken in a particular genre or area of interest: nonfiction, fiction, poetry, professional writing, or rhetoric.

Senior seminar:

WR 400: Senior Seminar: New Writers

The Interdisciplinary Writing Major

In the interdisciplinary writing major, students take a total of eight writing courses beyond WR 100: Effective Writing (the core curriculum writing requirement). Students also take seven to nine courses in another major (each department specifies the courses required). Interdisciplinary writing majors will spend an equal amount of time in two disciplines: writing and another subject.

Required courses:

- WR 200: Art of Nonfiction (or its equivalent WR 201)
- WR 220: Art of Rhetoric (or its equivalent WR 221)
- WR 230: Art of Poetry and Fiction (or its equivalent WR 231)
- WR 400: Senior Seminar

Elective courses (9 total):

- WR 301: Writing about Science
- WR 302: Wet Ink: Writing and Editing for Publication
- WR 303: History of Genre
- WR 305: Writing for the Web
- WR 311: Style
- WR 320: Art of the Argument
- WR 322: Gendered Rhetoric
- WR 323: Writing Center Practice and Theory
- WR 324: Speech Writing and Delivery
- WR 325: Rhetoric of Professional Writing
- WR 327: Civic Literacy
- WR 333: Writing Fiction
- WR 334: Forms of Fiction
- WR 335: Advanced Fiction: The Short Story
- WR 336: Advanced Fiction: The Novel
- WR 340: Writing Poetry
- WR 341: Poetic Forms
- WR 342: Advanced Poetry
- WR 343: Writing for the Stage
- WR 344: Fundamentals of Film Studies
- WR 345: Screen Writing for Film and Television
- WR 347: Comics in America: From Sunday Funnies to Graphic Novels
- WR 348: Writing about Music and Culture
- WR 350: Art of Prose: Selected Authors
- WR 351: Art of the Essay: Women Writers
- WR 352: Biography and Autobiography
- WR 353: Contemporary Essay
- WR 354: Writing about the Environment
- WR 355: Travel Writing
- WR 356: Writers in the Catholic Tradition: Selected Authors
- WR 357: Writing about Film
- WR 358: Literary Reviewing
- WR 385: Special Topics in Creative Writing
- WR 386: Special Topics in Rhetoric
- WR 387: Special Topics in Professional Writing
- WR 395: Fiction, Film, and Political Thought of the 1980s
- WR 401: Senior Portfolio
- WR 402: Writing Internship

References

Burke, Kenneth. 1973. *The Philosophy of Literary Form: Studies in Symbolic Action.* 3rd ed. Berkeley: University of California Press.

Core Review Committee, Loyola College in Maryland. 2005. "Interim Report of the Core Review Committee, 2004–2005." Baltimore: Loyola College in Maryland, April, 18.

Council of Writing Program Administrators. 2014. "WPA Outcomes Statement for First-Year Composition." *Council of Writing Program Administrators* 3. Accessed online August 2014.

Estrem, Heidi, Linda Adler-Kassner, Nancy Allen, Phillip K. Arrington, Steve Benninghoff, and Steven D. Krause, eds. 2007. "The Writing Major." Special issue of *Composition Studies* 35 (1).

Fulwiler, Toby, and Art Young, eds. 1990. *Programs that Work: Models and Methods for Writing across the Curriculum.* Portsmouth, NH: Boynton/Cook.

Giberson, Greg A., and Thomas A. Moriarty. 2010. *What We Are Becoming: Developments in Undergraduate Writing Majors.* Logan: Utah State University Press.

Loyola University Maryland. 2011. "Writing." In *Undergraduate Catalogue, 2011–12*, 317–24. Baltimore: Loyola University Maryland.

Loyola University Maryland Office of Institutional Research. 2010. *Loyola University Maryland Fact Book, Fall 2010.* Baltimore: Loyola University Maryland.

Mallonee, Barbara C., and John R. Breihan. 1985. "Responding to Students' Drafts: Interdisciplinary Consensus." *College Composition and Communication* 36 (2): 213–31. http://dx.doi.org/10.2307/357443.

McCarthy, Lucille P. 1987. "A Stranger in Strange Lands: A College Student Writing across the Curriculum." *Research in the Teaching of English* 21: 233–65.

McLeod, Susan H., and Deborah Balzhiser. 2010. "The Undergraduate Writing Major: What Is It? What Should It Be?" *College Composition and Communication* 62: 415–33.

O'Neill, Peggy, Angela Crow, and Larry Burton, eds. 2002. *A Field of Dreams: Independent Writing Programs and the Future of Composition Studies.* Logan: Utah State University Press.

Walvoord, Barbara E. Fassler. 1982. *Helping Students Write Well: A Guide for Teachers in All Disciplines.* New York: MLA.

Walvoord, Barbara E., and Lucille P. McCarthy. 1990. *Thinking and Writing in College: A Naturalistic Study of Students in Four Disciplines.* Urbana: NCTE.

Writing Department. 2011. Loyola University Maryland. Accessed December 30, 2011.

Writing Department Loyola University Maryland. 2011a. *Annual Report.* Baltimore: Writing Department Loyola University Maryland.

Writing Department Loyola University Maryland. 2011b. *Strategic Plan, 2008–2013.* Baltimore: Writing Department, Loyola University Maryland.

5

FIFTEEN YEARS STRONG
The Department of Writing at the
University of Central Arkansas

Carey E. Smitherman, Lisa Mongno, and Scott Payne

INTRODUCTION

The Department of Writing at the University of Central Arkansas (UCA) has been a standalone department or program since 1996. Although it is currently expanding programs in rhetoric and composition, creative writing, and linguistics, the department itself was established through many obstacles and reconfigurations. This profile shares histories and reflections from the founding faculty and administrators, illustrates the growth (and growing pains) the department has experienced since its inception, and looks forward to the plans we have made for the future.

PROGRAM OVERVIEW AND RATIONALE

UCA began considering the role of rhetoric and composition in the English department as early as 1979. During the next two years, the department hired three faculty members to seed interest in rhetoric, composition, and sociolinguistics. According to Dr. Margaret Morgan (2011), the three "rhet/comp" hires felt isolated in the department in the early 1980s. Not only did the other English faculty seem uninterested in composition pedagogy, but the rhet/comp hires began worrying about the evaluation of their activities in tenure and promotion practices. At the time, the English department offered a rhetoric and composition course, but it served as remediation for education majors. Still, Morgan reported, the English faculty valued composition insofar as it recruited majors and raised revenue for the department.

In the mid-1980s, those concerns were brought to upper administration. Led by the provost, a writing initiative began. This push spanned

DOI: 10.7330/9780874219722.c005

Department Name:	Writing
Institution Type:	Public, Master's L (awards at least 200 Master's degrees/year)
Institution Size:	11,700 students
Residential or Commuter:	Commuter
Student Body Description:	Diverse in terms of ethnicity, socio-economics, age, etc.; high percentage of full-time enrollment
Year Major Began:	1999
Official Name of Degree:	Bachelor of Arts in Writing
Number of Majors:	In year one: N/A In year three: 74 In year five: 87 Current: 146
Number of Full-Time R/C Faculty:	12

several attempts at improving the teaching of writing across campus. Without an official structure, however, these attempts ultimately failed, and the administration decided to create an independent writing program, one that would imitate the Schedler Honors College at UCA in its reporting structure.

Across campus, the creation of a writing program was seen as a further development in the forced split of growing departments (such as sociology and geology previously). The provost invited nine faculty members from various disciplines to join an ad hoc "writing program task force" in September of 1995. According to Dr. Francie Bolter (2011), he charged the task force with considering "the organizational structure, curriculum, and staffing needs of a writing program to be established for the purpose of improving the writing of UCA students. . . . In addition to having responsibility for the composition sequence, the program would develop and coordinate the writing/critical thinking across the curriculum effort, and any professional or technical writing courses to be initiated. It might also house courses in creative writing."

By the fall of 1996, the writing program was officially established under the provost. A new faculty member, Dr. Dave Harvey, was hired as director of the program. Although he would be working in the writing program, Dr. Harvey (2011) stated in an interview that he was originally hired as a tenured associate professor in the Department of Speech, Theater, and Mass Communication, a move that would foreshadow the eventual melding of writing and speech. The new program consisted of three tenured transfers from English; one tenure-track transfer from

English; two full-time, non-tenure-track instructors from English; three full-time, non-tenure-track instructors from transitional studies; and two new full-time, non-tenure-track instructor hires.

This combination of faculty made for an interesting structure in an independent writing program. Not only were compositionists part of this group, but also linguists, rhetoricians, creative writers, writing center theorists, and professional writing faculty members. Interestingly, including creative writing in this program was a strategic move on the provost's part. According to Dean Terry Wright (2011), a creative writing faculty member at that time, he realized that for this program to achieve his vision of a successful, independent entity, creative writing must be a key component—multiple genres of writing added strength.

Although English faculty originally continued to teach composition in the new program, there was a political schism and programmatic hostility in the air, even if individual faculty members got along well. In the end, disputes over the teaching of composition helped create the rationale for a new department, and the new department helped create the rationale for a major. As the program began hiring more tenure-track faculty, the "turf wars" became even more pronounced. In order to independently hire and tenure their own faculty, writing became a department in 1997 and voted to be housed in the College of Fine Arts and Communication (CFAC).

Not only did the move to fine arts avoid further conflicts with English faculty, but it also reinforced the concept of the writing department as being product-oriented (as in, the production of discourse). This emphasis on creation rather than analysis created a perfect fit for creative writing to join rhetoric and composition; a linguist joined the department in 1998. In 2000, the program became the Department of Writing and Rhetoric, and, in 2001, speech communication joined writing. Speech, public relations, and writing were housed in the same department until 2007. Although speech joined writing because they both fit under the umbrella of rhetoric, it later became clear that they would be better served as departments that were independent from one another. So, speech formed its own department in 2007 and is currently the Department of Communication.

IMPLEMENTATION NARRATIVE: INTERDEPARTMENTAL GROWTH
Majors and minors

Soon after its inception, the Department of Writing began to construct a writing major. As we considered this major, we wanted to ensure that it reflected the goals, values, and structure of the department itself. We established early on that our department believes in a comprehensive approach to communication studies. We promote students' development, both personally and professionally, through their ability to communicate effectively in a variety of modes and contexts. Our particular makeup of rhetoric and composition, linguistics, and creative writing faculty inspired these values, and we wanted the interdisciplinary trend of our faculty to be reflected in the major.

Since the writing major was established in 2000, the Department of Writing has expanded, offering an MFA in creative writing and three undergraduate majors and four minors. In addition to a brand new minor in professional writing, a major and minor are now available in writing, creative writing, and linguistics (the only linguistics major in the state of Arkansas).

As a part of each major and minor we offer, students have the opportunity to take a variety of elective courses in rhetoric and composition, creative writing (including poetry, fiction, scriptwriting, and nonfiction), professional/technical writing, and linguistics. Thus, students can, to a point, shape their own academic experience and gain an enriched understanding of how these disciplines intersect. In each new program, we continue to promote interdisciplinary activities and strive to support well-rounded and savvy communicators.

Throughout its tenure, the writing major has gone through some refinements (as all programs do). At present, however, we have just completed a significant revision of the major. We felt it was time to more specifically define what the writing major should accomplish, since the growth of the major led to the development of independent degrees in creative writing and linguistics; however, we did not want to lose the interdisciplinary flavor our department offers in the revision process. At present, the requirements of the major comprise thirty-six credit hours—twenty-one hours of core courses and fifteen hours of electives. The core requirements include seven courses. At the 2000 level: Introduction to Creative Writing and Introduction to Linguistics; at the 3000 level: Writing for New Technologies, Technical Writing, and Persuasion; and at the 4000 level: Contemporary Composition and Evolution of Rhetorical Theory. Students are then open to choose from a variety of electives in writing and rhetoric, creative writing, and/or linguistics. These requirements continue our vision for student access to a variety of genres.

Not only have our major and minor options expanded, but the number of students with a major in the Department of Writing has steadily increased as well. In the 2008–2009 academic year, we counted approximately 90 student majors in the department. In the fall of 2011, only three years later, we've seen a substantial rise to 146 majors. We attribute this success to both an increased definition of each of the three majors we offer, as well as a more sophisticated blending of courses in each major.

The students we serve

The writing major serves a variety of students. A number of writing majors are students who enjoy writing and know they wish to pursue a career related to writing in some way, but aren't sure which career would suit them best. The major provides students with the opportunity to build an array of writing skills while also exploring career possibilities. Additionally, the major serves students who are strongly interested in creative writing but wish to build their professional and technical writing skills in order to increase marketability for a variety of careers. Students who are interested in feature writing and some aspects of journalism, but who are not particularly interested in traditional news reporting, find a home in the writing department, where they can pursue some of these other areas of journalism and nonfiction writing without primarily focusing on news reporting. Furthermore, students interested in professional and technical writing can now take advantage of our newly implemented professional writing track (part of the general writing major) and/or our professional writing minor. Finally, because we are situated in the College of Fine Arts and Communication, and because our major is interdisciplinary, it tends to attract students from other areas of the college, particularly those in digital film and art. These students will often double-major or major in one discipline and minor in the other.

The writing major has served as an effective preparation for graduate school. A number of our majors go on to pursue graduate study in creative writing, linguistics, and law. While many teach, others work in the corporate world in technical writing and project management, and another significant portion combine their writing skills with personal passions and lead initiatives in the non-profit sector.

Programs in progress

As much as the Department of Writing has grown, we are continually looking for ways to offer students even more opportunities. Along with our revisions to the writing major, we have two new programs: a professional writing track option in the writing major, and an MFA in creative writing. These programs are an answer to our students' growing interest in both our department and in various types of writing.

The professional writing track situated within the general writing major was established in 2012. In a proposal written by Dr. Joanna Castner Post, she conveys that this track is designed for students interested in the multimodality of writing in contemporary society. The ideologies that influenced the structure of this curriculum include the following:

1. Rhetorical concepts provide a framework for determining a text's design, content, and delivery.

2. While traditional printed text continues to remain useful, digital technology has enlarged and altered the means by which we communicate.

Our vision for this track is to give interested students the opportunity to more specifically focus on movement between theory and practice. We designed the curriculum to include rhetorical theory, multimodal writing situations, and both service-learning and internship opportunities. Students graduating with this degree emphasis will not only bring valuable—and necessary—writing skills to today's workplace, but will also be capable of imagining innovations in communication.

We also offer a creative writing MFA, a writing-intensive studio program that prepares students for careers in both writing pedagogy and publishing and focuses on the study, practice, and teaching of creative writing from a non-English-department-based point of view. Building on the success of our BA in creative writing, this program promotes UCA's dedication to the arts and makes our institution more competitive. Assistantships in teaching creative writing and composition are available for our graduate students, and unique opportunities are now available for students to work for our cutting-edge publications, such as *Toad Suck Review*.

CONNECTIONS TO THE LARGER UNIVERSITY

The Department of Writing has connections with many entities across campus and in the community. Although some of them do not have explicit ties to the writing major, we feel all of these connections help shape the way we teach writing and view each of our three majors.

Connections with other departments and programs in the College of Fine Arts and Communication

Though many of the connections between the writing department and other departments and programs are informal, some of them are quite strong. The writing department shares many students in common with digital film; students often major in one department and minor in the other. To a lesser degree, there is also a fair number of art students who major or minor in writing or creative writing. Being housed in the CFAC and offering courses in scriptwriting, screenwriting, illustrative narrative, and children's writing (where illustration plays a major role), the writing department is in prime position to build connections with other programs in the fine arts. While the students themselves have sought such bridges by taking courses in multiple departments of CFAC, and often choosing a minor in CFAC as well as a major, the writing department has developed some formal arrangements with other CFAC departments in order to take advantage of our connections in fine arts and communication.

The department already has a formal agreement with digital film to allow their majors to take our Forms of Scriptwriting course without having taken Introduction to Creative Writing if they've completed digital film's Script Analysis course. Furthermore, digital film and writing are beginning to more actively search out collaborations that will benefit students in both programs. After the success of *Table at Luigi's*, an independent film produced by its Feature Filmmaking class, digital film is working on a new production, one for which involvement is sought from students in writing, art, and music.

Although there is no formal collaboration already established between the writing and art departments, the writing department sees strong possibilities for collaborating with art, both in its creative writing program (which includes two courses in illustrative narrative and two courses in children's writing) and its professional writing track (which offers multiple courses in digital media). The natural links between graphic design and professional writing are ones we look forward to exploring and developing.

At present, connections with the communications department (speech and public relations) are somewhat limited (after its separation from the writing department, communications took several years to find a long-term chair and begin to carve out its new identity); however, writing and communications do participate together in UCA's Cluster program. One instructor from each department partner each semester to offer a cluster consisting of a first-year writing course and a basic oral communication course. Not only do the courses consist of the same students, but the two instructors regularly interact with one another during the semester, providing shared instruction to the students in the cluster. Now that the communications department has an established chair, opportunities for collaboration are increasing. Most recently, the communications chair began a rhetoric discussion group in which both communications and writing faculty have participated.

Connections to the UCA campus and the community

The writing department actively pursues ways to reach out to the wider UCA campus and local community. In addition to its offerings in general education writing and linguistics, the writing department also works with degree programs in other colleges to assist with meeting student needs. Our entry course in technical communication has a long tradition of serving students in the health sciences and other disciplines. Our writing center, of course, provides support for the teaching of writing in all disciplines and at all levels through tutoring, classroom visitations, and consultation with professors across the curriculum. In addition, the writing center has partnered with the College of Education to assist their students in preparing for Praxis I. Our writing center also actively reaches out to students in our concurrent enrollment writing program. For two years now, high school students in the concurrent enrollment program have consistently taken advantage of our writing center services.

Our engagement with disciplines beyond CFAC is especially evident through our BA in linguistics. This is a highly interdisciplinary major. While the core courses consist of fifteen hours of writing department linguistics courses, the four tracks in the major (language, TESOL, computer science, and general linguistics) all require a number of courses offered in other colleges. The BA in linguistics is a collaborative degree involving four colleges and seven departments (the writing department and six departments outside of CFAC).

There are many advantages to being an independent writing department. One main drawback, however, is that the educational system for training public school teachers has not yet caught up with the growing trend for writing departments to exist independent from English—education departments are not in a position to provide content-area training in the teaching of writing. While we have found no strong solution yet in addressing this need, the writing department is currently making major strides in meeting the needs of existing language arts teachers. The writing department has just approved a plan to participate in the College of Education's MA in advanced studies in teaching leadership (ASTL) by offering a writing emphasis in their program. ASTL students, typically public school teachers, will take fifteen credit hours in education and fifteen credit hours in the writing department, including courses focusing on the pedagogy of composition, creative writing, and linguistics.

To meet the needs of teachers seeking additional training in the language arts, the writing department is also collaborating with the English department by helping support a new language arts track in the MA in English. This track consists of a mix of literature coursers and writing department courses in rhetoric and composition, creative writing, and linguistics.

Finally, while the writing department is already engaged with the community beyond UCA, in the next few years we intend to greatly increase that engagement for the benefit of both our students (providing them with professional and civic development opportunities) and the larger community. While we already have a number of students who serve as interns at local businesses and magazines, who are involved with the local community through a field research course in linguistics, or who are completing service learning for a special topics course, our goal is to eventually have all our students engage with the larger community through either an internship, a fieldwork course, or a service learning course. With the development of the professional writing track, we will be well on our way to achieving this goal.

REFLECTION AND PROSPECTION: HOLISTIC INTERPRETATIONS

In hindsight, it is clear that the writing department at UCA emerged from an interest in improving freshman writing. Administrative notions of writing across the curriculum seeded this development. Standardized test scores were not low, but UCA wanted to take on the mantle as a state leader in undergraduate education and continue the university's growing mission in that regard. As a result, an entire department has blossomed, featuring multiple majors, graduate programs and certificates, and collaborations across campus.

The writing department is the largest academic department on campus, with the most full-time faculty. It shares a beautiful new building with the communications department, even though the two had to split due to size (not philosophical difference). Freshman composition continues to flourish, and two of the full-time MA-level instructors have been finalists for the campus teaching award.

Curricular Summary: The Writing Major at the University of Central Arkansas

Within the writing major, students can choose one of two tracks: 1) general writing and 2) professional writing. The strength of the general writing track is its breadth. Students in this track take thirty-six credit hours in rhetoric, composition, creative writing, linguistics, and professional writing. As a result, students leave the program with a solid interdisciplinary understanding of the field of writing, including its creative, scientific, and professional aspects. The professional writing track is designed to give students theoretical and practical experience in information design. This track provides numerous substantive opportunities to work with community partners in designing and creating written products for print and digital delivery using the latest tools. As a result, students leave with a solid record of experience as writers and designers, evidenced by their important connections in the community and a portfolio of work. Students in the professional writing track take thirty-six hours consisting of core courses, required courses, and major electives.

MAJOR REQUIREMENTS (36 CREDIT HOURS)

Core courses:
  WRTG 2325: Introduction to Rhetoric
  WRTG 3305: Writing for Digital Media I
  WRTG 3310: Technical Writing
  WRTG 3390: Discourse Analysis

General writing track (8 courses total):
  LING 2320: Introduction to Language and Linguistics
  WRTG 2310: Introduction to Creative Writing
  One creative writing forms course
  One upper-division linguistics course
  One upper-division rhetoric or professional writing course
  Three additional courses from an approved list of electives

Professional writing track (8 courses total):
  WRTG 3306: Writing for Digital Media II (required)
  WRTG 4307: Practical Rhetoric (required)
  WRTG 4308: Writing for Change (required)

  Two additional courses from an approved list of electives (required)

  WRTG 3307: Introduction to Editing (elective)
  WRTG 4305: Contemporary Composition (elective)
  WRTG 4306: Writing for Digital Media III (elective)

WRTG 4309: Introduction to Publishing (elective)

WRTG 4320: Rhetoric and Cross-Cultural Communication (elective)

WRTG 4385: Internship in Writing (elective)

References

Bolter, Francie. 2011. Personal interview. Sept 7, 2011.

Harvey, David. 2011. Personal interview. Sept. 5, 2011.

Morgan, Margaret. 2011. Personal interview. Aug. 29, 2011.

Wright, Terry. 2011. Personal interview. May 21, 2011.

Writing Department, Loyola University Maryland. 2014. "Writing Department Curriculum: Learning Aims." Accessed online Nov. 2, 2014. http://www.loyola.edu /academic/writing/curriculum/learning-aims.

6

OAKLAND UNIVERSITY'S MAJOR IN WRITING AND RHETORIC

Lori Ostergaard, Greg Giberson, and Jim Nugent

INTRODUCTION

Oakland University is a doctoral research university (DRU) situated north of Detroit, Michigan. The vast majority of its 19,000 students are commuters, with no more than 2,000 students living on campus. The Department of Writing and Rhetoric (WRT) was founded as an independent department in 2008 and, as of 2013, consists of nine tenure-track faculty; three full-time, job-secured special instructors; and approximately forty-five other contingent faculty. Prior to the founding of the new department, the writing program existed as part of the Department of Rhetoric, Communication, and Journalism (RCJ). Although it took many different forms prior to RCJ and WRT, the writing program at OU has always been separate from the English department.

The major in writing and rhetoric was first offered in the fall of 2008, but it began as a series of program proposals written by senior faculty some ten years prior. Due to a variety of political, rhetorical, and contextual factors, these early proposals were unsuccessful in winning the required approvals from college- and university-level committees. In December 2007, the three newest faculty members in the rhetoric program—Greg Giberson, Lori Ostergaard, and Marshall Kitchens began work anew on the major initiative. Their new proposal was extensive and involved a nearly complete reworking and reconceptualization of the extant proposals, but the end result was received favorably by the university and won approval in relatively short order. Since its first semester, we have been pleasantly surprised—and logistically overwhelmed—by student interest in our program. While the major proposal projected twenty-five students by winter 2012, instead we could claim over sixty, with new students contacting us on a weekly basis to inquire about the major. We are pleased with the success of our program, and we are happy to share the following account of its rationale, genesis, and evolution.

DOI: 10.7330/9780874219722.c006

Department Name:	Writing and Rhetoric
Institution Type:	Public, Doctoral Research University (DRU)
Institution Size:	19,000 students
Residential or Commuter:	Commuter
Student Body Description:	Most students work part-time or full-time; they are diverse in terms of ethnicity, socio-economics, age, etc.; high percentage transfer from a local community college; high percentage are the first in their family to go to college
Year Major Began:	2008
Official Name of Degree:	Bachelor of Arts in Writing and Rhetoric
Number of Majors:	In year one: 15 In year three: 35 In year five: 45 Current: 45
Number of Full-Time R/C Faculty:	9

PROGRAM OVERVIEW AND RATIONALE

The mission of the Department of Writing and Rhetoric is to develop students' abilities to write independently and collaboratively; to become engaged participants in a democracy; and to be critical researchers, readers, and thinkers within academic, community, national, and global environments. Our full-time instructors are predominantly trained in writing and rhetoric and view rhetoric and literacy as academic disciplines that must be studied in the context of broader cultural and public interests. We are committed to offering students opportunities to write and read diverse kinds of texts; therefore, our courses integrate principles of academic inquiry and encourage students to become critical consumers and producers of texts. Because we view writing and rhetoric as forms of action worthy of careful consideration by students, teachers, and citizens, we affirm its ability to create common interests and foster understanding of differences. Our curriculum is ethically and intellectually grounded, requiring that students reflect on the forms and purposes of writing as well as on the ways written communication is shaped to suit particular rhetorical contexts inside and outside the university. In short, our department seeks to create thoughtful, informed, technologically adept writing publics, much as Kathleen Blake Yancey describes in her call for a "new curriculum for the 21st century" (Yancey 2004, 308).

We believe that OU's major in writing and rhetoric prepares its graduates to perform the kinds of collaborative work required for full participation in an increasingly global and technological society, whether they go on to professional writing in business, industry, and non-profits;

production work in new media; or pursue graduate studies in rhetoric and composition. All of our majors study rhetorical theories and gain experience in composing a variety of texts for multiple audiences, media, and contexts. Students individually pursue one of three tracks, which allows them to choose courses that fit with their academic and professional goals: writing for the professions, writing for new media, or writing as a discipline. Students who pursue the professional track take classes on writing within a wide range of professional contexts; those who pursue the new media track take classes that require critical engagement with the production and reception of digital texts; and those who pursue writing as an academic discipline take classes ranging from classical rhetoric to peer tutoring in order to prepare them for graduate study in rhetoric and composition. Unifying these three tracks is part of our program's intellectual and pedagogical commitment to rhetoric.

Our students learn to analyze the processes by which print and digital texts are produced within diverse contexts and communities. They also gain an understanding of the practices, conventions, theories, and ethics of written and visual communication, using that understanding to produce their own texts for multiple audiences and contexts. Central to this understanding is the ability to think critically about emerging forms of literacy and to adapt to the rhetorical demands of new technologies and new media. Consequently, coursework in the major involves immersion in online and digital forms of communication. Required coursework comprises three core courses: WRT 340: Issues in Writing and Rhetoric, WRT 342: History of Rhetorical Studies, and WRT 394: Literacy, Technology, and Civic Engagement. These courses are designed to emphasize the practical, theoretical, historical, and disciplinary place of writing and rhetoric in the university, in business, and in society. Students are also required to complete one of three gateway courses that introduce them to their chosen track: WRT 331: Introduction to Professional Writing, WRT 232: Writing for New Media, or WRT 329: Composition Studies.

During the proposal revision process, Greg, Lori, and Marshall thought as much about the common experiences they wished writing and rhetoric majors to have as they did about the unique experiences they felt should be offered in each of the three tracks. Thus, the core courses were developed to provide students with a solid foundation in disciplinary history, theory, and practice. WRT 342: History of Rhetorical Studies, for example, is described in the undergraduate catalog as an "examination of major Western rhetoricians and their cultural contexts." This course asks students to consider "the classical roots of modern rhetoric and the influences of rhetoric in other disciplines." As an introduction to the study of rhetoric, this course provides a theoretical and historical foundation for understanding contemporary rhetorical theories that are applicable across the major. Because all of our majors will need to deal effectively and critically with evolving technologies, WRT 394: Literacy, Technology, and Civic Engagement engages students in the critical "exploration and application of technology in the discipline of Writing and Rhetoric." The catalog further describes this course as one in which students examine "the uneven shifts from oral to print to digital literacy and how those shifts affect the production of knowledge, social relationships, and opportunities for civic engagement." This course unites our department's dual focus on new media technologies and civic engagement, which helps students to recognize, theorize, and make sense of these elements in all of their other coursework.

Each of the gateway core courses introduce students to their specific track and guarantee some consistency in their understanding of and experiences within that track. WRT 331: Introduction to Professional Writing is grounded in rhetorical theory and prepares students to write effectively in a variety of contexts. It examines the professional identity of professional and technical writers, and it prepares students to consider the social and ethical responsibilities of professional writing in practice. Students pursuing the new media track are introduced to the theories, technologies, and practices of writing for new media in WRT 232: Writing for New Media. Students enrolled in this course explore the rhetorical, ethical, stylistic, and technical principles of creating personal, observational, and ethnographic narratives through digital composition. Finally, students pursuing the writing as a discipline track begin their study with WRT 329: Composition Studies. As described in the course catalog, this course offers "a survey of composition-rhetoric as an academic discipline, including an examination of the history, theory, research, curricula, and practices associated with composition-rhetoric in the university." Our majors who plan to pursue graduate study in the field receive an introduction to both the history of composition and to contemporary programs and curricula through this course. The electives offered for each track occasionally overlap, but students are encouraged to focus their coursework on those classes that most relate to their chosen field of study. A breakdown of the core and elective offerings for each track is provided at the end of this chapter.

After completing their core and elective coursework, our students take part in either a senior thesis project or a semester-long internship that synthesizes the knowledge and skills they have gained in the course of their studies. Each internship is tailored to both the student's track and their career goals. For example, one of our first professional writing majors completed his writing internship at Beaumont Hospitals working on internal and external relations texts and public relations speeches for hospital administrators (he was hired full-time upon completion of his internship). One of our new media students worked as an intern for the writing and rhetoric department by compiling resources, research, and approaches for a special topics course in video game culture that is now taught regularly by the tenured faculty member who mentored the project. And finally, one of our writing as a discipline students completed an internship assisting with the collection of oral histories for the Rochester Oral History Archive, a project that aims to record and archive oral histories from members of the surrounding community.

Our department recognizes the importance of providing our majors with the practical, yet guided, experience of an internship. Nevertheless, OU students work an average of seventeen hours per week, which requires us to consider alternative experiences for our majors who are already working in their chosen fields while pursuing their degrees. Thus, our students who elect not to complete an internship for their capstone experience are required to compose a senior thesis that synthesizes the work they completed in the major or addresses some issue related to their elective work in one of the three tracks. The major curriculum—comprising core courses, gateway courses, track-specific electives, and an internship/thesis—all reflect our program's commitment to the theories and practices of rhetoric and to helping students become critical consumers and producers of texts.

IMPLEMENTATION NARRATIVE

Although it adapted some material from earlier, unsuccessful major proposals, the vision for the major that eventually won approval by the university was the result of countless revisions and reconfigurations on the part of Greg, Lori, and Marshall. The earliest major proposal submitted by our department included only one new course: a course on style. This first proposal also contained no individual tracks that would permit students to tailor the major to their own personal and career goals. On account of its limited curriculum and program structure, this proposal failed to gain approval at even the first college-level committee it encountered. After Greg, Lori, and Marshall reworked the proposal in late 2007, it was met with significantly less resistance from various approving bodies. We believe the revised proposal won approval so quickly for a number of reasons, with the most important being that the authors' vision for the program was based on what would be best for students as opposed to what courses might make faculty most satisfied. As observed by the college dean in an email reflecting on the development of the major, earlier proposal drafts "were flawed by focusing on the faculty and the subject matter rather than the students. . . . Attending to the curriculum outcomes for students is a radical concept in an environment of self-perpetuating teaching schedules where the operative question is 'What do I want to teach?' rather than 'What do the students need to learn?'" (Sudol 2010). By shifting its focus to the intellectual needs and career goals of OU students, the proposal authors created a major whose function and fit within the university curriculum were largely self-evident to their skeptical audience of disciplinary outsiders.

As mentioned above, our major has enjoyed a great deal of student interest—much more, in fact, than originally anticipated during the proposal process. This growth is made all the more remarkable by the fact that we made relatively little effort to promote the program during its earliest years. Many of our students hear about the major in our FYC courses. However, based on our experience advising students who are interested in the program or who are already enrolled, it is safe to say that the vast majority of them have found our major while perusing their options on the OU website or through discussions with their peers and advisors. We have majors who declared before beginning classes as first-year students; we have majors who transferred to OU from other universities solely to enroll in this degree program; we have students that changed majors from disparate fields such as business, physics, and mathematics; and we have majors who migrated to our program from OU's English major.

Our increasing program strength and growing population of students has enabled us to expand the department and undertake curricular revision in more recent years. By the time the major had entered its fifth year in 2012, the department had hired two new specialists in professional writing, hired two new faculty in rhetoric and composition, and had begun a search for a third professional writing specialist. These increases in faculty manpower have allowed us to undertake a number of significant revisions to the curriculum itself. For the first three years of the major, for instance, the advanced FYC course WRT 160: Composition II was one of the three required core courses. As described in the original version of this profile appearing in 2010 in *Composition Forum* (Ostergaard and Giberson, 2010), placing WRT 160 in the core curriculum allowed us to (1) establish a connection between the FYC program and the major program, (2) move away from the strictly service *ethos* of the advanced writing course, and (3) to establish writing in a very visible way as an independent academic entity at our university. This curricular decision also played a role in marketing the major to the student body during our first years, since many students satisfied this requirement before signing on as writing majors.

Although this curricular arrangement served us well intellectually, politically, and materially, by 2011 the department agreed it was time to move WRT 160 out of the core and replace it with WRT 342: History of Rhetorical Studies. When Jim joined the faculty in 2008, one of his first tasks was to develop an advanced course in web design, which serves students in both the professional writing and new media tracks. The department also added a handful of other course electives: WRT 360: Global Rhetorics and WRT 334: Rhetoric and Video Game Culture. The former examines the history of rhetoric in non-Western cultures, while the latter—a popular elective in the new media track—explores the rhetorical and cultural dimensions of electronic gaming. Meanwhile, our previously defunct WRT 380: Persuasive Writing course was retooled and added to the elective curriculum of the professional writing track with the intent to "institutionalize" curricular innovation and become a test bed for new specializations such as grant writing, legal writing, and medical rhetoric.

With each of these new additions to the curriculum, the program has stepped incrementally closer to the mature and vibrant program envisioned by the proposal authors. For instance, WRT 342: History of Rhetorical Studies had been on the writing program's books for many years but was seldom, if ever, offered. Although the proposal authors recognized the value of rhetorical history and wove it throughout their description of the program curriculum, at the time it was not feasible to propose a standalone course on the topic. In addition to requiring a sufficient number of students to support its regular offering, it also required the energies of new faculty to revamp the course for the core curriculum. Similarly, it was not possible at the time of the proposal to suggest and develop the newer electives—let alone offer them—on account of insufficient student and faculty resources. As we discuss in the reflection below, this iterative program building approach may have led to some later compromises.

REFLECTION AND PROSPECTION

There are, of course, a number of things that we wished we knew when we began re-envisioning the major proposal five years ago. The revised major proposal included a plan for six new, upper-level writing courses to complement and strengthen the major: WRT 394: Literacy, Technology, and Civic Engagement; WRT 340: Issues in Writing and Rhetoric Studies; WRT 305: Advanced Writing; WRT 331: Introduction to Professional Writing; WRT 231: Composing Audio Essays; and WRT 233: Digital Storytelling. We believe attaching these new course proposals to the major proposal strengthened our argument to the university by providing curricular context for our more conceptual arguments. Upon reflection, we also suspect that many of these courses may have been approved, at least in part, because of their connection both to one another and to the major proposal. In other words, the individual courses made sense to our college's curriculum committee because they were able to understand those courses within the context of the proposed program and vice versa. Another possibility for the relatively easy passage of these courses is that there may have been a honeymoon period associated with a new major: a period when courses that might garner resistance from other departments can work their way through governance without much objection. For example, objections were raised when Jim proposed his course on web design the year after our major was approved—a course that was suggested in the original proposal as part of the new media track, but not developed as a full course proposal at that time. Submitted individually after the major was established, the course proposal was met with significant resistance from the Department of Art and Art History and the Department of Communication and Journalism. This resistance lasted nearly a year before our college curriculum committee finally settled matters and approved both WRT 232: Writing for New Media and the originally proposed course, under a revised title, WRT 332: Rhetoric of Web Design. While developing and submitting six new courses as a part of the major proposal added a significant amount of work to the process, we believe now that it would have been both beneficial and timesaving in the long run to include as many new course proposals as we believed were necessary during the process, avoiding much of the subsequent wrangling over academic turf as possible.

In retrospect, we also wish we had taken more time during the proposal process to think about program assessment. As with many colleges and universities, ours has made assessment an institutional priority in recent years. Had we considered the assessment portion of the proposal more during the revision process, we would have been more prepared to enact our assessment procedures, and we would have been spared from retracing many of the steps we took during the initial proposal process. Our first formal assessment of the degree began in August 2012, using the procedures we established in our major proposal just four years prior. Although we received valuable feedback from the university senate's assessment committee, which helped us to refine our assessment protocol during the proposal review process, we wish now that we had also met with the Office of Institutional Research and Assessment (ORIA) to confirm the viability of our assessment plans. Over the life of our major program, we have focused our efforts largely on developing new courses and recruiting majors, two time-consuming yet important occupations for any new degree. However, in retrospect, had we met with ORIA during the proposal process, we might have immediately established a department committee charged with guiding us through our first assessment of this new degree.

As discussed earlier, we were unprepared for the amount of student interest we received. Had we been prepared, we might have set up our administrative structures a little differently to account for the added departmental and administrative work that accompanies a fast-growing program. For example, we initially proposed separate independent studies courses for the internship/thesis requirement, allowing students to choose one or the other. But, as the number of majors increased, we realized that administering independent studies courses for a dozen or more theses and internships every semester placed an undue burden on our already overworked faculty. So, in the second year of our new major, we found ourselves revising our requirements to include a single capstone course that would meet regularly for all students pursuing the thesis or internship option. This change allowed a single faculty member to mentor each new group of students through their capstone experience as a part of their regular course load, thus easing the burden of advising these projects as independent studies courses, for which there is no immediate or long-term compensation.

Perhaps the final lesson we learned from this process is a lesson that is only now taking shape: when developing and implementing a writing major, it's important to remain flexible and open to incremental change. The more we work with our majors, the more we learn about what they need. And the more we learn about writing majors throughout the country, the more critically we evaluate our own curriculum. We have already begun to discuss further changes to the core curriculum. For example, we now wonder if a required research methods course might benefit our students. We are also thinking about adding electives in editing and technical writing, as well as additional 300-level courses in new media.

Developing a new BA program has provided our faculty with the opportunity to rethink every aspect of our department's work, from the ways we conceptualize FYC to the ways we interact with, support, and professionalize our faculty. Working with our students has, in many ways, helped us refigure how we work together and the result has united our department's mission, goals, and values. Looking back, it's clear to us that effective program building requires several things:

- a keen sense of what is possible within individual institutional contexts,
- a willingness to accept that which is not possible at the current moment within such contexts,
- an appreciation for the processes of incremental improvement that refine the program over time,
- a community of kind and capable colleagues, and
- a lot of work.

CONCLUSION

Given the ongoing student interest in our major and faculty support from our college, we anticipate continued, but slowing, growth in future years. We are already seeing signs of external recognition for our program: our majors have been highlighted for their work in the community, our students have delivered two full panel presentations at the College Conference on Composition and Communication (CCCC), and several of our graduates have been enthusiastically recruited into top graduate programs in rhetoric and composition. However, in order to maintain our program's visibility, reputation, and relevance in future years, we must continue our efforts to assess and meet student needs. As a program and a department, we have to remain open to incremental change, and we must continually reevaluate our courses, our curriculum, and our goals if we are going to do what is best for our students.

Curricular Summary: The Writing and Rhetoric Major at Oakland University

Students majoring in writing and rhetoric will learn to analyze the processes by which print, digital, and cultural texts are produced in diverse contexts and communities. Through a group of three required courses, students gain an understanding of the practices, conventions, theories, and ethics of textual development and dissemination, using that understanding to produce their own texts.

Writing majors also choose sixteen credits in one of three tracks: writing for the professions, writing for new media, or writing as a discipline. Students take an additional eight credits in elective courses and must complete a four-credit capstone project that consists of either an internship or a research project.

MAJOR REQUIREMENTS (40 CREDIT HOURS)

Core courses:
- WRT 340: Issues in Writing and Rhetoric (gateway)
- WRT 342: History of Rhetorical Studies
- WRT 394: Literacy, Technology, and Civic Engagement

Capstone (final requirement):
- WRT 491: Capstone: Internship or Thesis

Writing for the professions track (4 courses):
- WRT 331: Introduction to Professional Writing (required)
- WRT 335: Writing for Human Resource Professionals
- WRT 350: Community Service Writing
- WRT 380: Persuasive Writing
- WRT 381: Science Writing
- WRT 382: Business Writing
- WRT 386: Creative Nonfiction

Writing for new media track (4 courses):
- WRT 232: Writing for New Media (required)
- WRT 231: Composing Audio Essays
- WRT 233: Digital Storytelling
- WRT 330: Digital Culture
- WRT 332: Rhetoric of Web Design
- WRT 334: Rhetoric and Video Game Culture
- WRT 370: Special Topics

Writing as a discipline track (4 courses):
- WRT 329: Composition Studies (required)
- WRT 305: Advanced Writing
- WRT 320: Peer Tutoring
- WRT 360: Global Rhetorics
- WRT 364: Writing about Culture
- WRT 414: Teaching Writing
- WRT 497: Apprentice College Teaching

References

Ostergaard, Lori A., and Greg A. Giberson. 2010. "Unifying Program Goals: Developing and Implementing a Writing and Rhetoric Major at Oakland University." *Composition Forum* 22. http://compositionforum.com/issue/22/oakland.php.

Sudol, Ron. 2010. "Message to Greg Giberson and Lori Ostergaard." July 9.

Yancey, Kathleen Blake. 2004. "Made Not Only in Words: Composition in a New Key." *College Composition and Communication* 56 (2): 297–328. http://dx.doi.org/10.2307/4140651.

7

EMBRACING THE HUMANITIES
Expanding a Technical Communication Program at the University of Wisconsin–Stout

Matthew Livesey and Julie Watts

INTRODUCTION

In 2000, the bachelor of science in technical communication became the University of Wisconsin–Stout's first (and only) undergraduate writing major in its 100+ year history. UW–Stout is a comprehensive, career-focused polytechnic university located in Menomonie, Wisconsin, with a current undergraduate enrollment of over 8,000 students. Only three years after it was initiated, our technical communication program, which then enrolled eighty-five students, was the eighth largest out of over 100 programs of its kind in the country (Rainey, Dayton, and Turner 2005). However, enrollment in our program suffered a steady decline to fifty-six students in 2005, where enrollment numbers have remained, each semester's graduates being replaced with just enough new students to maintain that level. Although every other program Rainey, Dayton, and Turner listed experienced a similar drop in enrollment during this period—according to an informal 2008 email survey conducted by Matthew Livesey—our program came under unique administrative scrutiny. Because UW–Stout offers only forty undergraduate majors, programs routinely tally students in the hundreds. While technical communication programs across the United States frequently enroll fewer than fifty students, at UW–Stout a program enrolling "only" fifty students finds itself facing cancellation. Moreover, the recruitment of freshmen is a key measure of the success of a program; with few entering freshmen declaring the degree, most of our program growth came from students changing to technical communication from other programs, as well as from non-traditional students transferring from technical colleges.

DOI: 10.7330/9780874219722.c007

Department Name:	English and Philosophy
Institution Type:	Public, Master's L (awards at least 200 Master's degrees/year)
Institution Size:	9,000 students
Residential or Commuter:	Residential
Student Body Description:	Primarily traditional (18–22-year-old) students who live on campus; includes a small group of working adult commuter students
Year Major Began:	2000
Official Name of Degree:	Bachelor of Science in Professional Communication and Emerging Media
Number of Majors:	In year one: 40 In year three: 81 In year five: 48 Current: 103
Number of Full-Time R/C Faculty:	10

In part to address lagging enrollment, our program has undergone three major curriculum revisions since its inception. Program revisions in 2004 and 2006 deepened the curriculum by adding courses such as International Technical Communication and Writing for Content Management. However, these revisions updated rather than reimagined the program's approach to the field of technical communication. Moreover, they did little to remedy dire enrollment issues now plaguing the program—freshman enrollment languished at a level of no more than five students per year. The 2010 program revision was intended, therefore, to take a fundamentally different approach to the field of technical communication, with a goal of strengthening the curriculum by incorporating a more broadly humanistic approach, thereby bolstering enrollment, particularly that of first-year students.

PROGRAM OVERVIEW AND RATIONALE

As our field struggles to determine "what to call itself" (Dayton and Bernhardt 2004), programs obviously struggle as well (Spigelman and Grobman 2006). Yet the identity of a program has been shown to be a critical factor in its sustainability (Johnson 2009). We discovered that the more explicitly defined programmatic identity achieved through our 2010 revision has enabled our prospective students to better limn their intellectual and professional identities.

This 2010 program revision renamed the degree professional communication and emerging media (PCEM) and diversified it, offering concentrations in technical communication, applied journalism, and digital humanities. The name change was instituted for several reasons, all of which reflect the purpose for and nature of the 2010 program revision. The term "professional communication" more broadly and accurately encapsulates the program curriculum currently offered. As Russell Rutter (1991) has argued, the discipline is severely limited if one accepts the idea that technical communication is "technical because its content is technical" (32). Data gathered from teachers of high school English courses across Wisconsin and the Twin Cities metropolitan area fifty miles to the west confirm this view: prospective students believed "technical communication" meant a curriculum focused exclusively on technology and the documentation of technical processes and devices. While some of our graduates do indeed pursue careers in technical industries, many of them find jobs in fields ranging from marketing, web design, and interactive development to public relations and journalism. Thus, renaming the PCEM degree more accurately defines the program, both for prospective freshmen and graduates entering the job market.

The inclusion of "emerging media" in the name also highlights our program's commitment to the analysis and application of technologically-mediated communication in its courses. Careers in our field now routinely involve a host of communication practices far beyond the drafting of a printed user manual (Rainey, Dayton, and Turner 2005; Whiteside 2003; Williams 2010). Today's practitioners repurpose content for emerging media, collaborate across disciplinary lines, and face a never-ending learning curve as new technologies are developed. We prepare students for an ever-changing workplace by giving them a broader, more strategic skill set. We accomplished this in our 2010 program revision by broadening our focus to embrace the humanities.

Perhaps the strongest evidence of the humanities' importance in our program is the foreign language requirement. While foreign language study is often lacking in programs like ours across the country (Hayhoe 2006), all PCEM students must take eight credits (two courses) in a foreign language. We were the first degree program at UW–Stout to implement even this modest two-semester requirement, and it clearly signals our commitment to the humanities to faculty and students alike. A second way in which we encourage student participation in disciplines outside our own is through the "applied field," a seventeen-credit block in the professional core that students design in coordination with their advisor. Students may elect to take courses in an area relevant to their career interests in engineering, health care, tourism, or other disciplines offered on our campus; they may choose courses in specific competencies complementary to their major studies, such as creative writing, digital pre-press, or graphic design; and/or they may select a humanities discipline—such as literature, history, or philosophy—to study in greater depth. Functioning much like an informal minor, the applied field concept provides students with great flexibility in curricular focus, while giving them subject-matter expertise that is crucial to success in the job market.

To prepare our students to work across multiple media, engage with a variety of disciplines, and adapt to new technologies, our major requires that students choose a concentration in technical communication, applied journalism, or digital humanities, each of which is described below. This 21-credit concentration, together with students' 60 credits of core courses and 43 credits of general education, adds up to a 124-credit bachelor of science degree.

The professional core comprises classes in rhetoric, document design, international technical communication, writing and editing, ethics, and speech communication, plus a year of foreign language courses. Beyond the general education and professional core courses, the 21-credit concentration offers students focused, specialized coursework in their areas of primary interest. The technical communication concentration maintains the strengths of the earlier program, including courses in usability design and testing, content management, project management, interviewing, and a required cooperative learning experience in which students seek out, interview for, and then fulfill a paid position for at least 320 hours of work related to their professional interests.

The applied journalism concentration provides a degree opportunity not available before at UW–Stout, where previously only a minor in journalism was offered. To be successful in a competitive job market, journalists must be more than good writers—they need a much broader and more strategic understanding of how content is repurposed into different channels in order to reach and interact with mobile users, web surfers, and podcast listeners. The concentration in applied journalism emphasis prepares students to accomplish all of this by learning to use today's (and tomorrow's) cutting-edge technology. Students take courses in mass communication, writing for the media, graphic communication, and photography. Perhaps even more important than the focus on "emerging media" is the stress on "applied" journalism. It has become clear in recent years that, while general readership journalism offers ever fewer employment opportunities, trade and industry-specific journalism seem to be sectors of the profession that are still growing—publications that serve a specific profession or a narrowly defined market continue to employ journalists. The PCEM curriculum provides this focused instruction in courses such as ENGL 330: Feature Writing and ENGL 407: Seminar in Applied Journalism.

While the first two concentrations built on the previous major and a popular minor, the digital humanities concentration was entirely new, and it represents the program's most visible commitment to the humanities. It requires undergraduates to engage in substantive research and the development of a project in the emerging field of digital humanities. Students choose a humanities field of interest from any of those offered at UW–Stout (e.g., history, literature, language, philosophy) and take courses in that area, pairing those with courses in computer science and basing their study on a solid foundation in writing, design, and rhetoric. Students then enroll in research methods and proposal writing courses and spend two additional semesters bringing technology, their knowledge of a humanities field, and their skills in research, analysis, and communication to bear on a digital humanities research project. The culmination of students' research is a cutting-edge digital artifact that constitutes the centerpiece of their portfolio. This concentration helps students learn to use technology to investigate and communicate about an academic discipline that interests them, and it allows them to develop advanced competency in an emerging technology that impacts communication.

Renaming and restructuring the PCEM program to involve a variety of humanistic, professional communication activities (technical communication, journalism, and digital humanities), while thoughtfully incorporating emerging media in substantive ways, has resonated with students, especially prospective ones. The PCEM degree has invigorated program enrollment. Marketing and recruitment for the PCEM began in spring 2011, and, since then, the program has seen a nearly sevenfold increase in freshmen enrollment, from an average of three per year to twenty-two freshmen enrolled in fall 2011. As of this writing, program enrollment across the three concentrations totals more than one hundred students, and the numbers continue to grow.

IMPLEMENTATION NARRATIVE

The humanities are, by their nature, cross-disciplinary; however, realizing the cross-disciplinary promise of the revised program proved challenging. The administrative structure of UW–Stout would seem to support this effort, as degree programs are housed not in departments but instead at the college level. This structure allows the program to engage instructors from across campus in program coursework without regard to their "home" academic departments, and the current program consists of just that: besides the core group of eleven faculty from the English and philosophy department, our program offers required core and concentration courses taught by faculty from six other departments. The benefits to students are obvious: the PCEM curriculum is more varied than it would be if it drew only from one department's faculty.

However, though the rewards are great, collaborating with faculty from across the disciplines also has its challenges, which range from the logistical to the philosophical. First, it is simply more difficult to convene a meeting of various PCEM faculty, much less an extended cross-disciplinary working group, if faculty are scattered across campus. Arranging a meeting time that fits the teaching and service schedule of members of six other departments is nearly impossible. The second challenge lies in the academic tradition that majors "belong" to the department that offers the majority of the coursework required for the degree. Thus, faculty in other departments are likely to view PCEM courses as simply service courses, and consequently accord them a lower priority. Third, and perhaps most intractably, it must be recognized that faculty are evaluated for promotion and tenure primarily on the basis of their contribution to their discipline and its students. There are few incentives for faculty to invest effort in keeping a course current with the latest developments (technological, theoretical, and pedagogical) in another field, even a closely related one, if that effort is not to be considered as part of the tenure and promotion process.

Knowing the difficult terrain of academic collaboration, the 2010 PCEM program revision, especially its new concentration in Digital Humanities, pointedly reached out to faculty across the humanities, including those in the English and philosophy department. The intention behind such collaborations was not new; in fact, interdisciplinary aspirations have always informed our program, just as cross-disciplinary collaboration is a principle of the professional communication workplace. However, our previous experiences were, in many respects, a cautionary tale.

From the program's launch in 2000 and during its first four years, the relationship between UW–Stout's technical communication program and the English and philosophy department was rocky at best. In fact, the founding director of the program describes this relationship in a *Technical Communication Quarterly* article as an "interdisciplinary civil war" between program proponents and "literature specialists" (Maylath, Grabill, and Gurak 2010, 265–68). Happily, the program of today has moved beyond this "friction" and "entrenched resistance." This path from "civil war" to relative harmony was paved by changes in program and department leadership, and the 2010 program revision capitalized on and helped to instantiate this newly productive program–department relationship.

The resolution of these conflicts began in 2004, when a new department chair helped to promulgate tenure-track job searches for writing and literature faculty with specific teaching and research interests (albeit with varying levels) in the technical communication degree. In addition, more formalized and structured department requirements specific to advising and service also encouraged faculty to work with the program and its students. Maylath, Grabill, and Gurak (2010) identify both faculty hiring and service responsibilities as key issues in the program-department divide. Their claim that addressing these two factors would help bridge this divide proved to be absolutely correct.

While the new department chair began his work in 2004, a new program director (only the second in the program's history) was appointed in 2007. The director, who holds a PhD in literature, has over ten years of experience working as a technical communicator in the software industry, and thus inhabits both the humanities and the technical sides of the "interdisciplinary civil war." Perhaps more importantly, his perspectives about the relationship between English departments and technical writing programs was largely uncolored by its contentious history, a legacy richly described in technical communication scholarship (Connors 1982; Kynell 2000). Indeed, the article by Maylath and his colleagues relies quite heavily on this history to argue its claim. In particular, the relationship between UW–Stout's program and the English department is held up as evidence of its contemporary continuance: "entrenched resistance emerged early on and successively from a hard core of literature specialists—hardly a surprise to those who know the history of the English field as it has played out in the U.S." (Maylath, Grabill, and Gurak 2010, 266). In 2007, however, the landscape of this department began to change, and the new director was able to approach the diminishing program–department divide less as a self-fulfilling prophecy and more as an opportunity to leverage disciplinary diversity for the benefit of the students in our program.

While the primary factors contributing to the current relative harmony between the program and the department resulted from the changes in leadership noted above, the 2010 program revision also played an important part. This revision not only looked forward to imagining new ways to utilize emerging media in its curriculum, but it also broadened the scope of the program's communication activities to specifically include the humanities. For instance, the seventeen-credit applied field, which constitutes an important part of the core curriculum, could be comprised entirely of literature courses. If they so choose, students' final research projects—the culmination of several semesters of related coursework and six credit hours of proposal writing and research—could meaningfully contribute to literature and literary studies. Further, faculty specializing in literature were encouraged to develop course topics for ENGL 480: Seminar in the Digital Humanities. Thus, through its new curriculum, the 2010 revision also helped to bridge the divide between the PCEM program and English department.

Broader collaboration

The challenges of implementing a cross-disciplinary program have been noted above, especially regarding the logistical headaches of working across departments, the varying faculty and department investment in the program, and the problems with providing continual course updates and improvements given the existing promotion and tenure structure. But the collaborative effort is not limited to faculty. The PCEM program has established relationships with other partners both on and off campus, including the FYC program, the writing center, the campus newspaper, and businesses and organizations in the surrounding community and beyond. The goal of these collaborative efforts is to offer students opportunities to deepen their knowledge while engaging in community-based service learning. We see this activity as central to the "humanistic understanding" that is a core mission of the College of Arts, Humanities, and Social Sciences (University of Wisconsin Stout 2014).

Since at least 2006, the program director has initiated a yearly recruitment effort involving the collaboration of the FYC program and its instructors. Each spring semester, over 1,000 students are enrolled in ENGL 102: Composition 2. Program faculty visit each section to deliver a five-minute introduction to the major, describing the coursework and projects in which a PCEM student typically engages, in addition to discussing the range of employment opportunities available to PCEM graduates. FYC instructors are encouraged to follow up by emphasizing the career applications of the composition and rhetoric skills they teach. Since its inception, this recruitment effort has been quite successful, with at least a dozen new students transferring into the major soon after these introductions occur each year.

The UW–Stout writing center, operational since 2005, employs many tutors who are PCEM students. In fact, the PCEM program continues to be a pipeline for the center; since it began, almost one-third of all tutors have been PCEM majors. The writing center provides a good opportunity for PCEM students to practice their writing and editing, analyze the writing of others, and hone their interpersonal communication skills as they tutor fellow students. Tutors also learn about the varied nature of writing across the curriculum and the complexity of meeting the demands of academic writing.

Besides these tutoring opportunities, many PCEM students work for the campus newspaper, *Stoutonia*. The paper's advisor also teaches program courses, and PCEM students often comprise the majority of *Stoutonia* staff. Students have the opportunity to work as writers, photographers, and editors, as well as engage in such activities as advertising sales, ad design, and the production of both print and online versions of the paper. The editor-in-chief is nearly always a PCEM major. Students declaring the PCEM applied journalism concentration are required to enroll in ENGL 210: Journalism Practicum, which structures students' work experience in journalism, often with the *Stoutonia*.

Beyond the campus, the PCEM program strives to engage students in a variety of real-world professional communication activities. The program has helped to place all of its advanced students into cooperative learning experiences (co-ops), and it has collaborated with companies and organizations on class projects. PCEM majors who declare the technical communication concentration (formerly all technical communication majors) are required to complete the co-op program, which is facilitated by the career services office at UW–Stout. Students must complete 320 hours of paid work relating to their program of study. Co-op supervisors in the workplace provide our students with performance evaluations, and PCEM students are encouraged to present the lessons learned from their co-op experiences to their fellow students and program faculty during the program's advisement day, which occurs mid-term each semester. The co-op experience has benefited many PCEM students, with nearly half going on to full-time employment at their co-op site.

PCEM collaborations with industry and community organizations also occur outside of the co-op experience. Since 2007, PCEM faculty have coordinated class-wide projects specific to usability, document design, and content management. For example, in ENGL 425: Usability Design and Testing, previous students designed and executed a usability test of a major corporation's consumer service website. The students' report was helpful to the company in revising their site, and students learned a great deal about usability testing—from experimental design to the analysis and presentation of results. Subsequent usability testing will be enhanced by new lab equipment purchased by the program, including behavior analysis and eye-tracking systems. In another semester, multiple PCEM courses worked with a community-based, non-profit organization—ENGL 385: Document Design students redesigned the organization's logo and crafted a promotional print brochure. Our ENGL 388: Writing for the Internet students collaborated with the ENGL 430: Writing for Content Management students to revise the organization's website. This multi-course collaboration resulted in a co-op site placement for one student, who implemented this organization's final design and web infrastructure. By engaging with the campus community, and the larger community beyond, we encourage our students to apply both the technical and the humanistic skills they learn through traditional classroom activities. This competency—reinforcing theory through guided practice—is of strategic value to students as they enter the workplace.

REFLECTION

We learned that in order to remain relevant and current, and in order to recruit effectively, we needed to redefine our program to more fully embrace other disciplines, particularly those in the humanities: "mak[ing] a case not for 'spanning' the distance between the cultures of technology and literature and the humanities, . . . but rather for integrating them" (Knievel 2006, 67). While characterizing our discipline as humanistic has generated debate (Dombrowski 1994; Johnson 2009; Miller 1979; Moore 1996), particularly on a polytechnic campus, the PCEM program has seen numerous benefits. This characterization of our major has enabled us to dramatically increase our student enrollment, especially concerning entering freshmen, and has allowed us to encourage more faculty involvement, such as serving as research mentors in the digital humanities concentration in particular, and advising students. Faculty advisors who are not specialists in technical and professional communication find that both they and the students benefit from the advising relationship—it seems to broaden the experience of both.

We believe that changes such as these not only help to make our program stronger, but also encourage a refocus on students and their potential for success. An industry advisor/board member, who is also an executive for a major corporation that produces hundreds of custom-designed web properties each year, noted: "The previous program gave us students who knew how to use the tools and technology we have today. Graduates of the new program will be able to tell us what we need to be doing in five years." This comment helped us to articulate the link between a curriculum more firmly rooted in the humanities and job prospects for our graduates. Programs in technical and professional communication must find ways to revise and adapt their curricula, as well as to build bridges across traditional academic boundaries for the benefit of their students. It is important to view this broadening not as diluting the discipline, but as a way of giving it the vitality that can only come from the infusion of new perspectives and purposes.

Curricular Summary: The Professional Communication and Emerging Media Major at the University of Wisconsin–Stout

The bachelor of science in professional communication and emerging media prepares students to enter a dynamic and growing profession where their opportunities are endless. The program combines professional core courses with one of three possible concentrations: technical communication, applied journalism, or digital humanities.

Core courses include editing, design, and rhetoric—all of which prepare students to write clearly for a specific audience. Students also gain a solid background in intercultural communication, international technical communication, and foreign languages.

The concentration in technical communication gives students hands-on experience in cutting-edge technologies such as usability design, content management, multimedia production, and project management. Applied journalism prepares students for the new age in journalism by exploring multimedia, interactivity, and content repurposing. The concentration in digital humanities gives students the skills needed to recognize trends in technology and understand how technology affects the way people communicate, interact, and comprehend the world. All courses are three credits, unless otherwise noted.

MAJOR REQUIREMENTS (80 CREDIT HOURS)

Core courses:
- ENGL 121: Introduction to Professional Communication
- ENGL 125: Elements of Style for Professional Writers
- ENGL 225: Editing Processes and Practices
- ENGL 247: Critical Writing
- ENGL 312: Transnational Professional Communication
- ENGL 340: Structure of English
- ENGL 371: Strategies of Argumentation

- ENGL 385: Document Design
- ENGL 388: Writing for the Internet
- ENGL 425: Usability Design and Testing
- PHIL 235: General Ethics
- SPCOM 312: Intercultural Communication (2 credits)
- Foreign language courses (8 credits total)

Capstone (final requirement):
- ENGL 471: Professional Communication Capstone

Technical communication concentration:
- ENGL 215: Foundations of Technical Writing
- ENGL 349: Cooperative Educational Experience (1 credit), or
  ENGL 437: Technical Writing Practicum (1 credit)
- ENGL 430: Writing for Content Management
- ENGL 435: Writing Technical Manuals
- SPCOM 414: Interviewing (1 credit)
- SPCOM 425: Informational Interviewing Skills for Professionals (1 credit)
- Two elective courses chosen, in consultation with student's advisor, from fields such as project management, computer science, or marketing.
- Applied field courses in a professional area outside of English/communication (16 credits total)

Applied journalism concentration:
- ENGL 207: Writing for the Media
- ENGL 210: Journalism Practicum (1 credit), or
  ENGL 349/437: Cooperative Educational Experience/Technical Writing Practicum (1 credit)
- ENGL 218: Mass Communication
- ENGL 330: Feature Writing
- ENGL 350: Digital Storytelling
- ENGL 407: Seminar in Applied Journalism
- ENGL 418: Convergent Media
- Applied field courses that are aligned with the student's professional interests (15 credits total)

Digital humanities concentration:
- CS 141: Introduction to Programming
- CS 248: Web and Internet Programming
- ENGL 335: Critical Approaches to Digital Humanities
- ENGL 350: Digital Storytelling
- ENGL 480: Seminar in the Digital Humanities
- ENGL 495: Digital Humanities Undergraduate Thesis (taken twice, for 6 credits total)

- Applied field courses in the humanities that align with the student's research interests (13 credits total)

References

Connors, Robert J. 1982. "The Rise of Technical Writing Instruction in America." *Journal of Business and Technical Communication* 12 (4): 329–51.

Dayton, David, and Stephen Bernhardt. 2004. "Results of a Survey of ATTW Members, 2003." *Technical Communication Quarterly* 13 (1): 13–43. http://dx.doi.org/10.1207/S15427625TCQ1301_5.

Dombrowski, Paul M., ed. 1994. *Humanistic Aspects of Technical Communication.* Amityville: Baywood.

Hayhoe, George F. 2006. "Education for the Global Future." *Technical Communication* 53 (3): 281–2.

Johnson, Robert R. 2009. "Trajectories, Kairos, and Tulips: A Personal Reflection and Meditation on Programs in Rhetoric, Technical, Professional, and Scientific Communication." *Programmatic Perspectives* 1 (1): 45–58.

Knievel, Michael. 2006. "Technology Artifacts, Instrumentalism, and the Humanist Manifestos: Toward an Integrated Humanistic Profile for Technical Communication." *Journal of Business and Technical Communication* 20 (1): 65–86. http://dx.doi.org/10.1177/1050651905281040.

Kynell, Teresa C. 2000. *Writing in a Milieu of Utility: The Move to Technical Communication in American Engineering Programs, 1850–1950.* Stamford: Ablex.

Maylath, Bruce, Jeff Grabill, and Laura J. Gurak. 2010. "Intellectual Fit and Programmatic Power: Organizational Profiles of Four Professional/Technical/Scientific Communication Programs." *Technical Communication Quarterly* 19 (3): 262–80. http://dx.doi.org/10.1080/10572252.2010.481535.

Miller, Carolyn R. 1979. "A Humanistic Rationale for Technical Writing." *College English* 40 (6): 610–7. http://dx.doi.org/10.2307/375964.

Moore, Patrick. 1996. "Instrumental Discourse is as Humanistic as Rhetoric." *Journal of Business and Technical Communication* 10 (1): 100–18. http://dx.doi.org/10.1177/1050651996010001005.

Rainey, Kenneth, David Dayton, and Ron Turner. 2005. "Do Curricula Correspond to Managerial Expectations? Core Competencies for Technical Communicators." *Technical Communication* 52: 323–52.

Rutter, Russell. 1991. "History, Rhetoric, and Humanism: Toward a More Comprehensive Definition of Technical Communication." *Journal of Technical Writing and Communication* 21 (2): 133–53. http://dx.doi.org/10.2190/7BBK-BJYK-AQGB-28GP.

Spigelman, Candace, and Laurie Grobman. 2006. "Why We Chose Rhetoric: Necessity, Ethics and the (Re)Making of a Professional Writing Program." *Journal of Business and Technical Communication* 20 (1): 48–64. http://dx.doi.org/10.1177/1050651905281039.

University of Wisconsin Stout. 2014. "Mission and Vision Statements." Accessed online Nov. 10, 2014. http://www.uwstout.edu/admin/colleges/ahs/mission.cfm.

Whiteside, Aimee M. 2003. "The Skills that Technical Communicators Need: An Investigation of Technical Communication Graduates, Managers, and Curricula." *Journal of Technical Writing and Communication* 33 (4): 303–18. http://dx.doi.org/10.2190/3164-E4V0-BF7D-TDVA.

Williams, Sean D. 2010. "Interpretive Discourse and Other Models from Communication Studies: Expanding the Values of Technical Communication." *Journal of Technical Writing and Communication* 40 (4): 429–46. http://dx.doi.org/10.2190/TW.40.4.d.

8

BUILDING A WRITING MAJOR AT METROPOLITAN STATE UNIVERSITY
Shaping a Program to Meet Students Where They Are

Laura McCartan and Victoria Sadler

INTRODUCTION

At Metropolitan State University our undergraduate writing majors fall into three separate BA programs: creative writing; screenwriting; and technical communication and professional writing. For this writing program profile, we follow the lead of the CCCC Committee on the Major in Writing and Rhetoric by distinguishing between a writing major and a fine arts writing major. Consequently, this chapter will focus solely on our Technical Communication and Professional Writing (TCPW) major (a professional/rhetorical writing major as identified by Balzhiser and McLeod 2010).

Many students at our university, including our TCPW majors, have "blue collar" literacies (not validated by traditional academics), such as auto mechanics, assembly line work, and drafting; many are first-generation college students; and many are underprepared for higher education. New TCPW majors have often worked as professional writers for many years and want a degree to match their experience. This tension consistently brings to the surface an age-old institutional debate between "meeting students where they are" and "taking students somewhere better." Our students "are"—literally in terms of demographics, and figuratively in terms of first-generation(ness) and college-readiness—in many different places. Thus, the idea of "meeting" students is about program shaping, not lowering standards. These factors are responsible for the motivation and vitality of our student body, but they can also complicate programmatic decisions.

DOI: 10.7330/9780874219722.c008

Department Name:	Communication, Writing, and the Arts
Institution Type:	Public, Master's M (awards between 100–199 Master's degrees/year)
Institution Size:	10,000 students
Residential or Commuter:	Commuter
Student Body Description:	Most students transfer here after collecting credits from several different schools; most students work, at minimum, part-time; diverse in terms of ethnicity, socio-economics, age, etc.; high percentage are first-generation college students
Year Major Began:	2012
Official Name of Degree:	Technical Communication and Professional Writing
Number of Majors:	In year one: 80 In year three: N/A In year five: N/A Current: 94
Number of Full-Time R/C Faculty:	9

PROGRAM OVERVIEW AND RATIONALE

In 2010, the professional writing program conducted a self-review that led to the decision to separate from creative writing and later merge with technical communication. This decision resulted from the feedback we received from local professional writers, alumni, and current students; from reviews we conducted of similar professional writing programs across the United States; and from our consultations with other writing faculty. This self-review concluded that "the program should continue to emphasize what it always has: writing, editing, research, and critical thinking. However, with the tidal wave of technological change occurring within professional communication, it is essential that we prepare our students for the work of professional writers in the second decade of the 21st century" (Aronson and Nerney 2010, 4). It was also clear that creative writing could stand on its own as a major and that it differed significantly from professional writing. In addition, because the two were tracks in the same major, students needed special permission to major in one and minor in the other, so splitting the two made sense for many reasons.

Programmatic issues regarding the design and positioning of degree programs in technical communication and professional writing are often discussed in journals such as *Technical Communication Quarterly*, *Programmatic Perspectives*, and *IEEE Transactions on Professional Communication*. As Dave Yeats and Isabelle Thompson state in their study, "Our fundamental finding is this: the 'representative' technical communication program does not exist" (Yeats and Thompson 2010, 259). Add to this the debate over how *technical* writing/communication differs from *professional* writing/communication, and you might expect that combining these two majors would result in battles among our faculty. That battle never occurred, primarily because the professional writing faculty had determined that they needed to offer more courses with a technological emphasis, and an alliance with technical communication was the ideal solution. This partnership was bolstered when faculty members worked together to articulate the goals of a new major in technical communication and professional writing (TCPW), or, as we like to say loudly, "Tech Pow!" Almost a year of meetings culminated in these outcomes for the new program:

- Theory and practice of writing and editing in diverse genres and for diverse audiences
- Theory and practice of document design for electronic and print media
- Research skills that inform the creation of persuasive, professional communication
- Knowledge of digital media, tools, and resources
- Experience in real world writing and communication through a required internship
- Development of a professional portfolio

Our writing faculty believes that the ability to put complex thoughts into written form, to communicate in writing to a range of audiences, and to use writing to learn are cornerstones of success both in college and in the workplace. Offered by the Department of Communication, Writing, and the Arts, our writing curriculum offers these skills to students across the university through courses in general writing, business and technical writing, journalism, and creative writing. For students who wish to specialize in writing, we offer a number of programs: undergraduate majors in creative writing and TCPW; undergraduate minors in creative writing, environmental communication, and technical communication; and a master of science in technical communication.

IMPLEMENTATION NARRATIVE

On January 1, 2012, we replaced a BA in writing and a BA in technical communication with the TCPW major. Within TCPW, students choose a track to follow—technical communication or professional writing.

Technical Communication Track:

Students completing this track take classes in technical writing, advanced web writing and design, instructional design and related media, and trends in communication technology. The technical communication track prepares students for careers in areas such as web content development and design, online education and training, technical editing, technical marketing, and product documentation.

Professional Writing Track:

Students in this track take classes in writing for publication, as well as writing for social media and multimedia. They also choose from an array of electives, including courses in grant writing, freelance writing, book publishing, public relations writing, and screenwriting. The professional writing track prepares students for careers in such fields as magazine writing and editing, grant writing, writing for marketing or public relations, employee communications, web content development, and print and electronic publishing.

On the surface, the changes to our technical communication (TC) and professional writing (PW) programs may seem minor and merely pragmatic, but they represent changes in thinking about how to best serve our students, and the process has uncovered differing opinions of what "professional writing" connotes. To faculty in the TC program, PW is the study and practice of writing in a particular profession—law, medicine, science, healthcare, etc.—and is often partnered with TC. At our university, PW has been the rough equivalent to journalism or editing; students in this track typically see themselves as broadly choosing the profession of writing. Fortunately, this difference in perspectives does not harm the relationships among writing faculty, and it will be interesting to see what direction our new—and larger (130 students)—major takes.

A primary difference between the two tracks is that the PW track is less prescriptive of required courses than the TC track, allowing students with a professional writing focus to choose *three* elective courses rather than *one* in the TC track. The rationale for this is that a TC focus incorporates skills other than writing, particularly a greater emphasis on understanding how technology affects communication, on comprehending training principles, and on designing for usability. For this reason, students who choose the TC track take courses in Advanced Web Design, Online Education and Training, and either Usability for Technical Communication or Issues in Communication Technology.

They must also take a course in Technical Writing. Students in the PW track choose either Digital Newswriting or Writing for Magazines, and they take a course in Communicating with New Media, which teaches them how to write for blogs and other forms of social media. They are not required to take a class in Technical Writing or Business Writing, but quite a few of them take one of these in order to satisfy a general education requirement.

REFLECTION AND PROSPECTION

We believe that the reconfigured major in technical communication and professional writing will provide students with the writing, editing, research, and digital communication skills that are essential for writing professionals in industry, government, non-profit, and freelance careers. The core curriculum of the major immerses students in the kind of analytical, critical, and creative thinking that is at the heart of effective communication, and it contains courses that are designed to adapt to changes in technology. For example, we replaced a general Desktop Publishing class with one in Digital Tools, which focuses on students assessing their own skills (with input from instructors) and creating a learning plan supported by online tutorials in chosen software applications. This plan also serves as both an advising tool and a touchstone for students as they progress through the program and acquire more technical skills. Another change to the new major included requiring a more in-depth research class that incorporates interviewing skills, which we believe are too often overlooked, particularly by students who wish to become technical communicators.

We still grapple with the challenges presented by the large number of students transferring general education courses, such as lower-division writing, to their BA degree. Before taking any upper-division writing courses, students must complete their lower-division writing courses, but are not required to take them at Metropolitan State. Using the Minnesota Transfer Curriculum, students can satisfy the general education writing requirement at other schools and jump right into our courses. This means a student might come to us having taken basic writing classes a decade or two ago or a semester or two ago. We feel this impact at all levels of our writing curriculum, from FYC courses to advanced major courses. Integrating technology into the program remains a challenge—another area in which we must meet the students where they are. Several two-credit "technology workshops" provide resources to students (e.g., Lynda.com accounts) and simultaneously make students responsible for keeping their technical skills current. In addition, students must take two prerequisite courses (an overview of the career field and the above-mentioned Digital Tools class) before beginning a five-course core:

- INFS 315: Searching for Information
- WRIT 371: Editing
- WRIT 372: Document and Information Design I
- WRIT 373: Writing and Designing for the Web I
- WRIT 461: Capstone

To provide more flexibility in meeting students where they are, we offer advanced classes in all of the courses listed above (except WRIT 461: Capstone), and program advisors may approve course substitutions or waivers on a case-by-case basis.

CONCLUSION

A full-time advisor for our college tells us that our writing program loses potential majors to the individualized major (an interdisciplinary BA offered in another college) because our college's admission rules present an obstacle to students transferring what are viewed as "technical" credits. Ironically, these credits are often in academic areas that the TCPW program desires its students to have—for example, graphic design, biomedical technology, design software, and healthcare. Moreover, because our university only began offering first- and second-year courses in 1998, our curriculum lacks these types of skill-based, foundational courses. Consequently, over the past year we have initiated formal agreements with local community colleges (all of which belong to the Minnesota State Colleges and Universities (MNSCU) system, so alliances are encouraged and the programs have control over the content of the agreements) in order to create a pathway for graduates of biomedical technology, computer graphics and visualization, and informatics for healthcare to apply all of their program credits to our BA degree. This allows students to use many of their credits as "free" electives to meet the 120-credit requirement for the BA and, in some cases, to receive equivalent credit for courses in the major. Graduates of these associate degree programs will enrich our program and challenge us as they look to apply their earlier degree to a career in technical communication and/or professional writing. We are planning for that eventuality as we begin to sketch out courses in biomedical and healthcare technical communication, with an eye toward creating an informatics-related minor that would serve students in majors such as nursing, dentistry, natural sciences, and computer science.

Metropolitan State University is just over forty years old, and in many ways it is a school of improvisation, not well-rehearsed tradition. The mission of the university has changed, and its goals continue to adapt as political and demographic demands shape both our student population and the expectations placed on our academic programs. Our writing program is shaped by our students, by the job market, by academic resources, by professional standards, and by faculty expertise and pedagogy. All of these factors have contributed to our new BA in technical communication and professional writing, which is still a work in progress. We believe we are successfully shaping our program for the twenty-first century by recognizing the abilities of our students and pushing them to go beyond where they "are."

Curricular Summary: The Technical Communication and Professional Writing Major at Metropolitan State University

The major in technical communication and professional writing provides students with a foundation in the writing, editing, research, and digital communication skills that are essential for writing professionals in industry, government, non-profit, and freelance careers. Faculty who teach in the program combine academic and workplace experience to educate students in both ideas and implementation, principles and practice.

MAJOR REQUIREMENTS (46–48 CREDIT HOURS)

Prerequisites:
- WRIT 301: Professional and Technical Writing Careers
- WRIT 280: Digital Tools for Writing and Communication

Core courses:
- INFS 315: Searching for Information
- WRIT 371: Editing
- WRIT 372: Document and Information Design I
- WRIT 373: Writing and Designing for the Web I
- WRIT 350I: Writing Internship

Capstone (final requirement):
- WRIT 461: Writing and Technical Communication Capstone
  Technical communication track (5 courses):
- WRIT 271: Technical Writing (required)

- WRIT 573: Writing and Designing for the Web II (required)
- WRIT 574: Usability for Technical Communication, or
  MDST 580: Issues in Communication Technology (required)
- MDST 583: Online Education and Training (required)
- MDST 485: Communicating with New Media
- MDST 580: Issues in Communication Technology
- WRIT 531: Advanced Writing
- WRIT 571: Advanced Editing
- WRIT 574: Usability for Technical Communication
- WRIT 575: Environmental Communication
- WRIT 599: Special Topics in Technical Communication

Professional writing track (5 courses):
- WRIT 341: Writing the News in a Digital World, or
  WRIT 342: Writing for Online and Print Magazines (required)
- MDST 485: Communicating with New Media (required)
- WRIT 341: Writing the News in a Digital World
- WRIT 342: Writing for Online and Print Magazines
- WRIT 377: Writing Grants and Proposals
- WRIT 531: Advanced Writing
- WRIT 532: Writing about Place
- WRIT 541: Writing for Publication and Profit
- WRIT 571: Advanced Editing
- WRIT 575: Environmental Communication
- WRIT 583: Writing Major Projects
- INFS 338: The Craft and Commerce of Book Publishing
- COMM 380: Public Relations Writing
- MKTG 348: Advertising Design, Production, and Copywriting
- One four-credit creative writing or screenwriting course

References

Aronson, Anne, and Brian Nerney. 2010. *Professional Writing Program Review.* Internal departmental document. July 15.

Balzhiser, Deborah, and Susan H. McLeod. 2010. "The Undergraduate Writing Major: What Is It? What Should It Be?" *College Composition and Communication* 61: 415–33.

Yeats, Dave, and Isabelle Thompson. 2010. "Mapping Technical and Professional Communication: A Summary and Survey of Academic Locations for Programs." *Technical Communication Quarterly* 19 (3): 225–61. http://dx.doi.org/10.1080/105722 52.2010.481538.

9

WRITERS AMONG ENGINEERS AND SCIENTISTS
New Mexico Tech's Bachelor of Science in Technical Communication

Julie Dyke Ford, Julianne Newmark, and Rosário Durão

INTRODUCTION

While other technical communication (TC) programs may exist on the margins of a larger English department, the TC program at New Mexico Tech is the *only* professional degree-granting program offered from our Communication, Liberal Arts, Social Sciences (formerly named Humanities) department. Since our BS in TC is one of the only non-engineering or "hard" sciences programs within our entire institution, we certainly could have ended up on the margins. However, efforts by current and former faculty have ensured us a solid place in our institution, in large part as a consequence of the recognizable success of our students upon graduation and the strong research/publication records of our faculty.

Through the noticeable contributions of our longstanding corporate advisory board, plus those of a recently added e-journal and an established e-journal—all housed in our program—we have secured our status at New Mexico Tech. Ours is a program that recognizes the importance of maintaining a curriculum that blends theory and practice with problem solving and innovation. With this approach, we carry out the research mission so firmly embraced by New Mexico Tech, while at the same time letting its industrial ties and research components enrich students' curricular experiences.

In this chapter we detail the strategies that have helped us distinguish our program in an environment dominated by engineers and scientists. We've gone beyond merely holding our own in a STEM-dominated

DOI: 10.7330/9780874219722.c009

Department Name:	Communication, Liberal Arts, Social Sciences
Institution Type:	Public, Master's M (awards 100–199 Master's degrees/year)
Institution Size:	1,800 students
Residential or Commuter:	Residential
Student Body Description:	68% male, 32% female; majority of students are in-state; New Mexico Tech is considered a Hispanic-serving institution
Year Major Began:	1983
Official Name of Degree:	Bachelor of Science in Technical Communication
Number of Majors:	In year one: N/A In year three: N/A In year five: N/A Current: 25
Number of Full-Time R/C Faculty:	5

institution (science, technology, engineering, and mathematics)—we have become a program with nationally recognized innovations that attract a unique group of students who are eager to connect their interest in technologies of communication to the best practices of verbal, written, and visual communication in industry and government settings. In the next section we offer necessary background information about our curriculum and mission. Following that, we describe how the corporate advisory board, our emphasis on research in the curriculum, the *Xchanges* interdisciplinary e-journal, and the *connexions* international professional communication journal all enrich our program and support our standing at New Mexico Tech.

PROGRAM OVERVIEW AND RATIONALE

The technical communication BS degree became an officially recognized program on our campus when it was unanimously approved by the New Mexico Tech Board of Regents in 1983. At that time, technical writing was emerging as a profession, and the humanities faculty who spearheaded the proposal adeptly analyzed the institution's culture and environment. In their analysis, our faculty found much cause to successfully argue for a need for a humanities-based degree, one that placed technology at the forefront and could serve as a complement to the already-established engineering and science programs.

Our 132-credit curriculum combines courses from the following fields of study: technical communication, humanities, social science, and science and technology. This design has the following goals:

- TC courses develop the writing, speaking, and editing abilities of students and introduce them to document design, graphics, and online/multimedia computer documentation. Our curriculum has an appropriate mix of theory and practice and incorporates current industry issues and trends.

- Humanities and social science courses improve students' understanding and appreciation of history, literature, philosophy, psychology, and fine arts/human experience. Science and technology courses provide students with a background in one specific science or engineering discipline. Students are required to take twelve credit hours in a specific area of either science or engineering outside of the general degree requirements, which include calculus, physics, and chemistry. These requirements provide students with a firm foundation in basic mathematical and scientific concepts and are repeatedly commended by employers of our graduates, who note our students' abilities to "talk the talk" (or at least understand the talk) of scientists and engineers.

Hands-on experience through coursework and other requirements

In addition to required courses that emphasize writing, research, speaking, editing, visual communication, collaboration, and project management, students must also complete a community service requirement that involves using TC skills to produce communication deliverables for a client. A more in-depth requirement is the professional internship, which involves at least 160 hours of applied TC-related work.

Whenever possible and appropriate, we integrate client-based projects into our courses so that students gain additional hands-on experience and graduate with a professional portfolio well-stocked with a range of professional examples.

Program size

Our current enrollment of twenty-five majors and twelve minors has been fairly consistent over the last two decades. These numbers translate to small class sizes, which work very well given our curricular goals and integration of client-based projects. Currently we have two full-time faculty, one of whom serves as the TC program director. We also have a half-time faculty member who holds a joint appointment between technical communication and mechanical engineering. In addition to two dedicated TC faculty, four members of our department's writing faculty teach courses for the program.

IMPLEMENTATION NARRATIVE

Within the last decade, our program has experienced significant changes. While our curriculum has remained largely unchanged, a shift in faculty and closer collaboration with our corporate advisory board has allowed us to include valuable new opportunities for our students. In addition, our recognition that undergraduate research experience is valued in contexts outside of academia (and often not given enough attention in undergraduate TC curricula) has prompted us to further emphasize the role of research within our program. Because the advisory board has been such an asset to our program's evolution and advancement, in this section we provide further detail about the role this board plays in our program.

Corporate Advisory Board

Established in 1990, the program's corporate advisory board was founded as a joint effort between TC faculty and our institution's development office. The goals included identifying corporate or government organizations who had been supportive of the university in the past and establishing relationships with these industrial partners, who could:

- keep faculty abreast of trends in the industry while also creating the opportunity for faculty to "inform industry about developments in pedagogy and research" (Yee 1994, 206). Since most early faculty did not possess PhDs in technical writing, but instead in literature or composition, this goal was a valuable way to ensure our faculty had appropriate exposure to industry standards and trends;
- review and provide input about TC curriculum;
- offer support for equipment, scholarships, and grants;
- provide internship and possibly post-graduation employment opportunities for students;
- advise students on career options; and
- provide research opportunities and collaborations, such as "studies of usability testing, ethnography, and writing processes" (Yee 1994, 208).

During annual one-day meetings on the New Mexico Tech campus, the board and New Mexico Tech faculty and administrators (including the university president) engaged in discussions and shared presentations for the purpose of meeting the aforementioned goals. These collaborations became a valuable opportunity to educate high-profile members of our campus about the activities and direction of the TC program.

Early in its history, the board consisted of program faculty and three industrial representatives from Hewlett-Packard, Westinghouse, and the

NCR Corporation. The HP representative played a pivotal role in securing major equipment grants for the TC program, totaling over $100,000. These grants, which directly fulfilled the goal of equipment support, led to a fourteen-terminal computer lab dedicated to TC students and with the most current hardware and software. Later, the advisory board added representatives from the government-supported Sandia and Los Alamos national laboratories.

Claiming an advisory board as part of our program demonstrated to engineering and scientific disciplines that we valued the teaching of an applied curriculum. Interestingly enough, we were a leader in this domain—the TC program was the first academic program on our campus to establish an advisory board. Other programs, including many from the engineering disciplines, followed our lead and later established their own.

In the second decade of the board's existence, a dramatic shift in the annual meeting occurred. The early board meetings had very little student involvement, which board members identified as a problem. However, around 2000, TC students became significantly involved. Also during this period, the composition of the TC faculty shifted, becoming predominantly comprised of faculty with PhDs specifically in TC, many who also had industry experience. With this change, the early role of the corporate board was revised, as the board's prior role of educating faculty about current industry standards and trends was less necessary. Thus, there was more room to include students at board meetings. Students became involved via the delivery of presentations to the board about Society for Technical Communication (STC) student chapter activities, internship projects, and senior thesis projects. Board meetings also began including a job materials review session where students received feedback from board members on their resumes and professional portfolios. These changes to the board meetings increased interaction between TC students and board members and provided the opportunity for more students to receive direct feedback and valuable guidance from industry representatives.

In addition to building in opportunities for face-to-face collaboration, TC faculty also made efforts to incorporate the advisory board into programmatic and curricular events throughout the year (at a distance)—for example, requiring students in our freshman-level Orientation to Technical Communication course to interview a board member, document the discussion, and share the interview with the class. Another significant part of the enhanced interaction between board members and students arose in 2005, when board members began serving as mentors for TC students working on their senior theses. As one of the fruits of this interaction, a TC faculty member, a board member, and a student collaborated on a poster presentation at an academic conference and later published an article in a leading TC peer-reviewed journal.

The most recent strategy to better connect board members with both TC faculty and students is the use of social networking, something we would recommend to programs that have an existing advisory board or plan to create one. At our last board meeting, TC faculty and all four board members (professionals employed at Qwest/Century Link, Hewlett-Packard, National Instruments, and Sandia National Laboratory) decided to begin a Facebook group for the program, with the goal of having a forum where TC students, program alumni, faculty, and board members could communicate. So far, the Facebook group has been used by students to request or share job leads, by faculty to announce upcoming presentations and programmatic events, and by board members and alumni to share pertinent links, begin conversations about industry trends, and share ideas for curricular revisions.

The purpose of the board is to counsel, educate, advise, and mentor. These are certainly roles that faculty members play for students, but they are also elemental roles our corporate board has come to perform in our entire program. The fact that we have made this multidimensional relationship—between a university, its students, and the larger industry these students hope to join—a crucial part of our program signals our belief in this model as one that other programs might embrace.

Emphasis on research curriculum

In 2005, several of our faculty members attended the Council for Programs in Technical and Scientific Communication (CPTSC) annual conference, where Rachel Spilka served as keynote speaker and urged TC programs to do a better job of emphasizing research within undergraduate curricula. Over the course of the conference, while attending various presentations devoted to the role of research within curricula, we realized that our TC program was rare in our heavy emphasis on research. At one particular session, colleagues from other institutions were speculating about the value of incorporating senior thesis projects into curricula, something that we have done at New Mexico Tech since our program began in 1983. Our senior thesis model, while it has been modified throughout the last few decades, is designed to serve as a culmination of the skills TC students acquire throughout their time in the program. Through the senior thesis experience, our students engage in a comprehensive process requiring them to combine skills in reading, summarizing, analyzing, and presenting research. The final deliverables for the thesis sequence require students to showcase their abilities in writing, editing, producing graphics, project management, and oral presentation. While previous publications (Ford et al. 2009; Ford and Newmark 2011) have provided extensive detail about our two-semester senior thesis requirement, here we offer a brief overview of the main components of this capstone exercise and highlight the benefits this model offers.

Taught over an academic year, the Senior Seminar course (offered each fall) and the Senior Thesis course (offered each spring) require students to critically analyze, evaluate, discuss, and present prior technical communication literature and then propose and carry out their own independent research projects. Because fairly small class sizes (each course is capped at twelve students) allow for close student–faculty interaction, students receive plenty of individual faculty feedback.

While working on their proposals in the latter half of the Senior Seminar course, students are paired with a mentor from the corporate advisory board, with each board member agreeing to work with up to three students if necessary. Board mentors are not expected to provide graded evaluation or mere editorial suggestions; they instead offer students substantive feedback on documents, beginning with the proposal.

During the thesis drafting process, students submit biweekly reports to both TC faculty and their advisory board mentor. In these reports, students detail progress but also ask questions, note specific problem areas, and request directive feedback. Oral presentations include one to the advisory board during the annual meeting in early April, as well as a final presentation on campus to faculty, students, and invited guests.

Upon submitting a final printed version of their thesis to TC faculty, each student receives feedback for additional revisions, and, upon making those revisions, each student must submit the thesis for consideration for publication in a peer-reviewed TC journal. To date, four of our students have had their thesis work published in peer-reviewed journals. The majority of students have submitted their theses to *Xchanges* for consideration, a peer-reviewed e-journal housed at New Mexico Tech and described further in the following section. Whether students submit their theses to *Xchanges*, *connexions* (also described following), or another TC journal, they are expected to have created scholarly documents or electronic texts that address critical questions of interest to technical communicators within and beyond university settings. Students' ability to address an extra-institutional audience is one of their final demonstrations of proficiency in or mastery of a crucial desired outcome of our program.

Xchanges journal

Another major research initiative our program has undertaken has been the *Xchanges* journal. Through this initiative, we have situated the role of research within our program in a prominent way. In addition to creating an additional research source for our students, we have also attracted the attention of our institution's administrators by producing a peer-reviewed publication in our program.

Xchanges, now an integral part of our TC program, relocated to New Mexico Tech in 2008, when the journal editor joined the faculty. The inclusion of *Xchanges'* production within our technical communication major is part of our effort to improve students' rhetorical awareness through an applied dexterity. This dexterity is revealed by students' movement from *recognition* to *creation* of appropriate modes of communication for specific audiences. The applied dexterity that *Xchanges* furthers is a key objective of our program: to ensure that students can imagine and produce pieces of technical communication for audiences beyond their professors and fellow students.

Students interact with *Xchanges* on three potential levels: as interns who work one-on-one with the editor, as members of the Publications Management course, and as submitters of scholarship to the journal at the conclusion of their senior year. The first two levels of this interaction foreground *Xchanges's* role at our institution as an innovative client project, in which *Xchanges* offers a "best of two worlds" situation. The first of these worlds is the one outside of the students' university context. As journal staff, either in their capacity as interns or class-members, students become answerable to the journal's international readership and institutional and national stakeholders: a multifaceted and faceless "client." The other world, however, is of the university domain, which the students also serve by completing assignments that meet course requirements and program standards. These students not only want to please their extra-university client (the readers, writers, and other stakeholders of the academic journal) but also their intra-university evaluators (their professor and the program director). Thus, students' work on *Xchanges* allows them to have a visible product (the journal issues and related documentation) and a decidedly new audience (the journal's readers, submitters, and board members).

The Publications Management class is the most recently added level of student participation with the *Xchanges* project. The first iteration of this class was offered in fall 2010. In this course, a small group of TC majors saw a graduate-student issue of *Xchanges* from the very early stages of its production through to its release. Newmark and Ford (2012) examined the first-person impressions of these students by conducting course exit interviews. These insights illustrate that the students felt the journal production work allowed them to exercise the audience- and client-awareness skills they had studied as "theories" in their previous TC coursework.

As a consequence of TC students having the opportunity to engage with *Xchanges* as senior-thesis submitters or as stakeholders on the production-end of the journal (either as interns or Publications Management students), we have been able to record their feedback and examine how this addition to our program has enhanced and enlivened the major in new ways, alongside many other recent and/or expanded initiatives. The practices we have instituted might be successfully adapted by other programs, as we have installed unique versions of client projects, research initiatives, and corporate involvement with the goal of constantly updating our program to keep pace with current technologies and expanding TC audiences.

While we can point to limited funds as a constraint for *Xchanges*, and have hopes that in the future we can set even more ambitious goals for the journal—such as employing an editorial assistant in addition to interns—we also recognize that the responsibilities currently undertaken by our interns provide them with invaluable professional experience.

connexions—international professional communication journal

connexions, a peer-reviewed, open-access journal focused on international professional communication, provides faculty and students at New Mexico Tech with a forum in which they can publish and learn about communication related to work and civic activity in our increasingly complex, interconnected world. As the journal website explains, *connexions* was developed to bring together the American and European views of professional communication—the former centered on professional and technical communication, the latter on translation—to "researchers, practitioners, students, and emerging scholars from diversified backgrounds, interests, and nationalities" (*connexions* 2012). *connexions* focuses on the

> practice, research, pedagogy, methodology, and technology of efficient and effective written, oral, visual, electronic and non-verbal professional communication—academic, business, crisis, development, environmental, health, media, nonprofit, political, research, science, and technical communication—in local, national, international, and global work and civic activity settings. (*connexions* 2012)

In addition, the journal includes an editorial board composed of academics and prominent professionals in different fields and from different parts of the world. The journal's main publishing language is English, but it also includes manuscripts written in French, Portuguese, and Spanish with attached 500-word English summaries.

With its move to New Mexico Tech's Department of Communication, Liberal Arts, Social Sciences in the second half of 2012, *connexions* was able to place a greater emphasis on international professional communication in STEM disciplines. In fact, the journal's second issue focused on international engineering communication. This issue was co-guest edited by Julie Ford, director of New Mexico Tech's TC program from 2004 to 2012, who embodies the symbiosis between TC and STEM through her joint appointment in the mechanical engineering and technical communication departments. We expect and will encourage contributors to the journal to follow this lead and propose other guest-edited, STEM-related issues to our journal.

With *connexions*' move to New Mexico Tech, we were able to introduce some needed modifications to its content. Besides research articles, review articles, and teaching case studies, the journal now publishes focused commentary and industry perspective articles. For our students, this addition provides a further incentive to publish in the journal, as well as greater opportunities to become acquainted with the issues practitioners are now facing in international professional communication.

The journal recently recruited a student to serve as editorial assistant and engaged the services of a second student as online content manager. As a result, these students are making a decisive contribution to the smooth operation of the journal and gaining valuable cross-disciplinary and professional skills by applying what they have learned in their majors (primarily technical communication, but also computer science and engineering) to managing an international e-journal.

Beyond contributing directly to the operations and management of the journal, TC students (particularly those working on international and intercultural topics for their senior theses) can also propose and be published in *connexions*. In addition, many possibilities exist for integrating the journal's activities into class assignments—for instance, editing manuscripts in our Editing or Publications Management classes.

connexions provides a venue for faculty and students to publish and learn about the issues that are specific to professional communication on an international and even global scale, thus integrating the research mission of New Mexico Tech and its unique TC program into their professional lives.

REFLECTION

As we write this chapter, a new semester is about to begin at New Mexico Tech. This morning, each of us was multitasking between finalizing course syllabi, signing registration forms, and catching up with colleagues and students. In a few days, when classes begin, we will walk into our classrooms with the energy that always accompanies a brand new semester. Also responsible for this energy is our own awareness that our TC program at New Mexico Tech is solid in its commitment to providing students with an education that is in-depth and rigorous as well as relevant to the TC practices and trends in the workplace.

We are excited about the future of our program. Technical communication is a growing field, dynamic and changing as new technologies, communication strategies, cultures, and areas of the world are embraced by industry and studied by academia. Through the direction of our corporate advisory board, we expect to keep abreast of the TC industry trends and the changes and challenges we will face. Our students, through their rigorous foundations in science and engineering, will tackle these changes through research and application in their course of study. Furthermore, we expect to confront these changes ourselves through our own research and applied projects.

In conclusion, we recognize that readers of this chapter may or may not have a technical communication major or program at their own home institution. They may or may not be part of an institution that focuses on science and engineering. They may or may not be similar in size or scope to New Mexico Tech. Nevertheless, the lessons and insights we describe here have broad applicability—some of the successful strategies we have employed can be applied to writing programs of various types and in different contexts.

Curricular Summary: Bachelor of Science in Technical Communication at New Mexico Tech

The technical communication curriculum combines courses from three fields of study to prepare students for technical communication positions upon graduation.

- The TC courses introduce students to document design, graphics, and online/multimedia computer documentation. The TC courses also develop students' writing, speaking, and editing abilities.
- The humanities and social science courses improve students' understanding and appreciation of history, literature, philosophy, psychology, and the arts.
- The science and technology courses provide students with a background in one specific science or engineering discipline.

MAJOR REQUIREMENTS (32 CREDIT HOURS)

Core courses:
- TC 100: Community Service
- TC 101: Orientation to Technical Communication
- TC 151: Visual Communication
- TC 202: Editing
- TC 211: Media Studies
- TC 321: Internship
- TC 411: Persuasive Communication
- TC 420: Senior Seminar and
    TC 422: Senior Thesis (two-semester capstone course)
- TC 421: Professional Writing Workshop

Additional requirements:
- Six credit hours of technical communication electives
- Twelve credit hours of science or engineering courses in a single discipline outside of general education requirements
- Twelve credit hours of humanities courses outside of general education requirements and excluding TC courses
- Six credit hours of foreign language (one language)

References

connexions: International Professional Communication Journal. 2012. http://connexionsjournal.org/.

Ford, Julie D., Jennifer L. Bracken, and Gregory D. Wilson. 2009. "The Two-Semester Thesis Model: Emphasizing Research in Undergraduate Technical Communication Curricula." *Journal of Technical Writing and Communication* 39 (4): 433–53. http://dx.doi.org/10.2190/TW.39.4.f.

Ford, Julie D., and Julianne Newmark. 2011. "Emphasizing Research (Further) in Undergraduate Technical Communication Curricula: Involving Undergraduate Students with an Academic Journal's Publication and Management." *Journal of Technical Writing and Communication* 41 (3): 311–24. http://dx.doi.org/10.2190/TW.41.3.f.

Newmark, Julianne, and Julie D. Ford. 2012. "An Academic eJournal as TC Client Project: Enculturation, Production, and Assessment." *Technical Communication* 59: 286–301.

Yee, Carole. 1994. "Can We Be Partners? Industry/Corporate Advisory Boards for Academic Technical Communication Programs." In *Publications Management for Professional Communication*, ed. O. Jane Allen and Lynn H. Deming, 203–11. Amityville: Baywood.

10

WRITING AS AN ART AND PROFESSION AT YORK COLLEGE

Michael J. Zerbe and Dominic F. DelliCarpini

In my opinion, no [person] can be an orator complete in all points of merit, who has not attained a knowledge of all important subjects and arts.

— Cicero (1970), *De Oratore*

It is well for us to keep in mind that human events are dominated by Chance and Choice.

— Giambattista Vico (1990), *On the Study Methods of Our Time*

INTRODUCTION

The professional writing major at York College of Pennsylvania began accepting students in 2002. York College is a private, secular, mid-sized institution of 4,900 students located in a small, Mid-Atlantic city between Baltimore and Harrisburg. York offers pre-professional programs in education, nursing, and business, as well as other fields and programs in the humanities, the sciences, and the arts. About half of the students are from Pennsylvania, with most of the rest from surrounding states: Maryland, Delaware, New Jersey, and New York. Housed in the English Humanities Department, the professional writing major shares institutional space and resources with majors in literary studies, English secondary education, philosophy, Spanish, and Spanish secondary education, and minors in each of the non-education majors as well as in creative writing, film, religion, women's and gender studies, German, and French. The professional writing program currently has seventy-nine majors and about a dozen minors.

PROGRAM OVERVIEW AND RATIONALE

The professional writing major, which awards a bachelor of arts degree, reflects York College's dual emphasis on the liberal arts and

DOI: 10.7330/9780874219722.c010

Department Name:	English Humanities
Institution Type:	Private, Master's S (awards at fewer than 100 Master's degrees/year)
Institution Size:	4,900 students
Residential or Commuter:	Residential
Student Body Description:	Most students work, at minimum, part-time; middle class socioeconomically; high percentage first in their family to go to college; 50% from Pennsylvania and nearly all of the remaining 50% from surrounding Mid-Atlantic states
Year Major Began:	2002
Official Name of Degree:	Bachelor of Arts in Professional Writing
Number of Majors:	In year one: N/A In year three: N/A In year five: N/A Current: 79
Number of Full-Time R/C Faculty:	7

pre-professional programs. Even before they become active in the major, students complete a number of core and area distribution requirement courses that comprise the college's general education program. Then, within the major itself, professional writing students are required to take seven courses that we see as continuing their liberal arts education:

- Interdisciplinary Writing
- Rhetorical Theory
- Language and Linguistics
- Four English and humanities electives, two of which must be in literature

The students are also required to take five pre-professional courses:

- Writing in Professional Cultures
- Digital Writing: Theory and Practice
- Document Design: Theory and Practice
- Experiential Learning (internship)
- Professional Editing

Ultimately, of course, the liberal arts and pre-professional split is something of a false binary: liberal arts courses do cover issues and develop skills that are timely and crucial for both professional and academic success and civic and cultural engagement, as has been argued by Randy Brooks, Peiling Zhao, and Carmella Braninger. They note that "if we accept this assumption [of this binary], we do not believe that students need real-world experiences to practice their reading, writing, and publishing abilities" (Brooks, Zhao, and Braninger 2010, 36). Conversely, liberal arts traits such as synthesis, reflection, appreciation for the human condition, and the ability to understand and handle complex and unexpected situations have a place in both pre-professional courses and the professional workplace. In our professional writing major, students complete a number of courses that we think adroitly navigate this nebulous boundary:

- Advanced Composition
- Two writing electives
- Senior Seminar in Professional Writing

Professional writing students also complicate the liberal arts/pre-professional split by completing either a required minor or, if the student wishes, a double major. Our goal here is to try to help students channel their writing in a certain direction. The students may choose from any minor offered at the college, and over the years—since the professional writing major's inception—we have watched (with pleasure) our students select minors in business, the arts, various social sciences, natural and physical sciences, and the humanities disciplines.

IMPLEMENTATION NARRATIVE

The York College major in professional writing was planned and developed in 2000 and 2001, and, as mentioned above, was instituted in 2002. Building upon a few foundational principles—the most important being that writing was a skill that was greatly valued across disciplines and professions—the proposal for the major was nested within the *ethos* of a comprehensive college. A key argument was that students completing this program would have a number of career and educational options. In this way, the major was rooted in the mission of the college, which aims to offers its students "a broad range of majors in professional and career fields as well as the arts and sciences" that "reflect the enrollment emphases of the undergraduate curriculum and the professional development needs of the region." It was also consciously built upon disciplinary standards of post-graduate education. This attention to the institutional mission and goals, and the alignment of those goals with disciplinary standards, positioned the program in several ways. It was able to favorably present itself to the likely student body through our admissions program, providing admissions personnel with a narrative that reflected both the essential nature of writing skills generally, and the marketability of such skills.

Thus, the proposed professional writing major was a good fit for the college as a whole. Seeking ways in which the liberal arts can be made relevant to today's career-minded students and parents, York College has embraced ideas and programs that strive to offer all of the advantages of a liberal arts education along with the relevancy to contemporary culture that students and parents seek.

Liberal arts in the professional writing major: a description of our courses

In our design of the professional writing major, we tried to ensure a balance of both liberal arts and pre-professional coursework and, as mentioned above, courses that complicate this boundary. In addition, we tried to structure the major so that students would experience such a balance at each course level—200, 300, and 400. At the 200 level, the liberal arts course is Interdisciplinary Writing. The goal of this course, following Cicero's (1970) counsel to orators to know everything, is to help students understand how discourse works in four disciplinary "families": humanities, social sciences, natural and physical sciences, and fine arts. Typically, the course opens with the instructor choosing a topic and then asking the students to learn about it from these four perspectives. Thus, if the topic is caffeine—a topic recently used by one of us—students may read historical, religious, and legal accounts of the substance (i.e., the humanities); economic, sociological/cultural, and psychological accounts (i.e., social sciences); physiological, toxicological, and botanical accounts (i.e., natural and physical sciences); and view artistic representations (art, music, theater) of caffeine, typically in the form of coffee, tea, or chocolate. For the humanities, social sciences, and natural and physical sciences, we move the students from popular nonfiction sources (e.g., *The World of Caffeine: The Science and Culture of the World's Most Popular Drug*) to scholarly, peer-reviewed sources in each family. For example, when we study from the natural and physical sciences perspective, students may read something like "Human Brain Metabolic Response to Caffeine and the Effects of Tolerance" from the *American Journal of Psychiatry*, and the humanities perspective gives us such scholarship as "Is Sipping Sin Breaking Fast? The Catholic Chocolate Controversy and the Changing World of Early Modern Spain" from the journal *Food and Foodways*.

Following this epistemological grand tour of the scope of human inquiry, which takes about a month, students choose their own topics to study, though the topic must lend itself to analysis from each of the four disciplinary perspectives. As a result of taking the course, students attain a holistic view of the range of human inquiry that is not fragmented into ever-more-specialized disciplines. As Giambattista Vico (1990) writes, "[a]rts and sciences, all of which in the past were embraced by philosophy and animated by it with a unitary spirit, are, in our day, unnaturally separated and disjointed" (76)—and to think that Vico wrote this in 1709.

The goal of requiring students to take a course in Rhetorical Theory, our 300-level liberal arts course, is to ensure they have some understanding of the "why" in addition to the "how" discourse works (or doesn't work, as the case may be). To this end, students are introduced to the history of rhetoric, starting with the Sophists, and to the system of rhetoric devised primarily by Aristotle. Students learn the five canons, artistic versus inartistic proofs, the persuasive appeals, enthymemes and examples, the three traditional forums for classical rhetoric, and *kairos*. Students in this class grapple with the epistemological and ontological questions associated with rhetoric—does language create knowledge and is language a part of reality or a reflection of it—through the Classical, Medieval, Renaissance/Enlightenment, Modern, and Postmodern periods. They join the debates surrounding the place of rhetoric in establishing and maintaining a democratic state or the best way(s) to teach writing—imitation/practice and/or study of grammar—and, as did the ancients, discuss the role played by natural talent (to the extent that it exists). Finally, our students learn about contemporary issues, such as the influence of discourse in forming and maintaining disciplines and the place of rhetoric in dominant discourses such as science.

Also at the 300-level, students take a course called Language and Linguistics that covers such topics as the structural components of language, the history of American English, and usage. This course helps our students understand how language works and how it is used on a broader sociocultural level than that found in our other courses. The students study dialects, fluency, translation, language innateness, slang and jargon, and language-related politics and power.

The final liberal arts-focused component of the professional writing major is the above-mentioned requirement for students to take four English and humanities department electives, two of which must be in literature and two of which may also be in literature or in any other departmental discipline—philosophy, foreign languages, film, religion, women's and gender studies, and writing. The rationale for having students take literature courses is that students learn just as much about good writing from reading as they do from writing, and studying literature provides students with an excellent opportunity to hone their stylistic skills and broaden their repertoire of schemes and tropes. For the other two required electives, professional writing majors have ventured into every corner of the English and humanities department; through academic advising, we have encouraged students to take electives that somehow connect with their writing and with how they see or foresee themselves as students, professionals, and citizens.

The (pre-)professional writing courses

While the professional writing major has an unmistakable liberal arts foundation and scaffolding, we also envisioned the program as a pre-professional course of study. Professional writing majors complete a series of five pre-professional courses that are, like the liberal arts courses, spread out across different levels of the program. These pre-professional courses are primarily genre, medium, and skill courses. Typically, students begin with our 200-level Writing in Professional Cultures course, which asks students to familiarize themselves with print and online types of memos, formal letters (including cover letters) and résumés, reports, proposals, instructions, brochures/newsletters, and press releases. Students in this class learn the generic, rhetorical, grammatical, and formatting conventions of each type of text and, in the case of press releases, the differences between academic/professional style and journalistic style.

At the 300-level, professional writing majors must take Digital Writing and Document Design to fulfill the pre-professional expectations of the program. Digital Writing introduces students to website design, and students must design and build their own websites, including both text and graphics. Our students also learn about online media, such as blogs, wikis, other new/social media outlets, digital photography, and various presentation platforms. We strive to keep the course up-to-date by asking each student to find and present a new online writing "tool." By the end of the semester, students have assembled a substantial online writing arsenal.

Document Design, another 300-level course, is our newest addition to the professional writing curriculum. Although we cover some aspects of layout and design in both Writing in Professional Cultures and Digital Writing, the increasing importance of these issues led our colleagues and us to propose a course that offered students more in-depth experience with topics such as fonts and font design, color, logo creation (and other basic graphic design tasks), and information architecture and management. In addition, the Document Design course has proven to be our most successful regarding client-based projects, with students designing and producing, for example, theater program playbills and departmental brochures.

At the 400-level, our professional writing majors take Professional Editing. The students learn copyediting symbols and practice by copyediting extensively. They also try their hand at comprehensive editing, focusing on content, organization, and overarching style issues. Class projects involve both print and online media, and the class covers such topics as editor/writer collaboration and editorial authority, style manuals, production, legal and ethical issues, editing in global contexts, and management. Depending on the semester, students in this course have worked with small groups of business administration majors, who write a lengthy company profile as part of their Operations Management course. Professional writing majors have joined these groups as editors.

Our most overtly pre-professional experience, the internship course, is officially called Experiential Learning. Like Professional Editing, it is offered at the 400-level, but the vast majority of students complete their internships as juniors in order to have internship materials to include in their Senior Seminar portfolios. Professional writing majors who have more than sixty credits and a 2.75 GPA or greater must complete an internship. (Students who do not meet these criteria complete an added professional writing course instead.) Before the internship begins, students complete a learning contract, which a supervisor at the internship site as well as the professional writing faculty internship coordinator must sign off on. They work a total of 120 hours for the sponsoring organization. Internship sites range from the York area to Harrisburg, Baltimore, DC, New York, and even overseas.

Complicating the boundary between the liberal arts and pre-professionalism

The split between liberal arts and pre-professionalism is, to an extent, artificial, and we believe that all of our courses cover both sides of this admittedly tenuous continuum. For example, both the Digital Writing and Document Design courses are subtitled "Theory and Practice"— they are not simply skills courses. Similarly, we make every effort to help students recognize the relevance of courses like Interdisciplinary Writing and Rhetorical Theory. However, we believe that three courses in particular exemplify the "both–and" (rather than "either–or") approach of our professional writing major. The first of these is WRT 315: Advanced Composition, which focuses on prose style. No other course in the major provides students with an opportunity to work with text at the sentence and word levels in the way this course does, and many students take great delight in learning the rich rhetorical tradition of figures of speech. We have discussed this course in detail elsewhere (DelliCarpini and Zerbe 2010). Advanced Composition is a liberal arts course in the sense that it is historical and concerns itself with matters of aesthetics; also, we cover grammar, one of the original liberal arts of the trivium. It is difficult to discuss elements such as word choice, coordination/subordination, and sentence structure without a working knowledge of parts of speech, phrases, and clauses.

A second way in which students blur the boundary between the liberal arts and pre-professionalism is by choosing their two required writing electives. Students have a wide range of courses to choose from. We offer special topics courses in rhetoric (e.g., Science in Rhetoric and Literature) as well as a number of creative writing courses. All of these courses, we believe, lean more toward the liberal arts side of the major. One of the most popular electives, though, is a course called Teaching and Tutoring of Writing, which is more pre-professional focused. Even professional writing majors who have no plans to pursue a career in teaching come to understand in this course that they will become a de facto language expert in whatever organization they will eventually work and that they will be called upon to share their expertise. As a result of this realization, students see Teaching and Tutoring of Writing as especially helpful, and earning a good grade in this course can lead to a paid writing tutor position in York College's Center for Teaching and Learning. Students also have the option of taking Print Media Writing, a journalism/public relations course in the mass communication program, or a grant writing course in the sociology program, both of which represent the pre-professional side of the major.

Finally, the Senior Seminar course perhaps best obliterates the liberal arts/pre-professional split. The course has an academic, liberal arts component centered on readings on a particular theme—recent topics have included the future of literacy and the life of a writer—and a major paper and poster session. However, the course also requires substantial pre-professional work in portfolio development, job or graduate school preparation, and freelancing instruction. For the portfolio, which typically has both print and online versions, we ask students to assemble a collection of their work for a well-defined audience and purpose. Our students must discuss this audience and purpose in a cover memo and explain why the works they selected help to achieve the stated purpose. We ask our students to save all of their major papers and projects from the time they enter the major so they can consider them for inclusion in the Senior Seminar portfolio. Discussion of freelancing has become more of an important issue as students explore ways to succeed and achieve financial independence in a difficult economy.

CONNECTIONS AS MISSION ALIGNMENT AT THE COLLEGE LEVEL

Since the professional writing program at York College was built with local exigencies and culture in mind, its place within the college as a whole has been more easily articulated, and its influence has allowed for the success and growth of both the major and its influence upon the status of writing across campus. As DelliCarpini (2007) has argued previously, and has been more recently noted by Tweedie, Courtney, and Wolff (2010), the amorphousness of what we call a "writing major" allows for greater attention to the shape that best fits its institutional mission.

This approach to building the major proved fortuitous—in 2008, York College used data collected in previous years by external environmental scans to build its brand around the concept of "professionalism." This scan of employers and other environmental factors revealed that among the most valued elements of York College graduates was their ability to function well within their professional environments. Consequently, the college, building upon this research, established its brand around the concept of professionalism, defining key characteristics of professionalism that would help guide the college ethos. The college's definition of "professionalism" includes:

- Commitment to the mastery of a field of endeavor and to lifelong learning to stay current in that field;
- Integrity in truthfully presenting ideas, products, or services to colleagues and clients;
- Working co-operatively with persons of diverse backgrounds;
- Capability and confidence to make independent judgments in one's area of expertise; and
- Engagement in civic affairs, community service, and charitable activities.

This definition of professionalism, now a college-wide standard, also led to the development of York's Center for Professional Excellence (Waldner 2011), which performs national research on what employers mean by "professionalism" and promotes "the capabilities that will enable students to be effective professionals in whatever career path they choose." Thus, the development of the professional writing major anticipated the direction in which the entire college would move, and it fulfills York College's comprehensive mission by including both liberal arts and pre-professional learning.

Below, we discuss some specific ways that the design and implementation of the professional writing major has positioned the program to play a crucial role in advancing the educational priorities of the college more generally. Among these exigencies are general education reform (including the development of a first-year experience), the integration of information literacy skills across the curriculum, working toward writing in the disciplines, experiential learning, and faculty development. These points of connection, as we illustrate below, demonstrate the ways in which the growth of writing majors can have a more global impact on higher education in the early twenty-first century if writing majors are developed in mission-driven ways.

Fifteen years into our current system, general education reform is one priority at York College that is driven by both local and national change. Claims about students' lack of higher order thinking abilities, the publication of books like Arum and Roksa's (2010) *Academically Adrift*, and current pressures for higher education to justify its value now omnipresent in the media all provide both a sharp need for reform and a real opportunity. Our professional writing major, as described above, negotiated between the Scylla of esoteric versions of the liberal arts and the Charybdis of vocational "training." By including a rich set of rhetorical and analytical learning opportunities, and tying those learning outcomes with real, demonstrable, and marketable skills, the professional writing major outlines a model that can likewise negotiate the large odyssey faced by general education reform. Rather than treating general education as a set of disconnected skills, the professional writing model included developing a course sequence that helped students integrate theoretical knowledge (rhetorical theory, grammatical understanding, and textual analysis) with practical skills (writing in professional cultures, document design, digital writing, and editing).

The professional writing major also serves as a model for developing first-year experience. The first-year experience program being piloted has its anchor in our FYC courses, into which we have infused attention to the "habits of mind" that are likely to assure success in both college writing and more generally (see Council of Writing Program Administrators 2011). Our pilot course for the first-year experience has consciously integrated the same principles of our major: connecting professional aspirations with liberal learning. To do so, we have included themes that allow students to be self-reflective about their professional goals while connecting those motives to the need for traditional liberal arts skills and habits of mind. We have also included requirements for attendance at—and written reflection upon—enrichment activities, co-curricular learning activities (through student affairs), and professionalism seminars (through our Center for Professional Excellence). Much like the design of our major, the first-year experience is thus an argument we make to students: liberal learning is not disconnected from "major" fields or career aspirations, but in fact drives the outcomes of a successful professional.

The integration of knowledge has also been advanced by the writing program's role in delivering information literacy skills at the college. For the past fourteen years, students at York College have been required to complete a two-credit information literacy course (IFL 101)—taught by library faculty—in order to prepare them for the need to find, evaluate, and incorporate information into their work at the college and beyond. However, as the concept of information literacy has continued to grow beyond that narrow envelope of concerns—the traditional tripartite description first offered by the American Library Association and the Association of College and Research Libraries—the standalone course has suffered from issues that are quite familiar to writing faculty. The "inoculation" method of teaching either information literacy or writing, a once-and-done approach, cannot serve the complexities of either outcome. As such, with the growth of the professional writing major and its faculty, as well as the attention of the major to issues of both technological and information literacy, a more integrated model is now planned for the delivery of information literacy across disciplines.

Likewise, the college has (as the professional writing major did earlier) committed to experiential learning. The academic senate endorsed the college's commitment to offering at least one course whose main emphasis is experiential learning. In doing so, the college has acknowledged the same conclusion as the writing program—knowledge is best activated by praxis. In this way, the professional writing program, along with many other programs at the college, can be a model for this college priority.

Perhaps one of the central ways the writing program can align and connect with the institutional mission is through faculty development. This connection is both a direct element of the professional writing major—which was built upon a model of ongoing pedagogical excellence—and a fortunate byproduct of the growth of the major and the concomitant growth of the full-time faculty in rhetoric and composition (which has now grown to seven from its original two before the major was developed). Additionally, growth is illustrated in the recent appointment of our writing center director as the director of our new Center for Teaching and Learning. Thus, the growth of the major has allowed for a rich set of resources for faculty development. (It is no accident that so many faculty development directors are appointed from our discipline, given the primacy of the scholarship of teaching and learning in our discipline.) Locally, this has led not only to the important role of the Center for Teaching and Learning director being placed upon a writing specialist, but also to inaugural initiatives through the center that have been led by writing faculty, including professional learning communities on writing in the disciplines, peer review, best practices in teaching and learning, and outcomes assessment.

REFLECTION AND PROSPECTION

In his 2006 CCCC Exemplar Award address, David Bartholomae (2006), who has devoted his career to the advancement of FYC, asked his peers (as he also did in his 1988 CCCC address) to avoid creating disciplinary boundaries that would cordon off rhetoric and composition from diverse interests and its core commitment to literacy education for all. This is perhaps the greatest challenge that faces the discipline as it continues to develop a strong disciplinary identity, as its majors continue to flourish, and as its faculty members become more specialized. The growth of exciting and attractive movements like the "writing about writing" initiatives led by Downs and Wardle (2007) make the decisions we face, both locally and nationally, particularly exigent and thorny. The local incarnation of that issue looks something like this: as our credibility and strength as a major grows, what is the role of the writing program as a service to the college more generally?

As we welcome our seventh full-time faculty member in the professional writing program, we look forward to positive growth in both size and curriculum: developing new technological learning opportunities, offering new document design courses, opening more areas of specialized disciplinary research, and implementing tracks within the major that student can pursue in lieu of an outside minor. Tracks under consideration include (but are not limited to) writing and technology, pedagogy, rhetoric, and/or technical communication.

At the same time, a whole array of deeper connections with institutional priorities exist, and the need to keep FYC and liberal arts education a priority remains. Specializations like those described above have the potential to lead to difficult choices about whether the professional writing major should continue to align itself with institutional mission and reform, or whether narrower disciplinary concerns should be prioritized. This is not to suggest that both are not possible. Indeed, as the history of our major seems to indicate, there are clear and available points of alignment that can indeed serve these multiple purposes, as well as an array of ways that the work of the national discipline can serve the needs of the local institution. However, these will require mindfulness and attention to the ways that other humanities fields have veered off course and become more esoteric (and hence expendable) parts of the academy. Surveying the many challenges to higher education—economic and otherwise—that now face us, it is crucial that we proceed carefully, knowing that the work that made us strong is also the work that keeps us strong. The double-edged sword we face is finding ways to avoid the impulse to become overly specialized, and thus insular, while also continuing to enrich our majors through our growing knowledge base. The environment around us is littered with humanities programs that have ignored that caveat by treating knowledge fields as somehow disconnected from one another. Successful professional writing majors generally, and ours specifically, have been responsive to institutional differences and missions, thus enjoying a central role in the new liberal arts. It is clearly possible to continue to offer the rich and pedagogically-centered work we do to advance the mission of higher education, and at the same time keep our majors responsive and student-centered.

Curricular Summary: The Professional Writing Major at York College of Pennsylvania

The professional writing major at York College of Pennsylvania is designed for aspiring writers who want to put their writing skills to work, and the program unites the best of the liberal arts and pre-professional traditions. There is a strong emphasis on the *professional* in professional writing; the major focuses on developing the ability to produce the kinds of writing that are valued in fields ranging from technical and business writing to creative writing and journalism. A professional writing major is also excellent preparation for students interested in work as editors, social media contributors/bloggers, web designers, and information managers, and in fields such as communication, publishing, journalism, law, information technology, government, non-governmental organizations (NGOs), insurance, non-profit and social service organizations, healthcare, finance, and the arts. Professional writing is also among the most valued courses of study for those interested in post-graduate education in English or rhetoric, law, technical writing, or creative writing.

The professional writing major provides students with:

- Marketable communication skills, such as editing, online communication (including web design and other new media), and collaborative writing
- Real-world learning through internship experiences
- A wide range of critical thinking and problem-solving skills
- A combined print and electronic portfolio of work that can be used in the search for a position as a professional writer or writing specialist, or as a way of publishing creative writing or obtaining a literary agent
- Background in the history and theory of language use
- Guided experience with a wide range of writing situations and stylistic options, such as document design and visual rhetoric

Because the professional writing program at York College supports liberal learning and studies the rhetorical tradition (past and present), all professional writing majors complete four English and humanities electives (twelve credits). Two of these electives must be literature courses. Three of the electives must be 200-level or higher, and one must be 300-level or higher. To support the specializations and professional aspirations of individual students, all professional writing majors declare and complete a minor (typically eighteen credits) that supports their area of interest. The minor can be from any college department, or it may be self-designed, and it is chosen or developed in collaboration with each student's academic advisor.

MAJOR REQUIREMENTS (30 CREDIT HOURS):
Core courses:
- WRT 210: Writing in Professional Cultures
- WRT 225: Interdisciplinary Writing
- WRT 305: Rhetorical Theory
- LIT 310: Language and Linguistics
- WRT 315: Advanced Composition (prose style)
- WRT 320: Digital Writing: Theory and Practice
- WRT 321: Document Design: Theory and Practice
- WRT 410: Professional Editing
- WRT 450: Experiential Learning (internship)
- WRT 480: Senior Seminar in Professional Writing

Electives (two courses):
- WRT 272: Introduction to Creative Writing
- WRT 275: Playwriting

- WRT 290: Teaching and Tutoring of Writing I
- WRT 372: Poetry Writing
- WRT 373: Creative Nonfiction
- WRT 374: Writing Children's Literature
- WRT 377: Screenwriting
- WRT 380: Literary Publishing
- WRT 382: Fiction Writing
- WRT 451: Experiential Learning II (internship)
- WRT 452: Teaching and Tutoring Writing II
- WRT 498: Independent Study in Professional Writing
- WRT 3*xx*: Special Topics in Professional Writing
- WRT 4*xx*: Special Topics in Professional Writing

References

Arum, Richard, and Jospia Roksa. 2010. "Academically Adrift: Limited Learning on College Campuses." Chicago: University of Chicago Press.

Bartholomae, David. 2006. "Exemplar Award Acceptance Address." Conference on College Composition and Communication, Chicago.

Brooks, Randy, Peiling Zhao, and Carmella Braninger. 2010. "Redefining the Undergraduate Writing Major: An Integrated Approach at a Small Comprehensive University." In *What We Are Becoming: Developments in Undergraduate Writing Majors*, ed. Greg Giberson and Thomas A. Moriarty, 32–49. Logan: Utah State University Press.

Cicero. 1970. *De Oratore*, ed. J. S. Watson. Carbondale: Southern Illinois UP.

Council of Writing Program Administrators. 2011. "Framework for Success in Postsecondary Writing."

DelliCarpini, Dominic F. 2007. "Re-Writing the Humanities: The Writing Major's Effect upon Undergraduate Studies in English Departments." *Composition Studies* 35 (1): 15–36.

DelliCarpini, Dominic F. and Michael J. Zerbe. 2010. "Remembering the Canons' Middle Sisters: Style, Memory, and the Return of the Progymnasmata in the Liberal Arts Writing Major." In *What We Are Becoming: Developments in Undergraduate Writing Majors*, ed. Greg Giberson and Thomas A. Moriarty, 177–203. Logan: Utah State University Press.

Downs, Douglas, and Elizabeth Wardle. 2007. "Teaching about writing, righting misconceptions: (Re)Envisioning 'First-Year Composition' as 'Introduction to Writing Studies.'" *College Composition and Communication* 58 (4): 552–584.

Giberson, Greg, and Thomas A. Moriarty, eds. 2010. *What We Are Becoming: Developments in Undergraduate Writing Majors*. Logan: Utah State University Press.

Tweedie, Sanford, Jennifer Courtney, and William I. Wolff. 2010. "What Exactly Is this Major? Creating Disciplinary Identity through an Introductory Course." In *What We Are Becoming: Developments in Undergraduate Writing Majors,* ed. Greg Giberson and Thomas A. Moriarty, 260–76. Logan: Utah State University Press.

Vico, Giambattista. 1990. *On the Study Methods of Our Time*. Trans. Elio Gianturco and Donald Phillip Verene. Ithaca: Cornell University Press.

Waldner, George W. 2011. "Strategic positioning of the College and professionalism definition." Memo sent to faculty and senior administrators, April, York College, York, PA.

PART II

English Departments

11

THEY COULD BE OUR STUDENTS
The Writing Major at Texas Christian University

Carrie Leverenz, Brad Lucas, Ann George,
Charlotte Hogg, and Joddy Murray

INTRODUCTION

As a cohort of faculty in rhetoric and composition, we share here our experience in shaping a writing major at Texas Christian University (TCU), a secular, private university of about 10,000 students in the country's fourth-largest metropolitan area. Our experiences were marked by both serendipity and strategy as we built upon existing resources, made the most of opportunities, and listened to our students—all the while respecting our colleagues and our own limitations. Beyond simply sharing our story, we hope that our insight can assist others who want to develop a major that accounts for, and emerges from, local contexts. Established in 2007, the TCU writing major has grown within our English department, alongside the literature-focused English major. And, though our path wasn't straightforward, we take pride in a major that deliberately reflects the culture of TCU: emphasizing the values of a liberal arts education in tandem with pre-professional study. While some new programs might require a large infusion of funding and faculty, we built our major with existing resources, adapting to changes in the campus climate and expanding the reach of our department by situating writing as a liberal art.

PROGRAM OVERVIEW AND RATIONALE:
OUR OWN RHETORICAL TRADITION

From the start, we have been lucky to have history on our side. Unlike many English departments, where writing courses—and too often,

DOI: 10.7330/9780874219722.c011

Department Name:	English
Institution Type:	Private, DRU (Doctoral Research University)
Institution Size:	10,000 students
Residential or Commuter:	Residential
Student Body Description:	Most students are of traditional age (18–21); roughly 60% are women, 40% are men, and 17% are minority; the most popular majors are pre-professional (business, nursing, engineering, communication); selective admissions (65% of students in the top 20% of their class)
Year Major Began:	2006
Official Name of Degree:	Bachelor of Arts in Writing
Number of Majors:	In year one: 17 In year three: 46 In year five: 52 Current: 64
Number of Full-Time R/C Faculty:	7

faculty—are relegated to a service role, our department has a long history of strength in rhetoric and composition. Once home to such field-shaping scholars as Gary Tate, Jim Corder, and Winifred Horner, TCU's English department has trained rhet/comp PhDs since the early 1970s. Additionally, since 1987, TCU has been home to the Lillian Radford chair of rhetoric and composition (formerly held by Horner, Susan Jarratt, and C. Jan Swearingen, and currently by Richard Enos). In 2006, when we began planning for a writing major, we started by capitalizing on TCU's own rhetorical tradition. From decades of catalog copy to a list of prominent alumni, we took stock of the hard work that had already been done on behalf of rhet/comp and recognized that the department had grown with this legacy, envisioning itself as a place where rhetoric, writing, and literature could productively interact.

This interconnection of rhet/comp and literary study was especially evident at the graduate level, where every PhD student took courses in composition theory and rhetorical history and where many dissertations incorporated both rhetoric and literature. This interconnection, however, didn't quite trickle down to the undergraduate major, though that had not always been the case. Throughout the 1990s, English majors could choose a concentration in literature or writing, and, over the years, many advanced courses in writing and rhetoric had been added to the catalog. But by 2000, the rhet/comp faculty numbered only three, and the English major had been revised, eliminating the writing concentration.

The English major that replaced the two-concentration system was designed according to a traditional period-and-coverage model that immersed students in literary study. In place of the five-course writing concentration students could once choose, only one writing course was required in the new major. Even with electives, English majors could take only a few writing courses. These constraints, however, ultimately helped our case for a separate major, rather than a return to the concentration.

Fortunately for us, existing courses in writing and rhetoric had not been eliminated with the writing concentration. The university catalog preserved a broad selection of courses, ranging from rhetorical history and criticism to technical and professional writing to magazine writing and creative writing workshops. By having this rich pedagogical resource, we could generate interest in a variety of writing courses simply by offering them—we did not have to justify their creation or shepherd them through several levels of curricular review. At first, these courses simply gave us teaching options, and we didn't consider them components of a coherent major. However, when we began designing a BA in writing, we saw that their very variety reflected the department's, and our own, commitment to a broad liberal arts mission. Thus, we did not consider the major as distinctly separate from English, nor did we imagine narrow definitions of writing that placed it in an exclusive category or defined it by instrumental ends. Rather, with the creation of a writing major, we hoped to expand our purview beyond composition courses and promote writing (symbol use) as a means of knowledge making. Our philosophy was this: writing is everywhere, belongs to everyone, and should be explored and practiced in as many forms as possible. Given our own broad training in rhet/comp, and the prospects for a major that could embrace writing in all of its forms, the exact shape and design of the curriculum was always secondary to our shared interest in promoting a culture of writing, reaching out to students beyond the English department, and preparing for the changes and challenges we knew were ahead of us.

TEACH IT AND THEY WILL COME

Long before seriously considering a major in writing, we were laying the groundwork to make a proposal feasible. We referred to our group as the rhet/comp "cadre," but we were not defined by a program affiliation or recognized as a department committee. Nevertheless, we met regularly to discuss course rotations, the needs of our graduate students, and ways to strengthen rhet/comp and its reach. Looking back, we might describe the years before the advent of our major as a period of strategic investments at opportune moments, a time when we concentrated on increasing the cadre's numbers and stimulating demand for writing courses, not just within the department but across the university.

We all shared an interest in being "program people," which inevitably led to our willing (albeit disproportionate) service to the department in administrative positions. During the period of strategic investment, three rhet/comp faculty in succession served as the director of undergraduate studies. The preponderance of rhet/comp faculty in administrative positions is widely acknowledged, but, in the context of building an undergraduate major, the costs of such work also come with benefits not so widely recognized. We garnered goodwill among our colleagues by demonstrating our commitment to the department as a whole. Perhaps more important, this service revealed ways that writing could play a larger role in the department. As the primary contact for students inquiring about the major, we had a clear sense that demand for writing was growing, especially from students in journalism and education, where changes in state certification requirements had led to some dissatisfaction. When we asserted that students wanted to take more writing courses, we could support our claims with enrollment patterns as well as comments students shared with us.

More writing courses would require more faculty, and our efforts to increase faculty lines in rhet/comp were aided by a number of circumstances. While only three strong in 2000, we have since grown to a cadre of seven tenure-track positions in rhetoric and composition (of twenty-three in the department), with six already tenured. This growth has resulted from steady increases in the undergraduate population at TCU, our dean's goal of having tenure-track faculty teach core curriculum courses, and our willingness to do so. In a typical five-course load, rhet/comp instructors generally taught two or three required composition courses. Another opportunity presented itself when our core curriculum went through a complete overhaul, designed primarily by the university's faculty, and we successfully advocated for retaining the requirements for both first- and second-year composition courses, along with two "writing emphasis" courses from any discipline that offered them. The new core curriculum thus reaffirmed the importance of writing at all stages—and potentially in all areas—of undergraduate study.

As new rhet/comp faculty joined the department, we began to offer a regular rotation of the writing and rhetoric courses that had, years earlier, supported the writing concentration. Our strategy was simple: if we teach it, they will come. And they did. Surprisingly, a number of these courses became requirements for other majors (e.g., education, political science), and, while it was a delicate balance to schedule these courses to meet other departmental needs, we were encouraged because we were making ourselves necessary—our courses had to be taught because they were in demand.

Beyond course offerings, we expanded our influence—and drew attention to writing on campus—through the creation of a New Media Writing Studio (NMWS). Funded by a university-wide grant initiative to promote innovation, the NMWS supports multimodal composing across the curriculum for all students and faculty willing to learn. As a program, the NMWS was independent of the English department, but it was created and managed primarily by faculty with rhet/comp backgrounds. By offering professional development workshops for faculty, ongoing consulting and lab support throughout the year, and opportunities for transdisciplinary exchange, the NMWS heightened not only the visibility and viability of writing, but also its central role in emerging technologies. Indeed, the very presence of the NMWS prompted questions from colleagues across campus as to why English faculty were facilitating new media endeavors, which, in turn, provided opportunities to tout our broad definition of writing. The rhet/comp cadre's investment in the NMWS inevitably influenced how we both taught existing courses and developed new ones, giving us the opportunity to redefine writing within, and beyond, our department. For example, in the English department, a capstone seminar for seniors included the creation of a digital portfolio as its major assignment, and new media assignments were increasingly naturalized in our writing instruction at all levels as well as emerging in courses across the university. With the rising demand for our writing courses, as well as a surge of interest and activity surrounding the NMWS and multimodal composition, many of our colleagues recognized that the digital tide was inevitably turning their way, and they saw us as capable of navigating these new waters.

LEAD, GROW, UNITE: COMMANDING
RESOURCES IN THE LIBERAL ARTS

In the years leading up to the writing major proposal, we shared a constant worry with our colleagues about the number of English majors, especially given the decline of undergraduate English majors nationally. This decline was noted specifically by an MLA committee, who introduced their 2003 report with this blunt opening sentence: "An academic field's ability to attract students affects its ability to command institutional resources" (Schramm et al. 2003, 68). Although our department courted prospective English majors by showcasing famous English majors and sending out personalized invitations to our best students, we saw no significant change in numbers. Many students, we learned, were reluctant to declare an English major either because they defined it narrowly (often based on secondary-school experiences) or had serious reservations about job prospects (reinforced, of course, by parental concerns about the return-on-investment for tuition costs). But these students loved to write, and, as we listened to them explain why they chose "practical" majors such as journalism or advertising, we realized that a major in writing could offer an attractive balance of the liberal arts and professional practice. This hunch was confirmed when, in a 2002 assessment survey of English majors, we learned that—while most were satisfied—students wanted more writing opportunities within the degree program.

Our students' calls for more writing mirrored a national trend. Rhet/comp was hitting its stride with the expansion of undergraduate writing majors and the affordances of new media composing championed by Kathleen Blake Yancey (2004) in her CCCC address. In addition to student interest and this national initiative, we found precedent for a writing major not only in the early curriculum models at TCU, but through a range of published scholarship. In 1975, and again in 1981, our predecessors at TCU—Tade, Tate, and Corder (1975), and Arthur Shumaker (1981)—argued for a writing major in the pages of *College Composition and Communication* and the *Journal of Advanced Composition. Rhetoric Review* documented the rise of writing concentrations through the mid-1990s, and the CCCC compilation of "Writing Majors at a Glance" in 2006 provided descriptions of forty-five different programs. Because TCU was the editorial home for *Composition Studies* in 2006, it was a pleasure to welcome guest editors from Eastern Michigan University, who prepared a special issue dedicated to "The Writing Major." Drawing from such scholarship and documenting the disciplinary landscape of rhet/comp, we could easily argue for the validity of a BA in writing, at least to our college- and university-level curriculum committees. Our challenge, however, was to make the case to the entire English faculty—and to do so with care, respect, and a genuine motivation to strengthen the department.

Because we were six faculty members trying to persuade a group twice our size, we wanted to avoid being threatening or divisive by emphasizing that the new major would not detract from the current undergraduate program or require additional resources—in fact, it could benefit the entire department. Consolidating our message, we prepared a hand-out, setting forth our rationale and a program of study for both a major and a minor. The rationale asserted that the department should "initiate a leadership role that emphasizes the liberal arts in writing instruction," should "provide an option for students who would not otherwise declare an English major," and should rest assured that the benefits from the new major would be realized by the department as a whole. ("The B.A. in Writing in the English Department" 2006)

In an effort to overcome resistance, we provided elaborations for the rationale, allowing us all to be literally on the same page: (1) no changes would be made to the existing BA in English; (2) existing writing and rhetoric courses would be enough to serve the major, displacing perhaps students from other majors taking the courses for elective credit; (3) our focus on both the liberal arts and professional practice would highlight "the critical difference between the English department and other fields that 'do writing'" on campus; (4) the writing major would require some literary study, just as the English major required some advanced writing and rhetoric courses; and (5) the college limit on courses in any one discipline was unfairly preventing students from taking more writing courses. ("The B.A. in Writing in the English Department" 2006)

We anticipated challenges via counter-proposals for a minor, a certificate option, or, most likely, a concentration or "track" within the English major (a return to the previously-eliminated model). With ample and fully-enrolled courses, and enough faculty to staff them and advise students, we argued for growth. Mindful of the students from other disciplines who loved our courses but were reluctant to major in English, we stood behind a basic assertion: they *could* be our students. But, if we wanted to bring majors to the College of Liberal Arts, anything short of a major called "Writing" would not appeal to those students—or their parents. In other words, if the new major still included "English" in its name, we were not likely to attract new students, nor command the institutional resources that would come with an increase in majors. Although we maintained that the new name of the degree would represent a more encompassing view of writing beyond the literary, we did concede that courses for the new major would retain the "English" course prefix (ENGL), thereby reassuring colleagues that the two majors would share a disciplinary home.

We likewise shaped the curriculum to emphasize the parallels between a major in writing and a major in English. In other words, by design, we presented a familiar structure for the curriculum, one that allowed students to choose within broad categories, thereby reinforcing the liberal arts dimension of the major. The English major required courses in four categories: American literature, British literature, theory, and writing. In turn, the writing major required courses in four categories: craft, rhetoric and culture, practical arts, and advanced study.

The categories themselves served both theoretical and practical purposes. From the beginning, we avoided the distinction of creativity implied by "creative writing" and opted for the broader term "craft" (a term inspired by Tim Mayers's (2005) *(Re)Writing Craft: Composition, Creative Writing, and the Future of English*). The second and third categories provided a tidy classification for existing rhet/comp courses: "rhetoric" with the added "culture" distinction to accommodate literacy and language-oriented classes, and "practical arts" to include advanced writing courses that complemented the offerings in craft. We avoided the term "composition" altogether to limit confusion with the two composition courses required in the core curriculum. The final category of "advanced study" included any coursework that looked beyond undergraduate classroom experience: directed studies, writing internships, or entry-level graduate courses available to seniors.

To ensure that students would have a broad foundation in the major, they are required to take one course from each category, then choose concentration electives (i.e., a student wanting extensive creative writing experience could take several "craft" courses). All writing majors are also required to take two upper division literature courses and two more electives in either literature or writing, allowing up to four courses in literature within the ten-course major. The English department voted to add a one-credit senior seminar as a requirement for both English and writing majors. Intended to provide students both a space for reflection on their work and an opportunity to prepare for graduate study or careers, Senior Seminar currently focuses on the production of a digital professional portfolio, thus showcasing the shared mission of these two majors within the English department.

IMPLEMENTATION NARRATIVE: THE ROAD SOMEWHAT TRAVELED, AGAIN

The writing major and minor were approved in March 2007, and, by December, two English majors had changed to writing majors just in time for graduation. We began attracting majors early and, at the time of this writing, have roughly one-third of the total number of majors in the department. TCU increased its undergraduate population by 7.95% from 2006–2010, despite a period of enormous economic downturn. Proportionate to the total undergraduate enroll-ment, then, the Department of English increased its overall number of majors (English/writing) by 25% over a four-year period. In terms of students in the College of Liberal Arts, English generated a propor-tionate increase of 41% over a four-year period. These numbers were undeniably in favor of the department's decision, and former skeptics became supporters.

This steady increase of writing majors affirmed that we were on the right track. From our perspective, the original structure of the major was working, requiring a broad writing experience while also allow-ing students a creative, academic, or professional specialization—or a combination—that they could easily translate into future goals. Our classes were filling, students were tracking through the writing major and graduating, and our faculty reported positive experiences in the sections they taught.

However, in the context of a department that considers its curricu-lum flexible and responsive to changing research, teaching interests, and student needs, we never intended for the major to remain static. Mindful of the initial structure's success, especially in recruiting writing majors from areas such as communication and business, by 2010, the rhet/comp cadre agreed that it was time to modify the major based on student feedback, faculty input, and institutional realities.

Through listening to our students and noting their questions about the curriculum, we learned that our categories of courses were not translating as well as we initially imagined. Identifying courses as "craft," "practical arts," "rhetoric and culture," and "advanced study" made good sense to us, but we recognized that more accessible categories would help students—and our colleagues—better understand the major. Further, the fourth category, the de facto "grab bag" of courses that comprised advanced study, presented a staffing challenge, and some stu-dents were disgruntled because the limited courses filled up quickly or were too narrowly focused to connect to their interests. Students often chose the internship because it was the only advanced study course offered every semester and had no enrollment cap—thus, it was always available, making long-term planning or last-minute enrollment easy. Ultimately, this curricular restraint proved to be yet another opportunity for change: as more students participated in increasingly diverse intern-ships, our writing majors—and we—came to see the internship as an important capstone experience.

As a consequence, in 2010 we revised the writing major to require the internship and galvanized the remaining coursework into three categories. First, we eliminated the "advanced study" category and replaced it with one simply titled "internship," including the original class but also adding a new course called Publication Production that focused on editing and production work on campus (e.g., TCU Press, the departmental newsletter, and an undergraduate creative writing journal). With this new category, students were now required to have some work experience related to writing, with options both on and off campus. We then reassigned the remaining classes in "advanced study" to the category that would be the best match based on subject matter rather than course level.

In reassembling course lists, we renamed two other categories accordingly: "craft" became "creative writing," and "practical arts" became "design and editing" ("rhetoric and culture" remained unchanged.) The new names resonated with students and faculty as more familiar, clear, and specific. The current, (slightly) revised major maintains our liberal arts orientation and a broad conception of the teaching of writing and rhetoric, and we expect to maintain such breadth as we add more courses that account for multiple genres, changing modes of production, and community engagement. As we do so, we also expect to continually negotiate which aspects of the major to expand: do we offer more creative writing, more new media, more of something else? That is, the very categories that together make up a liberal arts approach can, at times, seem to compete. Further, when students choose to concentrate their studies on "creative writing," "rhetoric and culture," or "design and editing," they also begin to customize the major to their own particular goals. And, as they do, they—and we—must navigate a perhaps inevitable tension between professional concerns and liberal arts objectives for our students, for us as faculty, and for our colleagues within and outside our department.

REFLECTION AND PROSPECTION: WE BUILT IT, THEY CAME—NOW WHAT?

As we reflect on the creation and revision of the writing major, our biggest challenge remains in maintaining our current success with existing resources. We have to offer enough courses in each category to ensure that writing majors can enroll in the courses they need. Because many of our courses meet core curriculum requirements, and sometimes requirements in other departments, demand typically exceeds our offerings. Additionally, with three of our seven rhet/comp faculty members partially diverted by administrative appointments, we are limited in the numbers of courses we can teach. Given such limits, the need to prioritize our teaching means we are unable to regularly teach required composition courses. This lack of opportunity to contribute to lower-division core courses is at odds with our professional commitment to those required courses, and is a source of tension within the department. Still, we continue to consider how to add new courses as the major grows in popularity, and we pursue structural adaptations that consider the institutional, cultural, and economic changes that are perennially part of a vibrant curriculum.

Looking forward, we aim to continue navigating the space between working within the constraints of current resources and presenting new initiatives to meet fresh opportunities. In doing so, we hope to foster growth that will, ideally, result in more resources for continued development (i.e., growing programs are generally the best positioned to add faculty). Outreach is one of our primary means for growth—for instance, increasing the major's visibility via our student journal of the arts (eleven40seven 2014), which showcases our students' work at the annual Undergraduate Research Festival; increasing internship opportunities; providing career information for prospective majors; and sharing efforts between our major, the NMWS, and programs such as study abroad and service learning. In hopes of recruiting interested students earlier in their careers, we have introduced new sophomore-level courses: Protest and Power, Writing Games, and Reading as a Writer. Ultimately, of course, our plans reflect a liberal arts ethic that we hope can be made stronger during a time when the national conversation on higher education among politicians, pundits, and management seems to be clamoring for a more vocational approach. To be responsive to these forces and the challenges yet to come, a flexible major—grounded in rhetoric and composition, with a broad understanding of writing—offers the best chance for its continued health and enduring strength, with the liberal arts as the cornerstone of undergraduate education.

Curricular Summary: The Writing Major at Texas Christian University

Writing is offered as a BA major and either a BS or BA minor. To earn the BA in writing, students must complete thirty-one credit hours in English; of these, at least twenty-five credit hours must be in upper-division English courses. All writing majors with senior standing and at least twenty-one hours in the major are then required to take a Senior Seminar course.

Each writing major forms a program of study in consultation with a faculty adviser in English. Students choose fifteen hours (six credits of electives) of course credit from the categories of creative writing, rhetoric and culture, and design and editing. In addition, students take six credit hours in literary and language studies and another six elective hours in any English course. A semester-long internship is required, along with completion of the senior-level seminar.

MAJOR REQUIREMENTS (31 CREDIT HOURS)

Core courses:
- ENGL 10803: Introductory Composition: Writing as Inquiry, or
  ENGL 10833: Introductory Composition: First-Year Seminar
- ENGL 20803: Intermediate Composition: Writing Argument, or
  ENGL 20833: Intermediate Composition: Sophomore Seminar

Creative writing concentration (one course):
- ENGL 10203: Introduction to Creative Writing
- ENGL 20103: Reading as a Writer
- ENGL 30233: Creative Nonfiction Workshop I
- ENGL 30343: Fiction Writing Workshop I
- ENGL 30353: Poetry Writing Workshop I
- ENGL 30363: Digital Creative Writing
- ENGL 30373: Drama Writing Workshop I
- ENGL 40133: Creative Writing Workshop II
- ENGL 40203: Fiction Writing Workshop II
- ENGL 40213: Poetry Writing Workshop II
- ENGL 40223: Drama Writing Workshop II
- ENGL 50233: Studies in Creative Writing

Rhetoric and culture concentration (one course):
- ENGL 20313: Power and Protest
- ENGL 20333: Language, Technology, and Society
- ENGL 30203: Urban Rhetorics
- ENGL 30213: Advanced Composition: Writing Genres
- ENGL 30243: Rhetorical Practices in Culture
- ENGL 30253: Rhetorical Traditions
- ENGL 30273: Argument and Persuasion
- ENGL 30283: Cyberliteracy
- ENGL 30663: Women's Rhetorics
- ENGL 30803: Theories of Cinema
- ENGL 40253: Propaganda Analysis and Persuasion
- ENGL 40333: Language, Rhetoric, and Culture

- ENGL 50243: Teaching Writing
- ENGL 50253: Classical Rhetoric

Design and editing concentration (one course):
- ENGL 20303: Writing Games
- ENGL 30223: Technical Writing and Information Design
- ENGL 30263: Style
- ENGL 30813: Books and the History of Print Culture
- ENGL 20103: Reading as a Writer
- ENGL 40163: Multimedia Authoring: Image and Hypertext
- ENGL 40233: Writing for Publication
- ENGL 40243: Professional Writing
- ENGL 40263: Multimedia Authoring: Animation and Film
- ENGL 40283: Editing and Publication

Additional requirements:
- ENGL 40273: Writing Internship, or
  ENGL 30390: Publication Production
- Two courses (six credit hours) from any of the concentration courses listed above
- Two literary and language studies courses (six credit hours) from any ENGL 30*xx*3 or ENGL 40*xx*3 not listed above.

References

"The B.A. in Writing in the English Department." 2006. Handout. Dept. of English, Texas Christian Univ., Fort Worth, TX, Nov.

eleven40seven. 2014. *eleven40seven: TCU Journal of the Arts.* Accessed online Oct. 31, 2014. http://www.1147.tcu.edu/.

Mayers, Tim. 2005. *(Re)Writing Craft: Composition, Creative Writing, and the Future of English.* Pittsburgh: University of Pittsburgh Press.

Schramm, Margaret, J. Lawrence Mitchell, Delores Stephens, and David Laurence. 2003. "The Undergraduate English Major: Report of the 2001–02 ADE Ad Hoc Committee on the English Major." *ADE Bulletin* 134–135: 68–91.

Shumaker, Arthur W. 1981. "How Can a Major in Composition Be Established?" *Journal of Advanced Composition* 2 (1–2): 139–46.

Tade, George, Gary Tate, and Jim Corder. 1975. "For Sale, Lease, or Rent: A Curriculum for an Undergraduate Program in Rhetoric." *College Composition and Communication* 26 (1): 20–4. http://dx.doi.org/10.2307/356794.

Yancey, Kathleen Blake. 2004. "Made Not Only in Words: Composition in a New Key." *College Composition and Communication* 56 (2): 297–328. http://dx.doi.org/10.2307 /4140651.

12

TWO STRIKES AGAINST
The Development of a Writing Major at West Virginia State University, an Appalachian, Historically Black College

Jessica Barnes-Pietruszynski and Jeffrey Pietruszynski

INTRODUCTION

Located in the heart of Appalachia and created by the Morrill Act of 1890, West Virginia State University's (WVSU) mission has always been a bit different than other, more traditional land-grant universities. The school was established as the West Virginia Colored Institute, and was charged with the education of black students. Early education of the students was based on the pedagogical style of Booker T. Washington, providing "real world" application of knowledge while instructing the first generation of freed men and women in a trade. Although this educational perspective was beneficial in the construction of the university as students created a self-sufficient campus by constructing the buildings and growing food, the overall prevailing thought was that the student body was not capable of the rigors of a "higher education." Nevertheless, throughout its history WVSU has challenged both those expectations and its students to create and recreate a student-focused university. Since its opening in 1891, WVSU has gone through many changes in both name and student racial makeup. However, what has not changed is its mission: to educate those people who would not otherwise have a chance at a college degree. In many ways, the writing option in the English degree reflects the growth of the school itself.

WVSU fully integrated after the 1954 *Brown v. Board of Education* decision without incident or violence, but this integration fundamentally changed the makeup of the student body as black students, formerly denied an education elsewhere, began to attend schools newly opened to them. No longer having a predominately black student population, the faculty's curricular focus moved from racial to class concerns. Many

DOI: 10.7330/9780874219722.c012

Department Name:	English
Institution Type:	Public, Baccalaureate Colleges-Arts & Sciences (Bac/A&S)
Institution Size:	4,000 students
Residential or Commuter:	Commuter
Student Body Description:	Most students work a minimum of part time; established Historically Black Colleges and Universities (HBCU); fully accessible; multigenerational population of students, mostly local Appalachian background; high percentage are first in their family to go to college
Year Major Began:	1982
Official Name of Degree:	Bachelor of Arts in English with a Writing Option
Number of Majors:	In year one: N/A In year three: N/A In year five: N/A Current: 33
Number of Full-Time R/C Faculty:	10

of the issues that came about because of the change in student makeup are illustrated, in a microcosm, in how the school's English department dealt with writing instruction. Serving a largely commuter student body, many of whom were first generation college students and often underprepared for college writing, the movement to identify and create a strong writing major was repeatedly hindered by the overwhelming need to concentrate on introductory writing classes. Through these struggles, the English department faculty created the writing major. Like the university, the writing major curriculum has gone through several changes, leading to its current incarnation. The most recent revisions have been greatly informed by the move of the institution from a state college to a state university. Currently offering a professional writing major, which includes a focus on technical and creative writing, WVSU's English department continues to revise its writing major to both reflect the needs of our student body as well as stay current within the field.

The current curricular changes at WVSU aim to break apart the major into different tracks: professional writing, technical writing, and creative writing. However, the English department is all too aware that the biggest focus of revisions to the writing curriculum must address both the current and future needs of the students themselves. The students at WVSU must navigate a variety of social, educational, and even political obstacles from outside the university, and yet most never get very far away from their Appalachian identity. This combination creates a unique situation in which the building of a writing curriculum is negotiated within the department while also reacting to what happens in the classrooms due to a statewide lack of educational development.[1]

In this chapter, we will explore the changes in how English, and writing in particular, has been taught at a historically black university in transition. From the initial conception of technical training to a modern push for an English studies model, we will demonstrate how the department has adapted its curriculum in each stage. Through the archival investigation of course catalogs, it becomes clear that the department has constantly had to walk a pedagogical tightrope between offering students much needed basic skills in English (reading and writing) and tackling the critical investigations of writing and literature.

IMPLEMENTATION NARRATIVE

To completely understand the current state of writing instruction at WVSU, it is important to understand its past. As we previously mentioned, WVSU began as a historically black college under the direct instruction of Booker T. Washington. His belief that classic literary knowledge needed to be taught alongside practical application became the foundation of the education philosophy of WVSU. In his autobiography, *Up from Slavery,* Washington posits that "The actual sight of a first-class house that a Negro has built is ten times more potent than pages of discussion about a house that he ought to build, or perhaps could build" (Washington 1963, 156). According to Washington, only by mixing practice with theory could recently emancipated slaves empower themselves and truly become "free." Booker T. Washington brought this educational philosophy to plantation land given to the state by its owner (herself a former slave) in the Kanawha Valley of West Virginia and helped create the West Virginia Institute for Colored People.[2]

Washington's theories of education inform this discussion of WVSU's writing curriculum in two very important ways. The first, as will be discussed later, involves the idea that identity (both actual and perceived) in a repressed, self-aware culture can be shared by Washington's descriptions of newly freed African Americans and by the Appalachian community. Second, Washington's idea of incorporating practical and theoretical knowledge into the higher education classroom became the foundation for writing education within the English department. By analyzing the courses offered in the early years of the school, we see that initially writing instruction came from a purely practical mode. Students were taught the writing skills that would most likely result in success in the workplace. Basic classes in handwriting, note taking, and, later, typewriting reflected the need to address skills that were practical in nature, as well as the ways in which students could be trained for entry-level service positions. Writing as a discipline of English, complete with theoretical underpinnings, took a back seat to practical knowledge, a trend that continued with the establishment of an on-campus community college.

In 1978, the state legislator of West Virginia created a community and technical school system in which faculty, administrators, and educational opportunities would be shared with "parent" state schools. In this new system, the West Virginia State Community and Technical College became attached to, and shared a campus with, WVSU. For the university (then West Virginia State College), this meant that the school had, essentially, an open admission policy. A student who did not qualify academically for a traditional university could come to WVSU through the community and technical college and learn skills important for success in college classes. The integrated system meant that instead of starting at a two-year college and transferring, one could simply move from one system to the next on the same campus. For the region, this was a good compromise.[3] Of course, this also complicated matters for the writing curriculum, as the lowest scores on entrance exams came in the areas of math and writing. More importantly, since the students were in an integrated system, it was not only the faculty at the community and technical college that had to develop ways to help basic writers in the classroom, so did the university faculty.

Before students could take college credit classes, they were required to either "test out of" or pass basic skills classes. Before 1982, four courses helped bring students to the level of writing proficiency that would be required to establish a standalone writing major. Two courses in reading (ENG 096 and 098) and two in writing (ENG 097 and 099) worked as developmental writing classes. Even though these courses were requirements for any student (both in and out of the major) who did not qualify for ENG 101: Effective Communication, they did not satisfy any general education or major requirements for students. These classes focused almost exclusively on the mechanics of writing: grammar and sentence structure. From this focus, one can surmise that writing classes were relegated to a secondary class, one in which practical skill was needed but further academic investigation was not warranted.

The writing option for the English major at WVSU did not exist until 1982. Old university catalogs show that, before this date, the English major focused primarily on literature. Although courses in writing and composition were listed in the catalog before 1982, they were not established as mandatory courses that lead to a defined academic plan for a writing major. Before 1982, the English major competencies included objectives like "The ability to use both oral and written English clearly, logically, forcefully, and appropriately" (West Virginia State College 1961). However, nowhere in the forty-two credit hours required for the major was the advanced instruction of writing designated. Instead, writing was seen as a service course for the entire college. ENG 101 and 102 were specifically designed as general education classes, and even upper-level writing classes were electives taught for students in other departments. For example, ENG 204: Business Writing is listed within the English department in older catalogs; however, the only students required to take the class as part of a course of study were business or finance majors. In other words, before the creation of a writing major, classes in writing were being created by the English department and taught by department faculty, yet were not offered to students who wanted to graduate with an English degree. It would seem that, even within the department, writing instruction took a back seat to the traditional literature degree.

In 1982, a new writing major was developed and courses that were once service courses took shape as part of a designated academic plan. However, even with the creation of this new major, evidence of a traditional literature degree program was evident in the department. For instance, students who decided to take the professional writing option of the major were still required to take several literature classes. In terms of writing versus literature, courses were disproportionately assigned. The writing option required seven literature courses (four in the 200–400 level), whereas students in the literature option were only required to take one English language course (Introduction to Linguistics, Traditional Grammar, History of the English Language, or Linguistics and the English Language). In addition, the writing major could be achieved in thirty-eight credit hours, whereas the literature major needed forty-two. Upper-level courses in writing were focused on practical application, such as ENG 420: Field Experience in Writing.

In the initial inception of the writing major, no theoretical courses (outside of literary criticism) were required. After choosing forty-five credit hours from a standardized list of general education classes, a student was able to enter into the writing option of the English major and take courses specifically designed for that area of emphasis. Lower-level classes focused on language or grammar. Students were required to take one class focusing either on the English language (ENG 230: Introduction to General Linguistics, ENG 401: History of the English

Language, or ENG 411: Linguistics and the English Language) or on English grammar (ENG 306: Traditional Grammar). These classes emphasized the history and nature of the English language and its application to writing. In addition to multiple classes in literature, students majoring in writing select five courses that help them determine which writing emphasis to specialize in.

Of the several courses students could choose from were classes that trained students via different "modes" of writing. Within the 1982 choices, ENG 212: Analytical Writing provided "systematic training of the students analytic skills: the ability to breakdown a complex object into its component parts" (West Virginia State College 1980, 141). ENG 214: Interpretive Writing again provided "systematic training," but this class was "designed to increase the student's ability to draw inferences, explain cause-and-effect, and utilize evidence in a convincing manner" (141). At the 200 level, these courses were clearly designed as precursors to more advanced writing classes, essentially building a foundation for more rigorous training. However, since no course sequence was specified, and no listing of them as prerequisites for higher-level classes appeared in the catalog, the notion of classes building upon one another did not exist. Instead, students were able to "pick and choose" which upper-level courses would be most beneficial to their professional careers.

These professional writing choices broke aspects of writing down into different "fields": business writing, journalism, writing for publication, and field writing. Classes like ENG 204: Writing for Business and Other Professions were "designed especially for students whose careers call for the writing of various kinds of business and technical reports" and focused their writing on "the fundamentals of language usage" with "some attention" to the writing of business letters (West Virginia State College 1980, 140). The use of prerequisites in these classes worked to establish the concept that writing knowledge was an ongoing process. For example, ENG 204 was a prerequisite for ENG 309: Technical and Report Writing, which stressed "a functional approach to business and technical reports" (141). Another possibility for the writing option included ENG 225: Journalism I and ENG 226: Journalism Practice. Again, each of these classes focused mainly on "practical experience" in writing as opposed to any theoretical underpinnings. The class that most reflected the practical nature of the original writing option was ENG 420: Field Experience in Writing. In this class, students were required to "spend a minimum of 60 hours in a writing assignment which will provide practical on-the-job training" (West Virginia State College 1980,

146). The assignment could take place at "a television or newspaper station, on a newspaper, in a business or industry, in a government or campus office" (146). This class was only open to English majors pursuing the writing option and is one of the earliest examples of a mounting awareness about what it means to pursue a major in writing.

Issues stemming from the initial creation of the professional writing option of the English major still resonate in the current English curriculum. Even though the number of students seeking the professional writing option is much greater than those in the literary studies option, there is still an unequal division of writing and literature classes, and several courses retain the same descriptions and objectives as in the 1982 catalog. Although more classes were added and a more traditional "core" was established for the writing option, the root of the degree still focused on teaching students "practical" skills as opposed to theoretical investigation. The next serious attempt at revision was not until 2005, when the department's composition specialists began to investigate the possible deficiencies in the degree and what revisions could be done to address them.

PROGRAM RATIONALE AND OVERVIEW

Currently, the writing major consists of a core of writing classes that every student must take regardless of emphasis. This core includes ENG 112: Technical Writing, ENG 204: Writing for Business and Other Professions, ENG 225: Journalism I, ENG 250: Introduction to English Literature, ENG 303: Expository Writing, ENG 304: Introduction to Creative Writing, ENG 315: Shakespeare, ENG 334: Principles of Literary Criticism, and ENG 477: Senior Seminar. This core has been developed to cover the integral aspects of both literature and writing, or, in other words, the basic principles every English major should know. There have been various discussions throughout the years about adding and/ or subtracting classes to better serve students majoring in writing. As the English discipline itself struggles with defining what students should know and read, we echo the problems of most English departments, particularly when exploring essential/nonessential knowledge and how each emphasis should be constructed.

Three of the nine core courses for our writing major are required literature courses. Also two of the five components—American Literature and Diversity—offer only literature options. This has become a valid concern for the faculty as we continue to revise and rethink the writing option. At the core of our discussion is this question: How does the study of literature lay a foundation for our writing majors? This question is central to the concerns of the English department as we consider what it is our students need to be successful. Addressing the need for more writing classes and designing a modern writing major are immediate concerns for the department, and several new upper-level courses have been developed to strengthen that program, specifically ENG 429: Writing for Publication, ENG 228: Introduction to Desktop Publishing, and ENG 410: Digital Literacies. Furthermore, the department is currently in the process of expanding writing options by offering a BA in technical writing.

The core writing courses seek to give students a foundation on which to build their specialization, as well as give an overview of the discipline itself. Technical Writing, Writing for Business and Other Professions, Journalism I, and Expository Writing attempt to provide students with a wide knowledge of different writing genres, which can help them choose their area of emphasis. The degree culminates in a capstone course, Senior Seminar, which encourages students to work on a capstone project that allows them to further explore—and showcase in open presentations—both how they see themselves within their major and where they see themselves going. Along with the traditional required class in language (either Introduction to General Linguistics, The Power of Language, Principles of Grammar, or History of the English Language) and classes within genre writing groups, students continue with nine more credit hours in their area of emphasis. To this end, and in an effort to better serve our students, the faculty continues to add upper-level writing classes in all emphasis areas. Expanding the writing major is a central concern of our department, and we continue to revise our curriculum to better serve our students both in and outside of the department, currently by implementing a BA in technical writing and developing classes in writing pedagogy and composition theory, which are aimed at both writing and education majors.

While still in its infancy, the development of a BA in technical writing will allow a more specialized emphasis for the writing major. Currently majors must, besides the core classes, take one course in each of two writing groups that allow students to explore the different emphases. The first writing group requires students to take one of four classes: ENG 227: Copy Editing and Makeup, ENG 430: Poetry Writing Workshop, ENG 431: Fiction Writing Workshop, and ENG 432: Creative Nonfiction. This group showcases the creative writing emphasis. Both writing groups continue to undergo revision as faculty members create and implement new courses. For example, Creative Nonfiction is a recently added class that seeks to address an increasingly popular writing option, both in mainstream publications and in academic study. The second writing group requires students to take one of two classes: ENG 310: Technical and Report Writing and ENG 429: Writing for Publication. While this selection seems restricted, it does not yet reflect the classes currently being implemented, such as two 400-level classes currently in committee and on track to be added within the year, a rhetoric studies course, and a course in information design that addresses the need for keeping technical writing classes current with the field. This class would also build on ENG 228: Introduction to Desktop Publishing. And, with the addition of a BA in technical writing, we will be able to continue to "beef up" our current writing offerings.

The transitions within our curriculum reflect a wider scope of transition across the entire campus. In 2004 the school was granted university status, and in 2008 new legislation separated the community and technical colleges from their parent universities. These changes came with new admission requirements—instead of a basically open admissions policy, the school now adheres to new and higher admissions standards. But, more importantly, this meant that we would continue to have students who need a "basic" or "developmental" writing class. Without a shared system allowing university students to attend classes within the community college and vice versa, as well as a new policy that admits a percentage of probation students who may have fallen short of the admission standards—the need for developmental writing classes became quickly apparent. The English faculty have been working for the past year to cultivate and implement a developmental writing class in conjunction with the West Virginia Developmental Education Task Force, a statewide task force charged with finding ways in which to retain developmental students in both community and four-year colleges. To this end, we offered ENG 090: Introduction to College Writing for the first time in the fall of 2012. We hope this will help serve our students who need additional writing classes.

Throughout these current endeavors, many of the historical problems with offering service courses and bringing struggling students up to a college level of writing and thinking have emerged. Though WVSU's student demographic is not traditional, the mission to educate is no less important, but, in some cases, is more difficult. Following the model for the initial construction of the university, the division between practice and theory once again dominates current models for revision of the major. Pedagogically speaking, we would like to be able to offer and teach advanced, upper-level writing courses that are in line with the new and exciting models for teaching writing; however, when the majority of students lack basic writing skills, new and innovative pedagogical methods are cast aside in order to instruct students in the fundamentals. As the university continues to grow and adapt to the needs of its population, the way the major shapes itself will also change.

Holistically, WVSU attempts to reflect on these issues by once again turning to Booker T. Washington's theories on education and combining the practical with the theoretical. University-wide, students are required to take a general education class, GED 200: Race, Gender, and Human Identity, an interdisciplinary course that looks historically and theoretically at the construction and struggles humans have endured because of identity markers, which include race and gender but also Appalachian identity. Specifically, the English department offers courses in Appalachian literature and advanced composition, which explore the theories of writing and allow reflection of what it means to write "correctly" versus finding an authentic authorial voice, particularly when that voice is devalued. A course in linguistics and the history of language is also a required class for all literature and writing majors. The study of how language is constructed and privileged as well as how linguistic markers pervade our social ideologies is an important aspect, particularly for our students who are learning to wade through this linguistic minefield. The concern for placing identity in the midst of a practical and theoretical practice of education continues to inform and influence the creation of new classes and the revision of the curriculum itself.

CONCLUSION

In *The Violence of Literary*, Elspeth Stuckey (1991) argues that we must understand literacy as "a system of oppression that works against entire societies as well as against certain groups within a population and against given people" (64). This is especially true in writing classroom, which are too often seen as gatekeeping classes, where the writing instructor is tasked with allowing only "correctly literate" students through to the academic pursuits of the rest of the university. However, this becomes a problematized position when the vast majority of students are exactly the type that many traditional critics think do not belong within that space, particularly people of color and people of a lower economic class.

In many ways the "back to basics" social movement of the 1980s is still in operation as students themselves see the importance of fluency in a particular dialect, even at the expense of their ability for full expression. Many of these students would agree with critics, who argue that non-standard dialects have no place in the university or perhaps the world at large. John Simon's (1980) argument in *Paradigm's Lost* is representative of many current ideologies that urge writing teachers to be even more vigilant gatekeepers, making it more difficult, not less, to access higher education. Simon and other critics are often very vocal about who should be left outside of the gate: "[A]s for 'I be,' 'you be,' 'he be,' etc., which should give us all the heebie-jeebies, these may indeed be comprehensible, but they go against all accepted classical and modern grammars and are the product not of a language with roots in history but of ignorance of how language works" (165–66). But what Simon and others ignore is the fact that the population they deride as linguistically deficient has endured centuries of forced illiteracy and geographic and social isolation. This knowledge is the center of all discussions about writing major revisions and will continue to be a touchstone for all future revisions—we always must be aware of the importance of our institution's history and the diverse makeup of our student body.

Curricular Summary: The Writing Major at West Virginia State University

Courses offered by the department prepare students for reading and writing throughout the college curriculum, for communication in business and other professions, for the advanced study and teaching of English, and for careers in professional writing, publishing, and related fields. The bachelor of arts in English has a core of courses in language, writing, literature, and critical theory. Students may choose to pursue the more traditional literature option, which prepares them for graduate study and professional school, or the professional writing option, which prepares students for a variety of writing careers.

Professional writing students must take six credit hours in the same foreign language at the 200-level or above, excluding courses on foreign culture that are taught in English. They also take nine credit hours in either a single discipline or a set of related disciplines, to be designed and approved by the student's advisor (twelve credit hours for those who entered before fall 2003).

Technical writing students must also take six credit hours in the same foreign language at the 200-level or above, excluding courses on foreign culture that are taught in English. Additionally, they pursue twelve credit hours of study in either a single discipline or a set of related disciplines, to be designed and approved by the student's advisor.

MAJOR REQUIREMENTS (42 CREDIT HOURS)

Core courses:

- ENG 112: Technical Writing
- ENG 204: Writing for Business and Other Professions
- ENG 228: Introduction to Desktop Publishing
- ENG 477: Senior Seminar

Professional writing track:

- ENG 225: Journalism I (cross-listed with COMM 225)
- ENG 250: Introduction to English Literature
- ENG 303: Expository Writing
- ENG 304: Introduction to Creative Writing
- ENG 315: Shakespeare
- ENG 334: Principles of Literary Theory, or
    ENG 441: Contemporary Critical Theory
- ENG 230: Intro to General Linguistics, or
    ENG 255: The Power of Language, or
    ENG 306: Principles of Grammar, or
    ENG 401: History of the English Language
- ENG 316: American Literature to 1860, or
    ENG 317: American Literature, 1840–1940, or
    ENG 408: Contemporary American Literature
- ENG 337: The Black Writer in America, or
    ENG 338: Black Novelists in America, or
    ENG 339: Black Poets in America, or
    ENG 340: Readings in African Literature, or
    ENG 342: Women Writers, or
    ENG 343: Appalachian Literature and Culture
- ENG 227: Copyediting, or
    ENG 430: Poetry Writing Workshop, or
    ENG 431: Fiction Writing Workshop, or
    ENG 432: Creative Nonfiction Workshop

Technical writing track:

- ENG 160: Practical English Grammar and Usage
- ENG 310: Technical and Report Writing
- ENG 311: Editing for Technical Writers
- ENG 410: Digital Literacies
- ENG 412: Information Design
- COMM 285: Web Design and Digital Media
- ENG 250: Intro to English Literature, or
    ENG 315: Shakespeare, or
    ENG 402: Early English Literature through the Fifteenth Century,
      or
    ENG 403: The Renaissance, 1500–1660, or

> ENG 405: Literature of the Restoration and the Eighteenth Century, or
> ENG 406: English Romanticism, or
> ENG 407: The Victorian Period, or
> ENG 409: Modern British Literature

- ENG 316: American Literature to 1860, or

> ENG 317: American Literature, 1860–1940, or
> ENG 408: Contemporary American Literature

- ENG 337: The Black Writer in America, or

> ENG 338: Black Novelists in America, or
> ENG 339: Black Poets in America, or
> ENG 340: Readings in African Literature, or
> ENG 342: Women Writers, or
> ENG 343: Appalachian Literature and Culture

- ENG 320: Literature of the Western World, Part I, or

> ENG 321: Literature of the Western World, Part II, or
> ENG 350: World Literature: Classical Era, or
> ENG 351: World Literature: Modern Era, or
> ENG 413: Development of the Novel, or
> ENG 414: The Modern Novel, or
> ENG 415: The Modern Drama

Notes

1. The woes of the K–12 educational system in West Virginia have been well documented. Most recently, West Virginia ranked last in the American Legislative Exchange Council's *Report Card on American Education* with an overall D+.

2. Washington's influence was so important in the creation of the West Virginia Institute for Colored People that he was asked to become the first president. Although he turned down the position to fill the same role at Tuskegee University, he went on to become the first commencement speaker.

3. As Chenoweth and Galliher (2004) discuss in "Factors Influencing College Aspirations of Rural West Virginia High School Students," students did not feel prepared for the rigors of higher education—both academically and culturally—so an open-admissions community college that transitioned into a four-year university allowed for a controlled integration and better chance for success.

References

Chenoweth, Erica, and Renee V. Galliher. 2004. "Factors Influencing College Aspirations of Rural West Virginia High School Students." *Journal of Research in Rural Education* 19 (2): 1–14.

Simon, John. 1980. *Paradigms Lost*. New York: Penguin.

Stuckey, J. Elspeth. 1991. *The Violence of Literacy*. Portsmouth: Boynton/Cook.

Washington, Booker T. 1963. *Up from Slavery: An Autobiography*. Garden City: Doubleday.

West Virginia State College 1961. "1960–1962 Catalog."

West Virginia State College. 1980. "1981–1982. Catalog."

13

"WHAT? WE'RE A WRITING MAJOR?"
The Rhetoric and Writing Emphasis at the University of Wisconsin–La Crosse

Marie Moeller, Darci Thoune, and Bryan Kopp

INTRODUCTION

The University of Wisconsin–La Crosse (UW–L) is a regional campus in southwestern Wisconsin. Enrolling approximately 9,000 undergraduates and 1,000 graduate students, UW–L is part of the Wisconsin state higher education system. The English department at UW–L currently houses twenty-four tenured and tenure-track faculty and eleven instructors. Of those tenured and tenure-track members, sixteen are literature specialists, seven are rhetoric and writing specialists (including two creative writers), and one is a linguistics specialist. Instructors in our department teach primarily general education writing courses, though several do teach literature general education requirements on an as-needed basis. Students can choose from three different tracks in our English department: rhetoric and writing (R/W), literature, and education. In addition, we offer minors in professional writing, creative writing, and education. As of fall 2012, we have forty-six literature majors, fifty-six education majors, and ninety-three R/W majors.

PROGRAM OVERVIEW AND RATIONALE

The R/W emphasis at UW–L has a long and tenuous history, one rooted specifically in the English field's long-standing, tumultuous relationship with power and legitimacy. For example, in the late 1980s, such tensions became public knowledge for our university when one of our senior faculty members published "The One-Sided Tripod and the New Pedagogy of Writing," in which he lamented the elimination of literature from freshman composition, the "incredible popularity of process theory,"

DOI: 10.7330/9780874219722.c013

Department Name:	English
Institution Type:	Public, Master's L (awards at least 200 Master's degrees/year)
Institution Size:	10,000 students
Residential or Commuter:	Commuter
Student Body Description:	Most students work, at minimum, part time; high number of international students; substantial percentage of first-generation college students; 58% female
Year Major Began:	2004
Official Name of Degree:	Bachelor of Arts in English, emphasis in Rhetoric and Writing
Number of Majors:	In year one: 5 In year three: 10 In year five: 40 Current: 93
Number of Full-Time R/C Faculty:	6

and the "unphilosophical temper of the age" (Voiku 1987, 24). North and Voiku (1988) replied, "You've had some bad run-ins—intellectual and pedagogical fender benders, if you will—with 'process' people, and you have good reason to be annoyed. . . . At the moment, you look like me at my angriest: sitting in an empty parking lot, windows steamed up from imprecations still being muttered long after everybody else has gone home" (74). Although a hyperbolic example of affective responses to larger disciplinary shifts, this history is one that also permeates local interactions in our department—and at times with our university at large—in a myriad of ways. A historical lack of hiring despite growing need, the numerically skewed ratio of faculty specializations, writing specialists' inability to teach courses for R/W majors because of the overwhelming need for broader writing courses throughout campus, an overwhelming reliance on instructors to teach FYC, and other examples such as these illustrate how our history—despite all best intentions to counteract it (of which there have been many by many)—still makes difficult the work of sustaining a R/W major.

While the above issues might make our work challenging, we also acknowledge that some R/W faculty (us included) created additional difficulties by virtue of circumstance(s). For example, recognizing that, historically, work within the English department to promote writing as a discipline was not gaining much traction, R/W faculty and staff sought support for writing outside of the department and developed WAC programs. From 1989–91, the committee built a writing emphasis requirement into the new general education curriculum, requiring all students to take freshmen composition plus two designated writing emphasis courses. Although many people across campus then chose to participate in "writing" in the "major," there was still no talk of a "writing major." In hindsight, we theorize that R/W specialists approached growing the writing portion of our department by creating need outside of the department; such pressure, it seems, was to assist R/W faculty in establishing a more robust writing presence at UW–L. The hope, then, was that such a focus would meld into the English department. While widespread institutional support for writing grew across campus (thus increasing our workload and further reassigning time for campus-wide writing initiative work), this move did not necessarily manifest itself in support for writing within the department (e.g., additional tenure-track hires for our department, release time for administrative work, etc.).

Unfortunately, in other words, we backed ourselves into a corner where we were increasingly responsible for the holistic presence of writing on our campus but were lacking local resources. In retrospect, while the development of WAC and WID programs was undeniably a good move for the institution, it was not necessarily a good move for R/W faculty—we essentially reinforced the idea that writing works in service of others, and not in service to itself. In addition, that extra workload translated to an inability to work on more pressing departmental issues, such as developing a writing major, developing and teaching new courses, or even teaching the courses already on the books because of the administrative needs of managing such an initiative. As a result, it has only been within the last seven years that we have begun to see the shift in hiring and administrative practices that will allow writing a greater presence in the English department. However, within those seven years, we not only maintained our commitment of service to the university and the English department, but we also began the slow work of creating a writing emphasis in English that also services the intellectual work of writing.

IMPLEMENTATION NARRATIVE

The opportunity to begin the development of a R/W emphasis presented itself during the 2003–2004 academic year. Its creation, oddly enough, was the result of a decision to overhaul the curriculum of the UW–L English department. These revisions began in literature, with a restructuring of course offerings and the addition of an introduction to literary studies course. In reshaping the literature major, several courses were removed for a myriad of reasons, including a lack of connection between the course goals and the goals of the restructured literature major. Those outlying courses became the basis for the R/W emphasis in the English major at UW–L.

As discussed previously, the initial move to reform the English major was not to integrate writing into the program; rather, the focus was on how to better organize literary studies into introductory and advanced courses. In fact, writing courses were conspicuously absent from the newly proposed English major. The department's writing committee noticed that upper division R/W courses, including a recently developed course in rhetoric and writing studies, were not included as requirements, let alone as electives. Committee members viewed this omission as an opportunity for growth and change. Rather than creating an entirely new emphasis that would require us to map out new learning goals and an alternative English curriculum (for which there was neither time nor resources), the committee looked at what was left out from the new literature-based major and attempted to connect the dots. In other words, the rationale for the new R/W major was simple: why not bundle these remaining courses into an emphasis? The unstated alternative—make room in the new literature-based major for rhetoric and writing courses—was unappealing because so much time had been spent wrangling over which combination of skills, periods, genres, authors, etc., made the best undergraduate literature experience. At the time, the other faculty did not seem very concerned by or interested in the proposal from the writing committee; it passed the department with little debate and was approved by the University Curriculum Committee for implementation in 2005.

These courses existed already and served diverse student populations. Included on the list were: "service" courses required by other major programs across campus, as part of the previously mentioned WAC work; courses focused on journalism, inherited from a dismantled mass communication department; and courses in the creative writing and professional writing minors. Curiously, some of these courses also served students who earned less than the minimum required grade in their FYC course, as stipulated in general education requirements. This grab-bag also resembled the minimally-structured professional writing minor of the time, which was essentially a list of these courses with a few other electives. There was no discussion of what constitutes "advanced writing," though the committee knew further work was needed to revise and coordinate upper-division offerings.[1]

Therefore, without acknowledging it, the committee had defaulted to a generalist definition of writing imported from the professional writing minor (at that time) and from the general education courses they mostly taught. Promotional materials asserted that "a degree that demonstrates your written communication skills will be an asset for practically any job position." The list of career paths, however, turned out to be a fairly accurate prediction of the types of interests students would bring to the program once they could declare themselves as R/W majors. At that point, faculty began to ask questions of the major and themselves, the most important being "How can a program equally serve the needs of such diverse students?" We are still trying to answer this question, remaining mindful that whatever successes we have achieved to date have been in part because of our willingness to be flexible and inclusive.

Early on, the major had quite a few successes—enrollments were good (even now, enrollments are substantial with eighty-seven majors); our graduates were having success in the job market and in graduate school; and, most importantly (especially on an institutional level), the department was given the go-ahead in 2008 to hire their first official writing program administrator (and first R/W faculty member in several years), something UW–L had never had before. Certainly, WPA work had been conducted in the department and on campus prior to this hiring decision; however, it had not been associated with any kind of course release and was largely done for free. In fact, the writing committee frequently engaged in and promoted the work of composition in the department. Interestingly enough, the heart of most of the writing work in the department evolved (and continues to evolve) from a valuing of FYC and writing pedagogy.

That support and recognition illustrated that writing mattered, not just around campus, but also in our own department. Both the administration and the department recognized that R/W faculty, without reassigned time, could no longer be asked to administer a general education program and simultaneously administer a major. This was a step toward campus-wide legitimacy for R/W faculty—if the university and the department could recognize that running a first-year writing program took an expert, then perhaps the writing culture really was changing.

REFLECTION AND PROSPECTION

In the process of investigating the formation of our R/W emphasis, we've had to unpack principles and cultural values in the department that have all led to the moment when the emphasis could form. Even now, many of the courses included in the emphasis are courses designed through a FYC lens—meaning they are predicated on the work being done in FYC. By emphasizing pedagogy and process, these courses fit rather neatly into the learning goals established in the "WPA Outcomes Statement for First-Year Composition" (Council of Writing Program Administrators 2008). The adaptation and adoption of this statement for our FYC course occurred contemporaneously with the development of the R/W emphasis; therefore, it is perhaps not surprising that the outcomes for the emphasis partially build off of the FYC outcomes. Whereas other writing majors may evolve from graduate school curricula or trends in the field, our program is the result of the influence of FYC and the creation of a WAC program, which, we imagine, is an unusual approach.

Consequently, the relatively late decision to hire a WPA is worth further reflection. The writing committee, responsible for both FYC and the new R/W emphasis, was reaching a point where it could no longer manage a general education course—and the various responsibilities inherent in such courses—and still focus on the development of the emphasis. In some ways, this was unfortunate. The committee that spent so much time supporting the work of FYC now had more work than ever. The new WPA, noticing that, in the development of the emphasis, FYC had been de-emphasized in committee conversations, created another committee, the composition committee. While this committee has been successful in designing assessments for FYC, providing professional development opportunities, and creating a community for our growing number of adjunct faculty members, it has also heralded a new era in our department: the proliferation of committees. Whereas once there were primarily two curriculum committees—in addition to the regular committee work of tenure, promotion, and retention—there are now many new committees that reflect the changing values of our program. However, and this is likely the same in other departments, the members of these committees largely overlap, making it more and more difficult to focus on one or two directions.

Adding a WPA to a program that already had a core of faculty invested in the work of composition was a complicated move. While there was clearly a need for a faculty member with reassigned time to focus specifically on FYC, this also meant reshuffling or renegotiating the work of three other R/W faculty members. And, while our emphasis has been successful in terms of recruiting majors, R/W faculty still exist largely as a minority group in our department. Although most faculty members teach FYC, this has largely been a solitary endeavor, with the exception of conversations taking place, historically, in the writing committee and among a few other committed instructors. As the visibility of

FYC continues to increase in the department, so has the visibility of the R/W emphasis, which is increasingly viewed as a threat to the more traditional, literature-based English major.

Furthermore, the shifting culture of FYC in our department has had an effect on the R/W emphasis in that the writing committee is increasingly focused on the business of running an emphasis. There are fewer conversations about writing pedagogy and more conversations about meeting the charges of a curriculum committee. With relatively few R/W faculty—most of whom are engaged in a variety of administrative work in addition to teaching—within a primarily literature-focused department, the work of composition remains important, even (maybe especially) from the margins.

Clearly, all these pieces come together to form a very complicated puzzle, and an even more complicated explanation of where we are now. For example, even with the addition of a much-needed WPA, the R/W faculty still faces deep challenges in terms of staffing. Furthermore, with so many majors and four of our six faculty having reassigned time for administrative duties, other, more systemic complications arise. Logistically, scheduling courses and ensuring we are offering them as often as needed is nearly impossible. In addition, creating new courses, working on revising the major and its related minors, and developing student learning outcomes for several existing courses all mean more time from faculty who are already stretched to the limit. Current political climates within the state, the institution, and even the department have also made more complex the department's ability to fill or create lines for faculty with specialties in R/W.

Along with, or perhaps connected to, the political climate in the department and the state, there have also been recent departmental proposals to eliminate the emphases within the major (R/W and literature, in favor of an English studies model). This would be devastating to the R/W faculty and their work, the place and strength of writing on our campus, and, most importantly, our eighty-seven majors. It will be interesting to see if such proposals gain any traction. If we are not careful in our approach and understanding of these ideas, our willingness to accommodate all parties in the department may complicate such a proposal, as well as inevitably work against us.

CONCLUSION

As can be seen from our previous discussions, the R/W emphasis at UW–L is in flux and will continue to be revised long after we have left academia. With that in mind, our discussion of where we go from here recognizes both the limitations of our own positionalities, as well as that we are only three of a larger contingent of rhetoric and composition faculty here on our campus. In addition, we also recognize that we are currently situated in a department that, while shifting, is still entrenched in a historical trajectory that places our respective disciplines within hierarchies of power. While such hierarchies have historically stymied growth, we are hopeful that as our department continues to shift, such shifting will subsequently alter the work and efficacy of the R/W faculty here at UW–L. We also recognize that change in any institution is slow to come about, and, at best, difficult to sustain and enact. We are grateful for the space in which we have to work, and look forward to doing even more work in the future.

Our most important trait, we believe, is highlighted in our discussion of how truly complex the situation is within UW–L's community, within our English department, and within the R/W major. There are many, many stakeholders (or shareholders) within this system, and recognizing that our major, while a separate entity, is also tied directly to FYC and WAC both disciplinarily and in practice (in terms of being a large focus of study within our field, being committed to general education and writing, and being connected to our faculty's administrative workload and commitment to understanding and furthering the study and practice of writing and rhetoric). Moving forward, we recognize that these shareholders, while at times complicating the work of the major, also create opportunities to find connections throughout the university in a way that perhaps evades other majors. Therefore, while difficult, we welcome these goals and challenges. We also recognize how lucky we are actually to have a major—as this collection illustrates, many will be looking toward the difficult but rewarding work of establishing a R/W major. We are fortunate that, while the path has been a difficult one, we have this major within our department. We are so grateful for its presence, for our students, and for our colleagues who share our commitment to writing and rhetoric.

Having worked with the existing emphasis for a few years, we are continually adapting and revising the major to better serve our students and participate in disciplinary conversations. While we are very pleased with the participation in our emphasis—as of fall 2011, the department had 206 majors among literature, education, and R/W, with 87 of those being R/W majors (42.2%)—we also recognize that in order to continue to respond to and grow with demands, we must diversify our offerings, hire more faculty, address workload issues, and continue to recruit students.

All of these goals surfaced for us in the fall of 2010, as we were revising our professional writing minor. Ironically, the professional writing minor was the initial, though at times problematic, model for our approach. It gave us what we now see as a genesis, however problematic, with which to establish and justify a major. And now, several years later, we are revising the professional writing minor in the hopes that it will help us reframe the major again.

This is not to say that the professional writing minor is in any way more important than our major; rather, through revising the minor, we have learned that we must consider more fully how our pieces fit together, and how the choices we make in one can inform and shape the other. We found we needed to ask ourselves questions such as: How do the student learning outcomes in each of our courses overlap with our major outcomes? How do our major learning outcomes reflect what we really value in our R/W emphasis and our minors? How do we see the R/W major fitting into our larger English department? How do our courses—as well as the practices of writing theorists and practitioners—support, or not, a view of writing not as a service action but a site worthy of study in and of itself?

In our previous approach to designing the major, we settled on practicality and service because of the tenor of the university and the department. The development of the professional writing minor has encouraged us to, once again, see a part for the whole, and in that synecdochal turn, to reconceptualize our work in the minor and the major simultaneously. Therefore, we wish we would have realized throughout this process that it is sometimes better to move from part to whole, rather than whole to part, when it comes to revision strategies for implementing change in our major. In other words, it sometimes takes a piece outside of the major to cast light on potential effective revisions within the major.

In addition, we wish we would have focused more on student learning outcomes from the outset of the major. What we have found that binds us together as a major is, of course, our commitment to particular major outcomes. However, while there are major outcomes, there is little discussion about the student outcomes in each of our courses that work toward achieving the major outcomes. Without student learning outcomes for all courses, continuity throughout course offerings can be difficult, and thus our major outcomes are more difficult to attain.

Finally, while we recognize the difficult positions that R/W faculty— and the R/W major itself—inhabit, both within the English department and across our campus, we also know that from those difficult positions often comes great opportunity. We are hopeful that we will continue to grow as a major, that administering and continually revising this major will lead to less accommodation of other groups and more work and revisions on our own terms.

Curricular Summary: The Rhetoric and Writing Major at The University of Wisconsin–La Crosse

An undergraduate English major with an emphasis in rhetoric and writing deepens students' understanding of a range of writing situations, improves their writing abilities, and provides a solid background for a number of career paths, including professional writing, teaching, creative writing, journalism, linguistics, graduate studies, and other communication-related fields. As students explore connections among language, culture, and power, they learn to use the art of writing to inquire, collaborate with others, and act in context. Students in our major learn to use effective composing processes for various audiences, purposes, and genres. Ultimately, a concentration in rhetoric and writing empowers our students to examine and shape their world through language.

MAJOR REQUIREMENTS (37 CREDIT HOURS)

Core courses:
- ENG 301: Foundations of Literary Study
- ENG 333: Introduction to Rhetoric and Writing Studies
- ENG 313: Prose Style and Editing
- ENG 497: Seminar in Rhetoric and Writing
- ENG 363: Shakespeare I, or
  ENG 364: Shakespeare II
- ENG 330: The English Language, or
  ENG 332: Modern English Grammars, or
  ENG 432: Intro to Linguistics
- One 300- or 400-level literature course

Capstone (final requirement):
- ENG 413: Capstone: Portfolio

General electives (three courses):
- ENG 304: Writing in the Arts and Humanities
- ENG 305: Creative Writing
- ENG 306: Writing for Teachers
- ENG 307: Writing for Management, Public Relations, and the Professions

- ENG 308: Technical Writing
- ENG 309: Writing in the Sciences
- ENG 325: Reporting and Copy-editing
- ENG 326: Feature and Specialized Writing
- ENG 327: Publication Production
- ENG 330: The English Language
- ENG 332: Modern English Grammars
- ENG 334: Language Studies for Secondary Teachers
- ENG 337: The Rhetorics of Style
- ENG 343: Creative Nonfiction
- ENG 355: Critical Theory
- ENG 403: Individual Projects
- ENG 416: Seminar in Advanced Fiction Writing
- ENG 417: Seminar in Advanced Poetry Writing
- ENG 432: Introduction to Linguistics
- ENG 434: Classical Chinese Discourse
- ENG 446: Forms of Poetry
- ENG 449: Forms of Fiction
- ENG 450: English Internship

Writing electives (one course):
- ENG 304: Writing in the Arts and Humanities
- ENG 305: Creative Writing
- ENG 306: Writing for Teachers
- ENG 307: Writing for Management, Public Relations, and the Professions
- ENG 308: Technical Writing
- ENG 309: Writing in the Sciences
- ENG 325: Reporting and Copy-editing
- ENG 326: Feature and Specialized Writing
- ENG 343: Creative Nonfiction

Note

1. The new R/W emphasis was distinctly different than the literature emphasis, with the following courses added:

   - ENG 333: Introduction to Rhetoric and Writing Studies
   - ENG 313: Prose Style and Editing
   - ENG 413: Writing Portfolio
   - ENG 497: Seminar in Rhetoric and Writing Studies

   Whether it was to prepare well-rounded English majors, to build a common core experience in the English department, or to minimize any perceived threats to literature course enrollments, the committee agreed to include the following courses in the original proposal for a R/W emphasis:

- Foundations in Literary Studies (4 cr.)
- Shakespeare (3 cr.)
- Literature elective (300- or 400-level) (3 cr.)

To more broadly prepare students, three credits in "language and grammar" were also included, with students selecting from these courses:

- The English Language (3 cr.)
- Modern English Grammars (3 cr.)
- Introduction to Linguistics (3 cr.)

For "advanced writing," students were asked to choose a course from our 300-level array of writing courses, selecting from the same list as part of their nine credits of electives:

- Writing in the Arts and Humanities (3 cr.)
- Creative Writing (3 cr.)
- Writing for Teachers (3 cr.)
- Writing for Management, Public Relations, and the Professions (3 cr.)
- Technical Writing (3 cr.)
- Writing in the Sciences (3 cr.)
- Reporting and Copy-editing (3 cr.)
- Feature and Specialized Writing (3 cr.)
- Creative Nonfiction (3 cr.)

Rather than confront the lack of equivalence in these courses, the committee made the case that such diversity (1) provided a solid background for a number of career paths, and (2) allowed students to specialize in one of the areas below, if desired, by taking the following recommended (not required) courses:

- Professional Writing
- Journalism
- Creative Writing
- Teaching (non-certification)
- Linguistics
- Graduate Studies
- Communication-Related Fields (e.g. business, grant writing, web design, public relations, graphic design, sales, research, marketing, publishing, and promotions)

References

Council of Writing Program Administrators. 2008. "WPA Outcomes Statement for First-Year Composition v2." Available online.

North, Stephen, and Daniel J. Voiku. 1988. "A Response to Daniel Voiku." *ADE Bulletin* 89 (Spring): 72–4. http://dx.doi.org/10.1632/ade.89.72.

Voiku, Daniel. 1987. "The One-Sided Tripod and the New Pedagogy of Writing." *ADE Bulletin* 86 (Spring): 24–8. http://dx.doi.org/10.1632/ade.86.24.

14

A MATTER OF DESIGN
Context and Available Resources in the Development of a New English Major at Florida State University

Matt Davis, Kristie S. Fleckenstein, and Kathleen Blake Yancey

INTRODUCTION

Implemented in August 2009, the Editing, Writing, and Media (EWM) track in our undergraduate English major currently enrolls over 700 students. Its success, we believe, stems from a curricular design that is both contextually sensitive and multi-resourced, drawing on (a) knowledge of and practice in twenty-first century literacies, (b) programmatic strengths of the department, and (c) experience with the university system. Our chapter describes the design of our EWM track, noting particularly the changes made between the first (failed) proposal and the second proposal leading to the major. We also highlight the importance of contextual sensitivity in both programmatic revisions and the subsequent success of the EWM track. We conclude with a reflection on current and forthcoming challenges.

PROGRAM OVERVIEW AND RATIONALE

Context isn't everything, but it matters: in 2005, the English department at Florida State University (FSU) committed to rebuilding a graduate program in rhetoric and composition, which led to the hiring of three tenure-track faculty and the recruitment of graduate students at both MA and doctoral levels—and it also led to the Editing, Writing, and Media major. When the new faculty moved to FSU in 2005–2006, we certainly knew we didn't have a major—what the English department had were *many* students, over 1,600 English majors divided between a literature track and an equally popular creative writing track. At the same time, we in rhetoric and composition (R/C) seemed to have the *makings*

DOI: 10.7330/9780874219722.c014

Department Name:	English
Institution Type:	Public, Very High Research Activity University (RU/VH)
Institution Size:	40,000 students
Residential or Commuter:	Mixed
Student Body Description:	Women account for 54.8% of enrollment; minorities total 27.2%; average age for undergraduate students is 21.1; students from all 50 states and the District of Columbia attend, and over 130 countries are represented
Year Major Began:	2009
Official Name of Degree:	Bachelor of Arts in Editing, Writing, and Media
Number of Majors:	In year one: 300 In year three: 700 In year five: N/A Current: 700
Number of Full-Time R/C Faculty:	7

of a major, specifically through the elective courses in rhetoric and composition that seemed a good fit with a more capacious writing track. We offered an upper-level course in composing theory, for example, and another 4000-level course in rhetorical theory and practice, as well as several 3000- and 4000-level courses—called "Essay and Article"—that lent themselves to a range of approaches, from multimedia composition to creative nonfiction. In addition, we planned a peer-tutoring course that would be connected with our writing center.

Given the infrastructure of the FSU major—that is, with two tracks, one with a writing label—it made sense to see if we could enlarge the writing major to include R/C offerings. Such hopes were, however, short-lived: even for us, the idea of expansion ran into some very real ideological and epistemological differences. On the ideological side, those of us in rhetoric and composition were interested in a writing program that would foster agency and egalitarianism; however, our colleagues in creative writing were more interested in maintaining a limited program more attuned to the aesthetic. On the epistemological side, we believed that writing makes knowledge in a communal context, while our creative writing colleagues think of writing as the expression of individual talent. Consequently, while it might have been possible to create a set of courses that would constitute a more capacious writing major, we didn't have sufficient intellectual coherence to make such a major actually work. And it's worth noting that our interest in a *coherent* major wasn't necessarily shared by colleagues in the other two programs.

Where we did find common interest was in an intersection between writing and editing, and that too linked to departmental interests. We have a tradition of editing scholarship among the faculty, and, in 2003, a graduate editing and publishing certificate was developed. In addition, undergraduates often completed editing internships, some of which involved assisting faculty with their projects. Overall, this context seemed hospitable. Our proposed new major, then, was developed by a small ad hoc group representing two of the three areas of the department—creative writing and rhetoric and composition—developing a proposal we called the Editing, Writing, and Media Track:

> The Editing, Writing, and Media Track engages students in the history, theories, and practices of textual formation. Students have the opportunity to take writing-intensive courses devoted to a variety of forms of nonfiction writing for a wide range of audiences and media, as well as practical courses in editing and internships in publishing. They will also study the history and theories of editing, publishing, visual rhetoric, and electronic media. The track is designed for students interested in pursuing careers in editing, publishing, journalism, and the teaching of writing. It is also ideal for students interested in undergraduate training in rhetoric, composition, the history of the book and media technologies, and other related fields.

In addition, we highlighted four distinctive components of the major.

- First, it included two introductory courses, "Introduction to Rhetorical Theory" and "Writing and Editing in Print and Online," which together were intended to introduce students to key terms and intellectual frameworks as well as to writing practices keyed to print, screen, and the network.
- Second, students were required to choose three courses from a set of five that included historical approaches to textual production and reception; editing practices, again with specific reference to print and online; contemporary publishing theory, including theories of authorship and intellectual property; theory and practice of genres, with attention to the role of technology in fostering certain genres and dissuading others; and visual rhetoric in a digital age.
- Third, each student was required to complete an internship of his or her own choosing, which provided a social apprenticeship as a complement to the classroom curriculum.
- Fourth, each student would be required to complete a capstone course focused on texts, both in theory and practice, culminating in a final project or portfolio (print or electronic) demonstrating their ability to theorize about texts and textuality as well as to write and edit numerous kinds of texts.

Prepared with this structure and these descriptions, we took our proposed EWM track for approval to the final annual department meeting. As the discussion began, resistance surfaced quickly, with creative writers concerned that the track might reduce enrollment in their major, and the literature faculty anxious that the major wasn't congruent with their understanding of a humanities major. Given the possibility of a negative outcome, we did not ask for a vote.

We didn't give up: our second iteration began in the context of that departmental discussion. We needed to develop a major that was clearly distinctive—one different from the creative writing major, but also familiar enough that it *looked* to our colleagues like an English major. Fortunately, our chair brought together another ad hoc group of faculty, this one including literature colleagues who were amenable to participating in the major. These colleagues seemed aware that, increasingly, students are interested in media, an observation that, in part, had already contributed to the literature program's new History of Texts and Technologies (HOTT) program, which is basically a program on the history and remediation of the book. In addition, the HOTT program has provided for several new hires, who, with an EWM major, would have new and interesting undergraduate courses to teach. In sum, from both intellectual and pragmatic perspectives, our literature colleagues were interested in making common cause.

The major we've designed, which we describe below and which builds on the earlier four-part structure, has three gateway courses, an array of upper-level courses that students sample, and—as before—the internship and the capstone. Moreover, it offers three distinctive curricular features: it is foundational, modular, and programmatic.

The three gateway courses provide the foundation for the major: one in rhetoric, one in the history of texts and technologies (HOTT), and one in writing and editing in print and online, this last a historical course in the relationship between technologies and texts ranging from petroglyphs to Google. More specifically, the course descriptions included readings and references that both distinguished them as EWM-specific and communicated them as traditional in sensibility. For example, the gateway course in Rhetoric "introduces students to key concepts and frameworks useful for analysis of texts, events, communication, and other phenomena ("Rhetoric" 2009). Put simply, these concepts and frameworks provide what rhetorician Kenneth Burke (1937) described as way[s] of seeing and of making meaning." Likewise, we identified the frameworks (e.g., Bitzer 1968, Bakhtin 1992) and pointed to other rhetoricians—Aristotle, Henry Louis Gates, Sonja Foss, N. Katherine Hayles, and George Lakoff—whose work we planned to include. This course, in other words, is a theory course; though the particulars may be new to our colleagues, its tenor feels familiar.

Similarly, the HOTT gateway course brought some historical and literary perspective to the major: "it provides an introduction to the history of the changing technologies that humans have used to record and transmit memories of their experiences across time and space. Beginning with cuneiform and other early textual innovations, this course surveys the history of forms that artificial memory storage has taken, including tattoo, inscription, scroll, . . . and digital multimedia." ("History of Texts and Technologies" 2009) In this course, students explore textual technologies, particularly in the context of the social, institutional, and cultural conditions that both produced and were created by texts. Here, too, sample texts are identified, in this case ranging from Sappho and the Koran to Margery Kempe, the Declaration of Independence, Charlie Chapman, and Martin Luther King, Jr. Overall, the course focuses on how literary production, transmission, and reception shape and are shaped by the materialities of texts themselves.

The third gateway course, Writing and Editing in Print and Online (WEPO), is a writing course, to be sure, but it is a writing course *in* a theoretical context: "Today, writers compose for many spaces, sometimes for the page, other times for the screen, still other times for the network. In this course, students will compose such texts in the context of Bolter and Grusin's *Remediation*, which suggests that all media are in circulation, each informing the others; and of Faigley's and Haas's historical and contemporary observations about the materiality of writing." ("Writing in Print and Online" 2009) The outcomes for the course include working in and across all three spaces—print, screen, and network—and repurposing at least one text for another medium. Students conclude the course by creating a digital portfolio.

The 3000- and 4000-level offerings were also expanded: students choose three courses from six upper-level offerings: Visual Rhetoric in the Digital Age; Issues in Publishing; Editing: Manuscripts, Documents, Reports; Rhetorical Theory and Practice; History of Illustrated Texts: Illuminated Manuscripts to Graphic Novels; and Advanced Writing and Editing. In this sense, then, the program is modular. As figure 14.1 suggests, one version of the major emphasizes the visual nature of texts, including digital texts; a second version is keyed to proficiency in writing and editing; the third, more historical in nature, focuses on textuality itself. For those of us in R/C, one of the interesting aspects of the major is its modularity: how, by assembling different upper-level courses, we

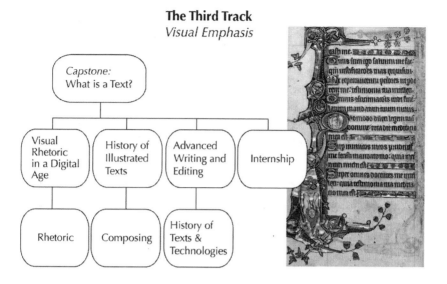

The Third Track
Visual Emphasis

Figure 14.1. A graphical representation of the "visual emphasis" option within the EWM track.

can offer new versions of the same major—which also creates an opening for new versions, one in creative nonfiction, for example.

The EWM major is also programmatic in design: it includes the gateway courses, an internship, and a capstone for *all* students. It's also programmatic in its six outcomes, which are divided into knowledge and performance outcomes, about equally divided between the two:

1. Students know theories and principles of rhetoric as well as ways to apply them and create with them.

2. Students know a general history of texts and the technologies/media influencing their development, as well as the literacies and agencies they have fostered or discouraged.

3. Students know theories of media and publishing in the context of cultural studies.

4. Students write with the style conventionalized within different genres—in public realms and in the academy—as well as against those styles.

5. Students can analyze, interpret, and evaluate the visual dimensions of various kinds of texts and create texts in visual environments (and those using the affordances of the visual).

6. Students can create a body of texts and explain their contexts, their attributes, and the ways in which they might be remediated and/or circulated more broadly.

When we—a group representing R/C and literature—brought this version of EWM to the department, it passed unanimously. In 2009, we introduced the major; since then, EWM has attracted over 700 students.

IMPLEMENTATION NARRATIVE

As we learned from the first proposal, the English department was the most immediate context and resource for the implementation of the EWM major. The success of the major depended on playing to and developing the existing intellectual infrastructure of the department. By locating the EWM curriculum vis-à-vis these various stakeholders, we designed a major in which each of our three programs had a significant investment.

The literature program, the largest of all of the programs at around thirty-five faculty members, provides EWM a grounding in both the traditional study of textual cultures and in the context of a new and exciting graduate interdisciplinary certificate program: the HOTT program. Combining faculty in English, history, religion, information science, modern languages, and library sciences, HOTT focuses on studying the materiality and technologies of textual production across a range of cultures and time periods. This program thus provides an advantageous context for the EWM major: one that values new, interdisciplinary approaches to the study of textual cultures, and that provides a developing intellectual infrastructure supported by new hires.

In redesigning the major, we incorporated HOTT approaches into EWM at two levels. Initially, students are required to take a History of Texts Technologies course to complement the writing and rhetoric core courses. Taught by HOTT faculty, this course introduces students to the study of textual materiality by emphasizing the changing influence of media on textual production and interpretation. Second, History of Illustrated Texts, an advanced course in the major, parallels the approach to textual study in History of Text Technologies but directs student attention to the role of visuality. The course often begins with the visual–verbal interface, and serves to complement other advanced coursework in visual rhetoric. Broadly speaking, in History of Illustrated Texts students look at the influence of images *on* texts, whereas in Visual Rhetoric in the Digital Age they examine images *as* texts. Crafting these courses as undergraduate HOTT courses, we were able to meet our new literature colleagues in the middle: focusing on rhetorically informed approaches to media in historical and literary domains of inquiry.

Creative writing, the second largest program in the department at around fourteen faculty members, also offered EWM access to significant intellectual infrastructure in the form of publishing experience. The creative writing faculty at FSU provides both graduate and undergraduate students access to a culture of textual production in many settings: public readings and author appearances, fundraisers, and the publication of *The Southeast Review*, a small but thriving creative writing publication run primarily by graduate students. *The Southeast Review* joins other publications within the department: faculty within the literature program edit the *Journal of Beckett Studies* and the *Journal for Early Modern Cultural Studies*, and the rhetoric program currently includes faculty who have edited several journals: *Assessing Writing* and *JAEPL: Journal of the Assembly for Expanded Perspectives on Learning*; special issues of journals like *ATD: Across the Disciplines*; and, currently, *College Composition and Communication*. These influential scholarly journals are complemented by smaller, local publications like *The Yeti*—an online and print alternative founded and staffed by FSU undergraduates—and *The Kudzu Review*—a journal of FSU undergraduate literature and art. Taken together, these publications form a productive publishing culture from which an undergraduate major, properly framed, can benefit.

Part of that framing, in our case, took into consideration how EWM could fit within and contribute to this culture in two ways. First, a course in Issues in Publishing leverages faculty knowledge to provide students with an opportunity to learn about the work of publishing by focusing on editorial practice in both print and digital media. Second, EWM requires an internship, for which there were several options already available: join departmental publications, take advantage of the established connections of the graduate certificate internship program (several of which are international), or seek commercial or non-profit internships in Tallahassee, Florida's capital city. Early indications are that students have completed all three varieties quite successfully.

Luckily for us, new approaches to textual study and production were not limited to the HOTT and creative writing programs. Indeed, a revived and growing graduate program in rhetoric and composition, now including seven faculty members, provided the main thrust for the EWM proposal, and EWM gives those faculty and graduate students an opportunity to merge scholarly inquiry and teaching. In particular, a recurring graduate course entitled Digital Revolution and Convergence Culture fosters interest in digital and visual rhetoric, multimedia and multimodal production and analysis, and the changing materiality of writing in the networked age. Different iterations of this course allow students in the R/C program to develop their interest in the study of print and online cultures, which in turn provides an intellectual resource for the major. For example, PhD students teaching sections of the WEPO course often draw from their experiences in the Digital Revolution and Convergence Culture course for readings and assignments. Some of these graduate students are now also teaching sections of the undergraduate rhetoric course, where they can pull similarly from their experiences in graduate rhetorical theory courses. In part, then, the continued success of the growing EWM major depends on our ability to leverage program expertise in rhetoric, especially because courses in rhetoric provide the backbone of the EWM major—they lay an epistemological foundation for the work students do in editing, writing, and media. It is important that graduate students can build on the groundwork put in place by the faculty in R/C so that these courses—focusing on the history, theory, and visuality of rhetoric at the entry and advanced levels—can continue to support students' exploration of how communication occurs, how knowledge is made, and how both of these are studied in various contexts.

In short, EWM is successful because it fits within the strengths provided by our specific department. Interfacing with the intellectual infrastructure in new areas of textual study, participating in publishing cultures, and merging rhetorical history and theory with the study of digital culture—these allowed EWM to emerge as a major in which our three programs all had a vested interest. In addition, while the success of the revised EWM proposal stems from a responsiveness to and reliance on the department's internal strengths, it also arises from our sensitivity to what Richard Selfe (2005) calls a "culture of support": an environment wherein institutional stakeholders, including the university itself, facilitate rather than impede change, especially technological change. Our assessment of the institutional scene played a significant role in the creation and success of the EWM option, especially in terms of the department's ability to fill curricular gaps, build on university attitudes, and tap into the power of FSU's advising system.

The first institutional element important to the success of our EWM major consisted of the university curriculum itself: we had to identify a need within that curriculum and create a new track responsive to that need. Perhaps one of the major obstacles to the development and approval of any new program—from a single course to a new degree—involves the perception of infringement. Academic units are justifiably protective of their intellectual territory, resisting efforts (or motives perceived as efforts) on the part of other departments to co-opt areas seen as necessary to their well-being or intellectual interest. Thus, a key factor in the development of our major entailed determining what curricular gap EWM could potentially fill—in other words, how could the new major fit within the overall university academic network of programs without overlapping or replicating other majors and courses? The first EWM ad hoc group identified two crucial gaps: FSU's lack of a journalism program, and the absence of any systematic or sustained education in professional writing and editing. For instance, despite a thriving student-run weekly newspaper, the *FSVIEW and Florida Flambeau*, the university offers no journalism program. Thus, students interested in mass media publications had no venue for formal instruction. Instead, they were forced to participate in journalism as an extracurricular activity, an experience important to their success after college, but certainly not sufficient for that success. In addition, despite a thriving and highly prestigious School of Communication—which features four undergraduate majors: advertising, media/communication studies, media production, and public relations—students interested in formal training in writing and editing had few options. EWM addressed those curricular gaps, and intersected with available programs in mutually productive ways. Thus, students currently in EWM can double major in communication, or they can take coursework congruent with their interests in other departments, such as Introduction to Website Design, which is popular among our EWM students but offered through FSU's Program in Interdisciplinary Computing. Rather than siphoning resources away from established majors, EWM opened up a new territory that enhanced those majors.

The second aspect of the university's culture of support important to the success of our EWM option consisted of institutional attitude, which served as a powerful sponsor of EWM. Kenneth Burke (1937) defines attitudes as "frames for actions," the ways in which we name a situation and prepare ourselves to act in alignment with that naming. The university's attitude toward digital technology and its advocacy for pedagogical and scholarly experimentation served as a crucial frame for action, especially for the new media aspect of our EWM option. The university's newly instituted technology fee, earmarked for technological support and innovation and one which all undergraduates pay as part of their registration costs, provides evidence of the university's support for digital technologies. Faculty members were encouraged to develop projects that would enhance students' engagement with technology, and to apply for internal grant money to support those projects. In addition, money was allocated to individual departments and colleges to be used for digital projects that would improve students' undergraduate experiences. Thus, the implicit and explicit message of the technology fee was that colleges, departments, and programs were to think in innovative ways about technologies, curricula, and pedagogies. This attitude, then, constituted a key incentive for positioning new media—as well as instruction in writing and editing across different technological platforms—at the heart of the EWM option.

Furthermore, the university, especially the College of Arts and Sciences, perceived the English department as a good site for activities involving new media, which we leveraged to garner support for the EWM option. This attitude was essential for moving the EWM major through the university approval process and acquiring the resources necessary to support it. Traditionally, English departments are classified as sites for print-based pedagogy and scholarship—English is quintessentially the realm of the book. However, at FSU (and especially within the College of Arts and Sciences), the English department had gained a reputation as a prime location for projects exploring the issues of textuality that are central to twenty-first century literacies, principally because of two initiatives. First, the HOTT component, described above, featured pedagogical and scholarly projects that attended to the role of media, including new media. Thus, faculty with proficiency in the materiality of book production complemented faculty with expertise in constructing digital databases. Second, the refounding of the doctoral program in rhetoric and composition in 2005 led to a graduate curriculum focused on digital issues in writing and rhetoric, as well as to student and faculty projects exploring the impact of twenty-first century literacies on classroom teaching. This support for new media research and pedagogy resulted in the creation of the Digital Studio in 2007, and an annual Digital Symposium in 2008, a center and an event within the English department that were designed to support new media projects. As a result of this concatenation of events, the university perceived the English department as working to integrate print and new media in scholarship and pedagogy—we were no longer simply a print-only shop. This attitude translated into enthusiasm for the EWM option.

Finally, the last element of the university's culture of support came in the form of its multilayered advising system. Developing and securing approval of EWM were only the initial, albeit complex, steps. The new major also had to be advertised to the incoming and transfer students, and the advising personnel were enthusiastic advocates and agents of this dissemination. For example, when the department was ready to roll out our first classes, the Director of Undergraduate Studies in English (DUGS) made presentations to Advising First, a university unit responsible for counseling first- and second-year students who have yet to declare a major. In that presentation, the DUGS answered three key questions: who the major served, what rationale organized the major, and what specific courses the major required. In addition to its own advertising efforts, the department also provided templates of course information that Advising First personnel could use as easy reference sheets in their meetings with students. Additionally, the Center for Exploratory Advising, which works with students without a declared area of interest, provided support for the new option by sharing information about the goals of the major, the required coursework, and the potential careers. Finally, our three departmental advisors worked not only with lower-division English majors who had not yet determined which option they wanted to pursue, but also with upper-division transfer students coming to FSU with an associate's degree and an interest in English, but no specific option in mind. Without these committed efforts of our advising units, we could easily have had a major without students.

REFLECTION AND PROSPECTION

As we write this, we are in the midst of the fourth year of our EWM option, and we now have a thriving program. While the response has been gratifying, the unexpected popularity presents a new set of challenges and opportunities, so we end our account of our EWM option by addressing various programmatic issues: providing media-rich spaces within the department, preparing graduate teaching assistants, and addressing the need for ongoing program assessment.

Even though all of the department's graduate and undergraduate teaching spaces include a screen, data projector, and computer set-up, before we created the EWM track we had only two technology-rich classrooms, each of which was equipped with twenty desktop computers. Those classrooms, however, were dedicated primarily to FYC courses. During fall 2009, the first formal semester of our EWM option, the DUGS applied for and received an internal grant of $64,000 to transform a conventional classroom into a laptop-ready classroom. The renovation included the installation of two SMART Boards and two data projectors with the capacity to display either four of the same images concurrently or four different images at the same time. Students also had the ability to plug their laptops directly into the SMART Boards. The success of that renovation led to a second grant in 2010 for a parallel transformation of a conventional classroom into a laptop classroom, yielding two media-rich spaces for the EWM program and inviting innovative teaching practices.

New classrooms, however, are only as good as the teachers who make use of their technology in pedagogically sound practices. To support teaching assistants assigned to courses in the major, the department developed and implemented a required one-credit pedagogy course. Any advanced-level graduate student interested in teaching in the program first had to apply to the DUGS for consideration and, second, had to complete the semester-long pedagogy course. That course focused on developing a syllabus, training in the new laptop classrooms, observing proficient EWM teachers, and beta testing potential assignments. In addition, the EWM pedagogy course instructor followed up with class observations of the students teaching in the program and with one-on-one conferences about the teaching experience. Not only did such commitment support quality pedagogy, but it also provided for a degree of coherence across many different courses, thus maintaining the major's identity and reinforcing EWM curricular goals.[1]

Finally, in order to assess the EWM major, a two-year review was built into the original proposal. During the spring semester of the major's first year, we began collecting information informally. We surveyed faculty teaching in the program, for instance, finding that most—but not all—were quite pleased with student motivation and the quality of work, and that the internships, as indicated by the portfolios students assembled, generated a wide variety of genres for students to write in and a rich diversity of experiences for them to synthesize. More recently, a review committee was convened to examine the EWM curriculum as a whole, a move particularly important given the unexpected and explosive growth of EWM majors. That committee is currently in the process of developing its agenda and collecting a variety of data. Like the committee that shaped the original proposal and reshaped it into the current successful program, the review committee is sensitive to the external exigencies that helped define the focus of the major, the internal strengths of the department that provide the intellectual grounding for the major, and the university's culture of support that offers resources for new growth. Through such sensitivities, we expect that the review committee will make decisions that ensure the health and strength of the EWM option.

Curricular Summary: The Editing, Writing, and Media Major at Florida State University

The Editing, Writing, and Media track reconceives the English major for the twenty-first century. It still preserves the traditional core of English—the creation and interpretation of texts—by combining practice in writing and editing with the study of cultural history and criticism. However, it transforms both writing practice and critical study to confront the new challenges of digital technology, visual culture, and the Internet. The EWM track aims to prepare students for leadership roles in twenty-first century culture, whether as intellectuals pursuing advanced degrees in book history, rhetoric, and critical theory, or as tech-savvy professionals equipped with editorial expertise and writing skill. EWM is not just a degree—it is a vision of the future of texts.

MAJOR REQUIREMENTS (36 CREDIT HOURS)

Core requirements:
- ENC 3021: Rhetoric
- ENC 3416: Writing and Editing in Print and Online
- ENG 3803: History of Text Technologies
- ENC 4942: Editing Internship

Capstone (final requirement):
- ENG 4815: What is a Text?

Electives (3 courses):
- ENC 4212: Editing: Manuscripts, Documents, Reports
- ENC 4218: Visual Rhetoric in the Digital Age
- ENC 4404: Advanced Writing and Editing
- ENG 3804: History of Illustrated Texts
- ENG 4020: Rhetorical Theory and Practice
- ENG 4834: Issues in Publishing

Additional requirements:
- All majors must also complete twelve credits in elective courses from any 3000- or 4000-level English courses.

Note

1.   We are researching various aspects of the major. Matt Davis's dissertation documents and theorizes students' composing processes, for example, while Kathleen Blake Yancey, Leigh Graziano, Rory Lee, and Jen O'Malley have co-authored "When Everything is New: Documenting and Learning from Writing in Print and Online (WEPO)" for *Reflection and Metacognition in College Teaching* (Yancey et al. 2013).

References

Bakhtin, Mikhail. 1992. *The Dialogic Imagination: Four Essays.* Austin: University of Texas Press.

Bitzer, Lloyd. 1968. "The Rhetorical Situation." *Philosophy and Rhetoric* 1: 1–14.

Burke, Kenneth. 1937. *Attitudes toward History.* Boston: Beacon Press.

"History of Texts and Technologies." 2009. File Syllabus. Department of English, Florida State University.

"Rhetoric." 2009. File Syllabus. Department of English, Florida State University.

Selfe, Richard. 2005. *Sustainable Computer Environments: Cultures of Support in English Studies and Language Arts.* Hampton: Creskill.

"Writing in Print and Online." 2009. File Syllabus. Department of English, Florida State University.

Yancey, Kathleen Blake, Leigh Graziano, Rory Lee, and Jen O'Malley. 2013. "When Everything is New: Documenting and Learning from Writing in Print and Online (WEPO)." In *Reflection and Metacognition in College Teaching*, ed. Naomi Silver, et al., 175–203. Washington, DC: Stylus.

15

RENEGOTIATING THE TENSIONS BETWEEN THE THEORETICAL AND THE PRACTICAL
The BA in Professional Writing at Penn State Berks

Laurie Grobman and Christian Weisser

INTRODUCTION

How do we teach the art of writing in everyday life? What do we owe students who need to find employment after graduation? Practical strategies, discursive techniques, and set routines may meet market demands for slick, persuasive communications, but how will learning such strategies equip young professionals with critical insight to face tough ethical problems? These questions have been central to the creation and continued development of the BA in Professional Writing at Penn State Berks. As we will explain, these questions have not led us to any easy or quick answers, but they have, in our opinion, helped create a program that attempts to balance the two seemingly disparate goals of theory and practice.

Our BA in Professional Writing is located at Penn State Berks, a branch campus of the larger university in east central Pennsylvania. The campus enrolls approximately 2,800 undergraduate students and offers fifteen undergraduate majors. The BA in professional writing is one of the mid-sized programs at the college, averaging approximately thirty to forty enrolled students per year over the past five years. Laurie Grobman and Candace Spigelman co-coordinated the major from its outset in 2001 until 2004. Grobman remained coordinator until 2006. Christian Weisser was hired in 2007 as an associate professor of English and coordinator of professional writing, a position he holds today. Grobman and Weisser have worked together in the continued evolution of the program, including curricular revisions, new course proposals, and research

DOI: 10.7330/9780874219722.c015

Department Name:	English
Institution Type:	Public, Baccalaureate Colleges-Diverse Fields (Bac/ Diverse)
Institution Size:	2,800 students
Residential or Commuter:	Commuter
Student Body Description:	Most students are local residents, with a high percentage of commuters; most students are enrolled full-time, but work either full- or part-time; approximately 20% of students are minorities; approximately 20% are considered adult learners; and 60% are female, 40% are male.
Year Major Began:	2001
Official Name of Degree:	Bachelor of Arts in Professional Writing
Number of Majors:	In year one: 10 In year three: 25 In year five: 30 Current: 30
Number of Full-Time R/C Faculty:	5

and assessment for the major's goals and outcomes, as well as in authoring this chapter. Collectively, they have played a central role in every major decision and development in the program's twelve-year history.

PROGRAM OVERVIEW AND RATIONALE

The program began its original development in September 2000. The professional writing major development committee consisted of five faculty with varied expertise in composition and literature and one administrator. At this time, few undergraduate writing majors existed (or were known to exist), and there was almost no scholarship available about undergraduate writing majors to assist the committee in creating one. By familiarizing themselves with research in technical, business, and professional communication, they came to see the committee's dynamic as part of the larger, ongoing debate that revealed repeated efforts to reconcile theory with practice and rhetoric with pre-professionalism in business and technical writing courses.

The committee decided to create a professional writing major that would emphasize the role of the rhetor in public and civic life, the kind of education David Fleming (1998) imagines in "Rhetoric as a Course of Study." Consistent with both classical and contemporary intentions, the committee believed that a rhetorically grounded curriculum would contribute to students' development as ethical, open-minded, intelligent, and civically-invested individuals, as well as foreground students' roles as active, responsible citizens and rhetors. The goal was to create a curriculum that combined traditional rhetorical principles, contemporary theories of language, and alternative rhetorics with contemporary professional discourse to promote practical and responsible workplace communication.

The professional writing major at Penn State Berks—like many of the undergraduate writing majors that have emerged in the past decade—has undergone continued reassessment, reevaluation, and transformation of its programmatic goals and objectives. The program continues to strive for the proper balance of coursework in liberal arts, rhetorical theory, practical application, and other key areas. The program has been supported by a strong faculty committee since its inception, and our colleagues play an active role in creating new courses, promoting and participating in special events and workshops, and assessing the strengths and weaknesses of all aspects of the program. We continue to meet regularly, though many of our discussions are informal.

The initial challenges in determining the program's focus have not vanished; they continue to permeate all aspects of what we and other faculty have done in (re)shaping the program. Efforts to balance the concerns of rhetoric—the ethical, the intellectual, and the pragmatic—with the development and redesign of the program's structure, course offerings, and course content is always fraught with tension and conflict. Yet, we firmly believe that an undergraduate writing major that combines the ethos of a liberal arts tradition with the practical skills needed by writers in workplace settings is both desirable and possible, but that it must be flexible enough to allow for ongoing curricular and philosophical negotiations to meet changing contextual demands. These competing agendas foster positive instability, fluidity, and adaptation, and thus necessitate flexibility and negotiation as ongoing aspects of the program. As a result, the professional writing major has undergone gradual reassessment and modification of the course offerings, categories, sequencing, and content.

IMPLEMENTATION NARRATIVE

The path to the development of the major was at times difficult. From the outset, most of the liberal arts faculty resisted the degree program, in part because of the title "Professional Writing." Many wanted to call the major "writing and rhetoric" to emphasize its ancient and ethical grounding as well as its commitment to a liberal education. Others argued that "professional writing" would elicit greater name recognition to prospective applicants. *Professional writing* is fraught with variable meanings and attendant implications, and, for many of our faculty members, the term smacked of vocational or pre-professional training. Others associated professional writing with either business or technical communication courses without disciplinary validation. In addition, reflecting the larger disciplinary debate about professional writing's place in English departments, many of our literature colleagues wondered why such a program would be housed in the liberal arts division of the college. Some of our colleagues were ardently committed to a course of study that would demonstrate the usefulness of writing in the "real" world; these faculty wanted courses that would teach skill sets and practical composing formulas free of theory or criticism.

As a result, debates among the program committee were often volatile, with composition and literature faculty pressing for a liberal arts ethos and other members resisting this pressure. Discussions were especially heated over the role of literature in the degree, as some of the more pragmatic-leaning committee members saw little connection between reading literature and writing in the workplace.[1] At times, the committee meetings became divided between those favoring practice-based courses and those representing the interests of literature. The committee finally compromised on a category that allowed students to choose two courses of upper-level literature *or* creative writing.

PHASE I: DEVELOPING A CURRICULUM

The initial curriculum that was approved and implemented in 2001 attempted to balance these competing goals and perspectives. It stressed both the production and consumption of texts, while positioning writing as the central object of study. The curriculum integrated the most salient issues of writing and language—authorship, collaboration and ownership, intertextuality, discourse communities, social construction, cross-cultural communication, ideologies, and others— throughout the program.

Since one of the primary goals included developing students' understanding of the role of writing and the rhetor in professional and civic life, the curriculum also incorporated rhetoric's longstanding intellectual tradition, with its emphasis on the development of ethical communication and character. In theory courses, students analyzed and explored written documents for their overt and hidden ideologies and values. They traced the social and political influences in both their own and others' writing. They examined texts representing a range of positions on contemporary debates in education—including conservative, liberal, feminist, multicultural, and moderate perspectives—studying rhetorical techniques while also considering the broader social implications of writers' positions. The curriculum focused not only on what graduates would do in professional life, but also on who they would become (Rutter 1991, 147).

As part of the degree program's ethical and political mission, the curriculum also stressed alternative rhetorics—issues of race, gender, class, and other categories of difference. Students studied both international and multicultural issues in professional discourse so that they might learn how to address diverse audiences in their written communications (Thrush 1993), become more attentive to non-egalitarian practices in their business writing communities (Lay 1992), and understand the unequal relations of power that underlie professional communication globally and within the United States (Grobman 2000).

The program's approach to technology was similarly designed to blend theory and practice. The required class in computer applications—web design, spreadsheet programs, editing graphics, Microsoft Excel, and Microsoft PowerPoint—was framed through the lens of critical theory. Students learned to both use the technology and think critically about the technology, including *who* uses technology (and who is excluded from using it), for what purposes, and at what costs.

But because much of the existing scholarship included critiques of programs so heavily invested in rhetorical or liberal educations that they failed to connect rhetorical study "to careers and jobs" or to clearly articulate the connections between employment and rhetoric (O'Neill et al. 1999, 274), the curriculum was designed to develop students' writing skills and offer them opportunities for practicing their craft under the direction of knowledgeable experts, mentors, and peers. To help achieve these goals, a diverse group of community members served on the program's advisory council. The council members worked in various jobs involving writing and communication, from journalism and editing to marketing and advertising, and the committee looked to them at first for input on the curriculum, and later for support with students' portfolios, internships, and employment opportunities. Although we set out to forge and maintain productive alliances with local business and industry, we often resisted the advice of our advisory council in favor of a more academic perspective. When, at our first meeting, one council member looked at our course offerings and stated, "I don't care about all this rhetorical and literature stuff; how will you teach them to write?" we refused this exclusively utilitarian sense of workplace writing in favor of our own goals as educators.

Several features of the phase I curriculum have carried through to the present time. From the outset, the program offered a gateway course to expose students to the central theories and pedagogies of writing. At the time, we used a defunct university course, ENGL 210: The Process of Writing, and adjusted it to the needs of our majors. The course evolved and changed over the years, but from the beginning it emphasized that students should view writing not only as a skill one must master but also as a complex object of study. The course exposes students to many of the central theories and subjects of writing studies, introduces them to key conversations in rhetoric and composition, and asks them to consider how these issues manifest in various professional contexts. These include, but are not limited to: authorship and ownership; writing processes; writing and ethics; writing history; writing and technology; and writing, race, class, and gender.

In keeping with the program's emphasis on the rhetorical tradition, the phase I curriculum required at least three courses in rhetorical theory. All students were required to complete ENGL 471: Rhetorical Traditions, which exposes students to rhetorical history and its relevance to contemporary communication. Students also chose two other rhetorical theory courses—for example, ENGL 474: Issues in Rhetoric and Composition. This course addresses contemporary rhetorical issues and subjects, though the theme varies from semester to semester. Throughout this course's history, instructors have taught according to their own scholarly expertise and research interests. The course has focused upon composition and the culture wars, working-class rhetorics, environmental rhetoric and eco-composition, and, most recently, visual and multimedia rhetorics. In the past several years, we have cross-listed these courses with other majors in order to offer community-based research in local history and bring an interdisciplinary nature to our rhetorical offerings. In 2011, two of our undergraduates presented their work on community-based research at CCCC.

Along with these theory-based courses, we continue to offer a collection of courses with a more pragmatic focus: Advanced Business Writing, Advanced Technical Writing, The Editorial Process, Article Writing, Advanced Nonfiction, Speech Writing, Advanced Expository Writing, and Science Writing, among others. While many of our courses had (and continue to have) a basis in either theory or practice, we have found it important to strive for praxis—the synthesis of theoretical and practical perspectives—within the overall program, without presuming the primacy of either approach.

As Balzhiser and McLeod (2010) point out, many undergraduate writing majors require either an internship or a portfolio in their capstone course—our program goes one step further by offering these as two separate, required courses. ENGL 495: Internship was included in our earliest curriculum and continues to be a foundational course in the program. Our internship course echoes Jennifer Bay's (2006) "applied course in rhetoric" (137) in that it combines regular class meetings, discussions, and reading assignments with internship fieldwork and contextualizes the internship through classroom discussion and rhetorical analysis. Similarly, the initial program offered an advanced editing course that was also used for student portfolios, but it was substituted with a new course in 2004, ENGL 491: The Capstone Course in Professional Writing, which includes a portfolio and several other assignments and activities designed to prepare students for their future careers as writers. This course focuses on the application of students' rhetorical knowledge; its overall purpose is to provide students with the opportunity to reflect upon and integrate academic coursework, co-curricular activities, and internship experiences through the design and development of print and electronic professional portfolios.

Throughout the years, we developed a rich *extra*curriculum that we think is vital to a successful undergraduate writing program. The professional writing major at Penn State Berks provides students with opportunities to interact with writers outside of the academic setting and apply their writerly knowledge in tangible ways. Many of the program's alumni had the opportunity to serve as peer reviewers and proofreaders for *Young Scholars in Writing: Undergraduate Research in Writing and Rhetoric*, an international undergraduate research journal founded by Laurie Grobman and Candace Spigelman.[2] Some have participated in the Writing Fellows program, in which they assist faculty across the campus with writing in their courses through workshops, peer tutoring, and mini-lessons on writing related topics. Writing fellows have also presented their research at scholarly conferences. ENGL 250: Peer Tutoring is required as part of the Writing Fellows (and current writing center tutoring) program, and this is just one among many of our courses that link professional writing to other majors and disciplines.

Additionally, other students work for the campus newspaper, earning credit hours while they write about important campus-wide issues and topics. ENGL 110: Newspaper Writing Practicum is open to all students, though professional writing majors often comprise the majority. And finally, professional writing students were exposed to a range of other examples of public or "real-world" literacy, such as guest speakers who held writing-related jobs and bus trips to various literacy events. Most recently, students and faculty constructed literacy-themed public displays and presentations together in support of the National Council of Teachers of English's (NCTE) National Day on Writing.

PHASE II: NEGOTIATIONS AND ADAPTATIONS

The phase I curriculum was created around a particular set of ideological assumptions, balanced by an ethical pragmatic. However, despite one of the program's guiding principles being that theory is requisite to practice, we discovered that students needed to know Quark and Adobe as much as they needed to study Foucault and Foss. What these students knew, as well as what they could do, had consequences for multiple invested parties. First and foremost were the students themselves, who, in an increasingly shrinking economic market, must be competitive for jobs and internships. Choices had to be made between (1) technical writing, newspaper practicum, and an array of other "hands on" courses using real-world scenarios or advanced technologies, and (2) theoretical courses in writing and rhetoric, rhetorical traditions, and text analysis. Even by pressing the maximums, however, an undergraduate major can require only a circumscribed number of credits. The greater the number of practical courses admitted to the major, the fewer spaces there are in students' schedules for rhetorical or composing theories.

While the initial curriculum was limited to preexisting courses within the Penn State system, new courses were later designed, created, and offered within the major in an effort to achieve a more appropriate balance of theory and practice. These courses included the aforementioned ENGL 491: Capstone in Professional Writing and ENGL 480: Communication Design for Writers (added in the summer of 2005). ENGL 480: Communication Design for Writers focuses on theory and practice in document design, and students analyze and use the latest software programs for creating documents. Moreover, a group of faculty at another Penn State campus had developed ENGL 420: Writing for the Web for a professional writing minor, and we added this course as an elective to our program's offerings.

The final phase II change—reducing the required number of upper-division rhetorical theory courses from three to two—resulted from further reflection and discussion about the roles of theory and practice within the curriculum. Thus, our phase II modifications leaned a bit more toward the pragmatic. This new "balance" served our students well for many years. However, by 2007, our enrollments were leveling off, while undergraduate writing majors were becoming increasingly popular across the United States.

PHASE III: DESIGNING AND REDESIGNING THE PROGRAM:

When Christian came on board as the program's new coordinator in 2007, we decided to reassess the curricular design and focus of the program. At this point, undergraduate writing majors were proliferating, and we had a large body of scholarship to draw upon. Laurie was a member of both the CCCC Committee on the Major in Rhetoric and Composition and the CCCC Undergraduate Writing Major Special Interest Group. After a year of learning about the program and its students, Christian led meetings with the professional writing faculty committee and we began to collaboratively redesign the program. At the same time, Christian began working with our campus' Office of Planning, Research, and Assessment (PRA) to conduct a more comprehensive assessment of the program than had yet occurred. After a series of meetings and discussions, the group decided to focus the assessment on what we saw as our program's main outcome: the increasing number of professional writing alumni. The first class of graduates had finished the program approximately five years earlier, and we wanted to know more about the professions they'd entered and how our program had prepared them—or failed to prepare them—for these careers. Christian, Laurie, and the PRA developed an alumni survey that was funded, in part, through a PRA grant. We also relied upon our campus' Alumni Relations Office, which helped us find contact information for those alumni with whom we'd lost contact. We sent email invitations to our sixty-seven graduates through SurveyMonkey, a survey-hosting website.[3] (See Weisser and Grobman 2012 for a fuller description and analysis of the survey results). A group of twenty-nine alumni—seventeen males and twelve females—completed the survey, for a response rate of 43%. This response rate is high for surveys solicited through email (Schuldt and Totten 1994).

This first survey consisted of forty-two questions divided into three categories: background and employment information; questions about the role of writing and rhetoric in their current profession or graduate program, including the genres and types of writing required of them; and more specific feedback about their undergraduate experiences in our program. These questions were intended to help us assess the strengths and weaknesses of various aspects of our curriculum, from the perspective of those who experienced it firsthand.

We were intrigued by our former students' rhetorical savvy as they carved out their career paths, and we realized they had a great deal to teach us about their professional identities, their professions, their professionalization, and their rhetorical proficiency. As a result, we conducted a follow-up survey in the summer of 2010. This survey, which also received IRB (Institutional Review Board) approval, consisted of questions that elicited longer, more descriptive responses. We asked sixteen questions, each of which stemmed from areas of inquiry we felt were broached in the first survey, yet were not explored in sufficient detail. For example, the follow-up survey asked the alumni about job searches and advancement, their use of rhetoric in the workplace, their perspectives on professionalism and ethics, and their future career plans involving the profession of writing. There were twelve respondents to these follow-up questions (out of our original group of twenty-nine), giving us greater insight into our alumni's proficiency with rhetorical techniques and the ways in which they have pursued their professional goals. The survey results convinced us to proceed with curricular modifications.

Consequently, we implemented several changes to the program. For example, ENGL 210: The Process of Writing had long served as the "default" gateway course to the professional writing major. However, given nationwide developments in undergraduate writing majors, we realized a course specific to our program was needed. We developed ENGL 211W: Introduction to Writing Studies as our new gateway course, also open to all students who met the prerequisites. As a result of a formal consultation with English faculty, this course was offered with or without the "writing-intensive" designation—we offer it in our program as a "writing-intensive" course.

We also replaced an introductory course in information technology (CAS 283: Communication and Information Technology) with a required senior-level editing course (ENGL 417: The Editorial Process). This change had much to do with the increasing computer aptitude of our students and with the findings of our survey. We recognized that fewer of our students needed to be introduced to the basics of computers. Similarly, we found that many students lack specific training in editing documents, which is a cornerstone of workplace writing. Our survey revealed that a growing number of our graduates go on to professions in which editorial skills are highly valued. We also introduced new category requirements into our curriculum that focused more exclusively on the genres of workplace writing. Four new categories—writing for publication, workplace writing, visual design, advertising and public relations—each require one course per category. These new categories provide better coverage of the principal subject areas that all professional writing graduates should know. Our survey results revealed that alumni from our program go on to a wide range of professions, often into positions that they did not initially plan to obtain while they were pursuing their degrees. Further, we found that their jobs can transform over time through promotion, downsizing, and other factors, and that some alumni change professions multiple times throughout their careers. We believe that these new categories help prepare students for the sometimes unforeseen directions of their later careers.

In addition, after long debates over the place of literature in a professional writing degree, we eliminated the literature requirement from the program altogether, but kept the requirement for one course in creative writing. We were bolstered in this change by the growing number of undergraduate writing majors, the growing body of scholarship in this area, and the emerging "legitimacy" of the writing major as an academic unit. We still see a vital connection to creative writing and its focus on the production rather than the consumption of texts. Consequently, students in our program learn valuable methods of invention and description, as well as other skills offered in creative writing courses, whether or not they see creative writing as a potential career choice.

REFLECTION AND PROSPECTION

As we look forward, we will continue to evaluate our program's goals and make curricular changes based upon our discussions with our colleagues and community members, emerging research about undergraduate writing majors, and feedback from our current and former students. We are particularly guided by the growing focus on professionalism both in the field of writing studies and in the feedback we receive from our alumni. As we have written elsewhere, we have come to understand a set of common and noteworthy attributes among our alumni, including their ability to: gauge their audience, employ effective rhetorical techniques and strategies, and convey a sense of professionalism, ethics, and adaptability in workplace situations and contexts. This *rhetoric of professionalism*, as we call it, is not unique to alumni of writing programs, yet we see a tangible connection between the rhetorically focused nature of our program and our alumni's ability to successfully navigate workplace environments. In other words, our analysis suggests that an undergraduate writing major grounded in rhetoric can provide an effective path to gainful and meaningful employment and success beyond undergraduate coursework.

As a result of our alumni surveys, we are considering the development of a course focusing on the concepts of "profession" and "professional" and the ways in which they impact the work of writers. For quite some time, "the professions"—such as engineering, law, medicine, and journalism—have been defined by "an ethic of service" (Rothblatt 1995, 195). Yet, Gardner, Csikszentmihalyi, and Damon (2001) in their book *Good Work: When Excellence and Ethics Meet*, suggest that ethical and responsible conduct are vital to many professions: "People who do good work, in our sense of the term, are clearly skilled in one or more professional realms. At the same time, rather than merely following the money or fame alone, or choosing the path of least resistance when in conflict, they are thoughtful about their responsibilities and the implications of their work." We see an important link between a rhetorically focused undergraduate writing major and this (re)emerging definition of a professional who embodies both expertise and ethical responsibility. In fact, this definition of professionalism reflects the curricular and programmatic debates that many undergraduate writing programs (our own included) have wrestled with as they've attempted to balance instruction in skills-based courses with ethically and rhetorically grounded perspectives. This is part of a larger debate on the currency of our programs within the field of English, and even within the liberal arts in general. We find it fruitful for undergraduate writing majors to aim for alumni who do the type of "good work" implied by Gardner, Csikszentmihalyi, and Damon (2001), work that combines expertise, ethics, and responsibility.

CONCLUSION

In (re)designing and administering a professional writing program, we have learned that there can be no "ideal" balance of philosophical and practical concerns. Rather, we must continually renegotiate the intellectual, ethical, and practical in response to our student population, faculty expertise, administrative goals, and market demands. Acknowledging that debates about the nature, value, and obligations of professional writing programs have been ongoing for at least twenty-five years, we understand that competing perspectives and methodologies may be reconciled temporarily, but will likely never be resolved. However, as was true for Candace and Laurie in 2006, we hope that faculty and administrators who are considering developing or modifying professional writing degrees will find in our story that those enduring tensions—between the philosophical and the practical, intellectual investigation and useful skills, theory and practice—if approached with flexibility and openness to change, can enrich, rather than undermine, their programs.

Curricular Summary: The Professional Writing Major at Penn State Berks

The professional writing major is intended to prepare students to write effectively in a variety of workplace and academic settings. Methods of instruction draw upon the strategies and techniques of practicing writers outside of the university, including workshops, peer conferencing, collaborative writing, portfolio preparation, and internships. At the same time, theory courses provide the necessary background to help students understand and appreciate the larger issues surrounding the writing and reading of texts.

As a liberal arts degree, the professional writing major is appropriate for students who wish to develop a set of applied communication skills to prepare for a wide range of professional positions or for graduate or professional schools. The degree differs from most current English majors in at least three ways: (1) a practical orientation prepares graduates for employment as well as post-graduate English studies; (2) a multidisciplinary focus integrates courses from the liberal arts, business, and information technology; and 3) a required internship ensures that students actively apply their skills.

MAJOR REQUIREMENTS (39 CREDIT HOURS)

Core courses:
- ENGL 211W: Introduction to Writing Studies
- ENGL 417: The Editorial Process
- ENGL 471: Rhetorical Traditions
- ENGL 491: The Capstone Course in Professional Writing
- ENGL 495: Internship

Writing for publication (one course):
- COMM 260W: News Writing and Reporting
- ENGL 215: Introduction to Article Writing

Workplace writing (one course):
- ENGL 418: Advanced Technical Writing
- ENGL 419: Advanced Business writing

Visual design (one course):
- ENGL 420: Writing for the Web
- ENGL 480: Communication Design for Writers

Advertising and public relations (one course):
- COMM 320: Introduction to Advertising
- COMM 370: Public Relations

Creative writing (one course):
- ENGL 212: Introduction to Fiction Writing
- ENGL 213: Introduction to Poetry Writing
- ENGL 415: Advanced Nonfiction

Rhetorical theory (one course):
- ENGL 472: Current Theories of Reading and Writing
- ENGL 473: Rhetorical Approaches to Discourse
- ENGL 474: Issues in Rhetoric and Composition

Additional writing courses (two courses):
- ENGL 110: Newspaper Writing Practicum
- ENGL 250: Peer Tutoring in Writing
- ENGL 416: Science Writing
- ENGL 421: Advanced Expository Writing
- CAS 214W: Speech Writing
- Any course listed in the previous six categories

Notes

1. Parts of this chapter appeared in Spigelman and Grobman (2006) and Weisser and Grobman (2012).
2. The journal moved to the University of Missouri–Kansas City in 2010, but students at Penn State Berks remain as peer reviewers. Laurie Grobman and Holly Ryan, assistant professor and writing center director at Penn State Berks, serve on the faculty editorial board.
3. According to our alumni office's records, the number of professional writing alumni totals sixty-seven.

References

Balzhiser, Deborah, and Susan H. McLeod. 2010. "The Undergraduate Writing Major: What Is It? What Should It Be?" *College Composition and Communication* 61 (3): 415–33.

Bay, Jennifer. 2006. "Preparing Undergraduates for Careers: An Argument for the Internship Practicum." *College English* 69 (2): 134–41. http://dx.doi.org/10.2307/25472198.

Fleming, David. 1998. "Rhetoric as a Course of Study." *College English* 61 (2): 169–91. http://dx.doi.org/10.2307/378878.

Gardner, Howard, Mihaly Csikszentmihalyi, and William Damon. 2001. *Good Work: When Excellence and Ethics Meet.* New York: Basic Books.

Grobman, Laurie. 2000. "Multiculturalism and Professional Communication Studies: A Response to Patrick Moore and Emily Thrush." *Journal of Business and Technical Communication* 14 (1): 92–101. http://dx.doi.org/10.1177/105065190001400106.

Lay, Mary M. 1992. "Gender Studies: Implications for the Professional Communication Classroom." In *Professional Communication: The Social Perspective*, ed. Nancy Blyler and Charlotte Thralls, 215–29. Thousand Oaks: SAGE.

O'Neill, Peggy, Nan S. LoBue, Margaret McLaughlin, Angela Crow, and Kathy S. Albertson. 1999. "A Comment on 'Rhetoric as a Course of Study.'." *College English* 62 (2): 274–5. http://dx.doi.org/10.2307/379023.

Rothblatt, Sheldon. 1995. "How 'Professional' Are the Professions? A Review Article." *Comparative Studies in Society and History* 37 (1): 194–204. http://dx.doi.org/10.1017/S0010417500019599.

Rutter, Russell. 1991. "History, Rhetoric, and Humanism: Toward a More Comprehensive Definition of Technical Communication." *Journal of Technical Writing and Communication* 21 (2): 133–53. http://dx.doi.org/10.2190/7BBK-BJYK-AQGB-28GP.

Schuldt, B. A., and J. W. Totten. 1994. "Electronic Mail vs. Mail Survey Response Rates." *Marketing Research* 6 (1): 36–9.

Spigelman, Candace, and Laurie Grobman. 2006. "Why We Chose Rhetoric: Necessity, Ethics, and the (Re)Making of a Professional Writing Program." *Journal of Business and Technical Communication* 20 (1): 48–64. http://dx.doi.org/10.1177/1050651905281039.

Thrush, Emily. 1993. "Bridging the Gaps: Technical Communications in the International and Multicultural World." *Technical Communication Quarterly* 2 (3): 271–83. http://dx.doi.org/10.1080/10572259309364541.

Weisser, Christian, and Laurie Grobman. 2012. "Undergraduate Writing Programs and the Rhetoric of Professionalism." *Composition Studies* 40 (1): 39–59.

16

FROM "EMPHASIS" TO FOURTH-LARGEST MAJOR
Learning from the Past, Present, and Future of the Writing Major at St. Edward's University

John Perron, Mary Rist, and Drew M. Loewe

INTRODUCTION

Founded in 1885 by the Congregation of Holy Cross, St. Edward's University is a private, Catholic, liberal arts institution in Austin, Texas. St. Edward's serves about 5,300 students of diverse backgrounds. The curriculum emphasizes critical thinking, moral reasoning, small classes, opportunities to study abroad, and internships. The university has grown dramatically since 1999, when its current president arrived.

Writing and rhetoric as an undergraduate major at St. Edward's University has a history dating back to 1975, when a writing emphasis was added to the English major to complement the literature emphasis. The English writing and rhetoric (ENGW) major is now the fourth largest on campus, and ENGW faculty hold key positions within the university and the School of Humanities.

The story of the ENGW major at St. Edward's is one of gradual change and revision. In 1999, ENGW had just seven tenure-track faculty members; currently, it has fourteen full-time positions, with three additional literature faculty holding joint appointments. All recent hires hold PhDs in rhetoric and composition or rhetoric and professional writing, except for the MFAs who teach in our creative writing specialization. Many of our graduates attend graduate school (MFA programs, law school, and programs in rhetoric and composition); obtain entry-level writing, communication, or publicity jobs; or seek teaching certificates. Over the years, we have adapted our course offerings and outcomes to try to make the best match we can between our students' need for practical experience and their need for disciplinary knowledge. The hands-on,

DOI: 10.7330/9780874219722.c016

Department Name:	English Writing and Rhetoric
Institution Type:	Private, Master's L (awards at least 200 Master's degrees/year)
Institution Size:	5,300 students
Residential or Commuter:	Mixed
Student Body Description:	Hispanic-serving institution (31.7% Hispanic/Latino in 2012); 82% of students from Texas; 8.4% international students; many domestic students have a connection to Holy Cross Catholic heritage; special programs for first-generation college students and students whose families are migrant workers
Year Major Began:	1987
Official Name of Degree:	Bachelor of Arts in English Writing and Rhetoric
Number of Majors:	In year one: N/A In year three: 155 In year five: 144 Current: 120
Number of Full-Time R/C Faculty:	10

experiential nature of many of our core and specialization courses fulfills our institution's mission to develop students' practical skills, while the program's emphasis on the (Western) rhetorical tradition provides a liberal arts perspective from which our graduates can continue to develop and critique these skills. In short, a blend of fiscal practicalities; continuous, multifaceted visibility; and targeted adaptations of the curriculum have provided strong *topoi* for inventing the arguments necessary to build and sustain our undergraduate major in writing.

While St. Edward's has grown in both size and selectiveness during the past ten years, it has not always been a university on the rise. Indeed, in the 1970s, the university nearly ceased to exist. In 1971, a debt crisis led the faculty to vote unanimously to ask the board of trustees to replace the university's first lay president. The board appointed a Brother of Holy Cross as interim president, later naming him president after a more extensive search (Dunn 1986, 319). In 1974, a Presidential Task Force mandate required freshman- and senior-level common courses: a) Freshman Studies, a lecture course integrating the study of topics from the liberal arts and the sciences (team-taught by faculty from different disciplines), with a rhetoric and composition course attached; and b) Senior Capstone, focused on the written analysis of controversial social issues. Crucially, from our perspective, the same administrators who were revamping the overall curriculum also endorsed growth in specialized writing studies courses. By 1975, the academic council and the board of trustees approved a structural

change to the English major: students could pursue a literature emphasis or a writing emphasis.

Even with this available emphasis in writing studies, though, the
major's core remained focused on the study and interpretation of literature. However, in 1982, due to the most persuasive force of all—student
demand—the English major was again revamped, this time resulting in
a writing studies "concentration," with the balance of required courses
now weighted more toward the study of rhetoric and writing than
toward the study of literary texts.

By 1987, the ENGW major had matured fully. Disciplinary and institutional legitimacy is demonstrated in course catalog abbreviations—by
1987, students could major in ENGL (literature) or ENGW (writing and
rhetoric), both separate degrees. While the ENGW major has always had
a core of required courses, in 2002, students could choose from among
coherent groups of elective courses that formed three "tracks": general,
professional writing, or creative writing. The three tracks allow students
to build on the core courses, but also shape their degree plans to suit
their interests and career or postgraduate goals. As of 2011, the core and
elective courses comprise twenty-four named ENGW courses, with three
additional course numbers for special topics courses.

PROGRAM RATIONALE AND OVERVIEW

The rationale for the ENGW major has always had three intertwined
strands:

1. A rhetorical focus on the production of texts, not just the interpretation
   of texts;
2. A focus on experiential learning; and
3. A developmental structure.

Focus on Production

The rhetorical focus permeated the curricular design of our major
from its earliest manifestation as an "emphasis," giving rise to specialized courses in argumentation, technical writing, and communication
theory. From FYC through the entire major, students study and write
for various audiences, purposes, and occasions, investigating "recurring
textual and discursive practices" (Schwegler 2000, 30) in a variety of
courses. The ENGW major inverts "the traditional hierarchy of English
studies," which, as Tim Mayers (2005, xv) has suggested, "privileges

interpretation over production." For example, in our Text and Discourse Analysis and Document Design courses—and in later courses such as Legal Writing, Media Writing, Writing Online, and Writing for PR/Publicity/Advertising—students participate in the discursive practices of a variety of fields and learn how writing mediates activities in those contexts. Thus, the ENGW major's focus on rhetoric is less about what Kurt Spellmeyer (2002, 278) calls "the ponderousness of The Classics" and more about what he calls "knowledge-ology"—that is, a study of how various disciplines and activities use language for particular purposes.

More recently, the major's focus on textual production has distinguished it from the university's newer communication major, where rhetorical criticism and business communication are also taught, but with a heavy focus on analysis and interpretation. Only recently, due to student demand, has the communication major begun offering courses that ask students to create and design texts as well as study them.

This privileging of invention and production in ENGW's history explains its relatively rare alliance of creative writing and professional writing. At St. Edward's, the two have been allied since the program's inception. Hesse (2003) and Mayers (2005) have argued for bringing creative writing into the fold of composition studies as a way of bringing composition's focus back to production. While our creative writing students sometimes chafe at the explicitly rhetorical focus of the major's core, some contact us years after graduation to say that Technical and Business Communication, Revising and Editing, or other core courses have proven most helpful in their post-graduation careers. Over the years, creative writing courses have been the link between the writing and literature departments. Literature faculty encourage their students, especially those who indicate interest in pursuing an MFA, to take our creative writing classes in order to gain experience writing in the genres they are studying. Creative writing faculty have also organized a Visiting Writers Series, which brings authors to campus for workshops and public readings.

Experiential Learning

In addition to emphasizing production and invention, the ENGW program has always valued experiential learning and writing beyond the university walls, both in internship opportunities and in course offerings. As early as 1975, students had the opportunity to participate in an internship for course credit, working with community organizations on writing projects. In 1982, when the writing concentration adopted its own core of classes, the credit-bearing internship became one of the required core classes and remains so today. Currently, students are encouraged to choose a second internship with a publisher, a local business, or a non-profit organization.

Beyond the internship, many courses in the ENGW curriculum also include an experiential component. For example, in Revising and Editing, students revise texts they have received at home, at work, or in other classes. Students in Technical and Business Communication work with local businesses and non-profits in developing user manuals or handbooks. More recently, students have also begun submitting work to Instructables (an online community for do-it-yourselfers). In courses such as Media Writing, Writing for PR/Publicity/Advertising, and Writing Online, students work with local clients to create websites, newsletters, and social media strategies. In our Grant Writing course, students work with local nonprofit groups to research and write actual grant proposals.

In addition to these formal requirements for experiential learning, ENGW students often develop experience by writing for the campus newspaper, editing the university's literary and academic journals, or tutoring other undergraduates. Our creative writing students participate in local readings and literary contests—such as the Austin Poetry Society's annual poetry contest, the *Austin Chronicle* short story contest, and National Novel Writing Month (NaNoWriMo)—and take advantage of the workshops and public readings offered through our Visiting Writers Series and the Texas Book Festival.

Developmental Structure

Finally, since the ENGW program began to manage its own core in 1982, it has been developmentally structured, with a large core of required courses in grammar/linguistics, style/editing, and discourse analysis/theories of rhetoric, in addition to electives focusing on creative and professional writing genres. St. Edward's seems unique among the undergraduate writing majors documented by the CCC Committee on the Major in Writing and Rhetoric in its focus on developmental structure. It has a much larger required core (twenty-seven credit hours; nine required courses) than the undergraduate majors Balzhiser and McLeod (2010) profile in their study of the committee's findings, or than the majors described in Giberson and Moriarty's (2010) anthology *What We Are Becoming*. The nine courses in the core of the St. Edward's writing and rhetoric major span all four years of undergraduate study.

Since the writing emphasis was added to the English major in 1975, the writing program has striven to be a curriculum designed, as Robert Schwegler (2000) urges, to "develop expertise and knowledge important to writers" rather than to be a "curriculum of writing courses" (27). Students enter the major in 2000-level courses such as American Grammar and Document Design, which have minimal general education prerequisites. In American Grammar, students study the basic phrase and clause structure of English, while mostly learning some of the specialized terms that will be part of their discussions throughout the major. In Document Design, students learn basic graphic design and typography principles by both creating and critiquing a mix of print and online documents. The other two required 2000-level classes, Revising and Editing and Text and Discourse Analysis, introduce students to discourse analysis and methods of rhetorical criticism.

These types of foundational courses are uncommon and almost never required—at least in the programs surveyed by Giberson and Moriarty (2010) and Balzhiser and McLeod (2010). Yet, many in our field have argued for the direct teaching of what Robert Connors (2000, 120) called "sentence rhetorics," what Doug Hesse (2003, 257) termed "writing as craft," and what DelliCarpini and Zerbe (2010, 177) refer to as the rhetorical canon's "middle sisters." For our program, focused as it is on students' producing many kinds of texts for many situations, these courses are essential, providing our students with a basis for understanding how design and linguistic style affect readability and how differing audience expectations in various genres affect the rhetorical success of particular texts.

Even students specializing in creative writing take nine core classes introducing them to rhetorical theory and practice, situating their creative and literary writing as one activity field among others in the discipline. Since 1982, when writing courses replaced literature courses in the core of the writing concentration, all writing majors have taken a course in Theories of Rhetoric and Composition. This course, like the undergraduate history of rhetoric course proposed by Richard Leo Enos (2000) in *Coming of Age*, provides students with a "more sensitive knowledge of the past" (81) and how discourse has shaped societies and cultures. In addition, the study of rhetoric's history, as Enos points out, allows students to see the relationships among various components of English studies—literature, creative writing, and professional writing. Building on this desire to have students see the relationships among the different approaches to writing studies, in 2008 the ENGW major developed a second required course: Current Theories of Rhetoric and

Composition. This second upper-division theories course, modeled on a graduate seminar, focuses on postmodern and contemporary rhetorics, including multimodal and online rhetorics.

The middle (3000-level) courses in the major are mostly professional and creative writing electives, with two required courses: Technical and Business Communication and Theories of Rhetoric. Technical and Business Communication (more an introduction to professional writing than a traditional technical writing course) acknowledges the necessity that most students will likely earn a living outside of the academy. It has experiential requirements and group projects designed to make sure all of our graduates have some experience in collaborative and non-academic/non-literary writing. The final required courses are the internship, the Current Theories course, and a senior seminar focused on portfolio and career preparation. The portfolio provides an opportunity for students to revise work they have already done, reflect on their growth as writers, and prepare writing samples, resumes, and personal statements for employers and graduate schools. Before portfolios are returned to students, ENGW faculty members evaluate them for the purpose of programmatic assessment. To encourage students to build their portfolios earlier and make them more visible to multiple audiences, we have now implemented an online portfolio system built using WordPress. Students begin the e-portfolio in their 2000-level Document Design course and complete it in their senior year. We intend for the e-portfolio to continue to serve two roles, as evidence of students' development and as a departmental assessment tool.

This large major (twenty-seven required credit hours and eighteen elective credit hours) requires students to take a variety of courses, while also allowing them to study some forms of writing in greater depth. The required courses permit St. Edward's to fulfill its commitment to its liberal arts tradition by introducing them to the rich history of rhetoric and the complexities of discourse-in-practice. Moreover, the required courses allow the ENGW program to promote the university's mission of serving first-generation and underrepresented students, many of whom need to work while in school and immediately upon graduation.

IMPLEMENTATION NARRATIVE

If a program's success can be measured in terms of its longevity and its enrollment, then the ENGW major has been quite successful. As the university began to see dramatic growth after 1999, the writing major became one of the most successful on campus—now the fourth largest major on campus with 155 students. We can point to several factors contributing to this success, some unique to our campus and history and others that can be replicated elsewhere.

Among the factors unique to St. Edward's, the program has enjoyed unusual administrative support from its inception in the 1970s. Once the writing program became a separate BA in 1987, it began to hire faculty with PhDs in rhetoric and composition. The administration also continues to support our major with curriculum and professional development funds. For example, in May 2011, we received internal funding to host a professional development workshop (led by Cheryl Ball) to encourage faculty to create assignments using multimodal composing technologies. ENGW teachers (both tenure-track and adjunct) received stipends for attending this workshop. Our FYC director held follow-up workshops to help our faculty share assignments and develop assessment methods.

The collegiality of the faculty has also been an asset, one not afforded to many of the writing programs whose histories have been recently documented. When it began in 1975, the English writing emphasis required five literature courses, so the literature faculty had no objections. The university's structure was also a factor in limiting internecine warfare: St. Edward's did not have discipline-specific departments, but instead had groups of disciplines—humanities, natural sciences, etc.—so there was no "Department of English" per se. By 1982, when the writing concentration revised its core to require writing rather than literature classes, the writing program had been in place for seven years and few faculty members objected. Hiring joint literature–writing faculty members in the 1980s and 1990s helped the writing program as well since those new hires were invested in the success of the writing program. That said, there are still occasional territorial skirmishes over curriculum decisions and hiring, especially for creative writing positions, where the writing faculty want new creative writing hires to have more than a passing familiarity with composition research.

While not all institutions will be able to offer the kind of support, both administrative and collegial, from which we have benefited at St. Edward's since the 1970s, other factors in the longevity and success of the writing major at St. Edward's are highly replicable. For instance, our writing faculty and our majors are woven into the general education, supplemental instruction, and extracurricular pillars of the St. Edward's experience—from Freshman Studies to Rhetoric and Composition II to the writing center to student publications to internships. Members of the writing faculty have also collaborated with the director of the Center for Teaching Excellence to offer faculty development workshops, often at the request of deans and faculty from other departments. The writing center, administered and staffed exclusively by faculty in the writing program (both adjuncts and full-timers), also offers class presentations and consultations for faculty on improving writing assignments. Its regular one-on-one consulting services are well used by students and highly regarded across campus. A new member of the ENGW faculty, with expertise in grant writing, is serving as a liaison to the Office of Sponsored Programs, the campus hub for faculty from all disciplines who seek external funding for research or development. Writing faculty also regularly serve on key university committees, including the tenure and promotion committee and curricular review committees. Writing faculty members participated in the 1992 redesign of the general education curriculum and currently serve on the General Education Advisory Committee. We teach Capstone and other general education courses, in addition to the FYC courses, as our schedules permit. So, while we have clearly benefited from already having departmental status, our visibility and service to faculty and campus committees have boosted our reputation on campus, and such activities can surely help writing departments on other campuses.

Like fledgling writing departments elsewhere, our long-standing program is always concerned with the recruitment and retention of majors. Proponents of writing majors, whether they propose brand-new programs or expansions to existing pilot programs, ought to research the numbers of writing majors at other universities and their contributions to tuition. Such numerical and fiscal realities constitute a major factor in the rise of ENGW at St. Edward's, and are strong grounds for an argument to initiate or expand a writing major. In 1999, our department enrolled forty-six majors. We began an effort to more than double the number of our majors by launching recruitment efforts that we continue today. While we recruit a number of incoming freshmen into the major, other students change majors after a semester or two. Most don't arrive on campus knowing they want to major in writing, but we have found that emphasizing the academic and professional creativity, practicality, and flexibility of our program helps recruit students who knew themselves to be good writers but did not know what they would do with an English major. To make sure that many students hear about the major, the tenure-track writing faculty use the bully pulpit of FYC courses to encourage strong writers to consider ENGW. We also began offering honors sections of Rhetoric and Composition II every spring, sections set aside for strong writers nominated by their Rhetoric and Composition I instructors. In addition to providing strong writers and conscientious students with a group of equally ambitious peers, these honors courses offer faculty another forum for recruiting strong students to ENGW. We now offer honors sections every fall as well, since many of the best writers come to campus with AP or dual-enrollment credit for FYC. These honors sections have proven to be a productive recruiting tactic.

These honors courses and our participation in the FYC program in general are by far our best recruiting tools, though we also participate in majors fairs for undecided students and we promote the major in courses (such as American Grammar or Information Design) that are cross-listed as required courses for students in other majors (such as education). For the last three years, we have also team-taught a one-credit-hour freshman experience course for students considering an English major, either literature or writing. We have found that students are impressed when they meet our faculty and visit with graduates, who discuss their current jobs and the internships they held while at St. Edward's. Giving students, as early and as often as possible, the sense that writing can be practical and useful as well as fun and creative has helped us turn dabblers in our creative writing or Revising and Editing courses into majors or minors. Since fall 2007, we have held steady with 140–155 majors, moving from the seventeenth largest department on campus in 1999 to the fourth largest in fall 2010.

Finally, we reinforce the sense of our major as practical and useful by our willingness to update our curriculum to reflect changes in our field. We have offered topics courses—for example, in Media Writing, Grant Writing, and Writing with Computers (now Writing Online)—that, once proven successful, have become regularly offered elective courses. More importantly, we have continued to update the core of the major based on both scholarship in the field and assessment results from our senior portfolios. In 2008–2009, we added Information Design (now Document Design) as a core requirement to ensure that our students have some familiarity with basic principles of graphic design, XHTML/CSS coding, and working with a content management system. We also replaced the last of the literature courses in our curriculum, Literary Criticism, with Current Theories of Rhetoric and Composition. Surveys of graduating seniors report that our majors are happy to have skills they see as up-to-date and practical as well as experience in thinking critically about rhetoric and technology. We would argue that our willingness to update our curriculum and replace retiring faculty with faculty able to teach these new courses is a major factor in our retaining majors and recruiting students from other majors in the humanities, some of whose curricula have changed little in the last twenty or thirty years.

REFLECTION AND PROSPECTION

Some readers may conclude that the St. Edward's ENGW major developed relatively easily, but ours is actually a story of gradual change and updating to suit students' needs and take advantage of our university's culture. By consistently seizing opportunities to enhance our disciplinary legitimacy within the university, and by evolving to keep pace with the ways in which writers produce texts of all kinds, we have built a program that balances the three strands of textual production, experiential learning, and developmental structure. In turn, other programs seeking to create or develop a writing major can take up those strands and weave them in ways that best suit their local needs.

Curricular Summary: The English Writing and Rhetoric Major at St. Edward's University

We all live in a world that writing built. The noted writer and educator Janet Emig contends that we live in a world that writing helps to shape and to make understandable "since writing either serves or actually represents so many of the functions that make us human, that make us civilized. Through writing, we can record, describe, explain, argue, justify, codify, discover, create, reflect, destroy, and build our own lives and the four worlds [private, public, college, and work] in which we live." (Lauer et al. 1991, 13) The writing and rhetoric major prepares students to function competently in these worlds. It provides a wide range of coursework for students wishing to prepare for careers involving writing, editing and other communication skills—law, government service, teaching, advertising, public relations, etc.—as well as those wishing to become professional writers.

Students take nine core courses (including a required internship) and six elective courses. Electives are determined by the student's chosen specialization (general, professional writing, creative writing). As of fall 2013, students also have the option of selecting a specialization in journalism.

MAJOR REQUIREMENTS (45 CREDIT HOURS)

Core courses (27 credits):
- ENGW 2320: American Grammar
- ENGW 2325: Text and Discourse Analysis
- ENGW 2326: Revising and Editing
- ENGW 2329: Document Design

- ENGW 3335: Technical and Business Communication
- ENGW 3336: Theories of Rhetoric and Composition
- ENGW 4341: Current Theories of Rhetoric and Composition
- ENGW 4344: Career Preparation
- ENGW 4350: Internship (students with three or more years of workplace writing experience may replace this course with an additional elective)

General writing track (six courses):

- ENGW 3324: Principles of Style (required)
- Two courses from:
  - ENGW 3332: Writing Online
  - ENGW 3333: Print Production
  - ENGW 4342: Magazine Writing
- Three additional elective courses offered by the department.

Professional writing track (six courses):

- ENGW 3324: Principles of Style (required)
- Two courses from:
  - JOUR 2321: Journalism I
  - ENGW 3301: Writing for Advertising, Public Relations, and Publicity
  - ENGW 3331: Media Writing
  - ENGW 3332: Writing Online
  - ENGW 3333: Print Production
  - ENGW 3337: Advanced Editing
  - ENGW 4342: Magazine Writing
  - ENGW 4345: Grant Proposal Writing
- Three additional elective courses offered by the department.

Creative writing track (six courses):

- Two courses from:
  - ENGW 2301: Poetry Workshop I
  - ENGW 2302: Fiction Workshop I
  - ENGW 2303: Playwriting Workshop I
  - ENGW 2304: Special Creative Writing Workshops
  - ENGW 2305: Creative Nonfiction Workshop
- One course from:
- ENGW 3307: Poetry Writing II, or
  - ENGW 3308: Fiction Writing II, or
  - ENGW 3309: Stage and Screen Writing II, or
  - ENGW 3310: Special Topics in Intermediate Creative Writing
- One course from:
- ENGL 3303–3305: Poetry Studies, or
  - ENGL 3306: American Novel to 1890, or
  - ENGL 3307: Victorian Novel, or
  - ENGL 3308: Restoration and 18th-Century British Literature, or

- ENGL 3312: Victorian Prose and Poetry, or
- ENGL 3335–3338: Drama Studies, or
- ENGL 3339: Special Topics in Literature, or
- ENGL 4310: Modern American Poetry, or
- ENGL 4319: Modern and Postmodern Literature, or
- ENGL 4322: Turn of the Century and Early Modern Novel, or
- ENGL 4327: The 18th-Century British Novel
- Two additional elective courses offered by the department.

References

Balzhiser, Deborah, and Susan McLeod. 2010. "The Undergraduate Writing Major: What Is It? What Should It Be?" *College Composition and Communication* 61 (3): 415–33.

Connors, Robert. 2000. "The Erasure of the Sentence." *College Composition and Communication* 52 (1): 96–128. http://dx.doi.org/10.2307/358546.

DelliCarpini, Dominic, and Michael Zerbe. 2010. "Remembering the Canons' Middle Sisters: Style, Memory, and the Return of the Progymnasmata in the Liberal Arts Writing Major." In *What We Are Becoming: Developments in Undergraduate Writing Majors*, ed. Greg Giberson and Thomas Moriarty, 177–201. Logan: Utah State University Press.

Dunn, William. 1986. *Saint Edward's University: A Centennial History*. Austin: Saint Edward's University Press.

Enos, Richard Leo. 2000. "The History of Rhetoric." In *Coming of Age: The Advanced Writing Curriculum*, ed. Linda K. Shamoon, Rebecca Moore Howard, Sandra Jamieson, and Robert A. Schwegler, 81–6. Portsmouth: Heinemann.

Giberson, Greg, and Thomas Moriarty, eds. 2010. *What We Are Becoming: Developments in Undergraduate Writing Majors*. Logan: Utah State University Press.

Hesse, Douglas. 2003. "Who Owns Creative Nonfiction?" In *Beyond Postprocess and Postmodernism: Essays on the Spaciousness of Rhetoric*, ed. Theresa Enos and Keith D. Mille, 251–66. New Jersey: Erlbaum.

Lauer, Janice, Janet Emig, Andrea Lunsford, and Gene Montague. 1991. *Four Worlds of Writing*. New York: Harper.

Mayers, Tim. 2005. *(Re)writing Craft: Composition, Creative Writing, and the Future of English Studies*. Pittsburgh: University of Pittsburgh Press.

Schwegler, Robert. 2000. "Curriculum Development in Composition." In *Coming of Age: The Advanced Writing Curriculum*, ed. Linda K. Shamoon, Rebecca Moore Howard, Sandra Jamieson, and Robert A. Schwegler, 25–31. Portsmouth: Heinemann.

Spellmeyer, Kurt. 2002. "Bigger than a Discipline?" *A Field of Dreams: Independent Writing Programs and the Future of Composition Studies*, ed. Peggy O'Neill, Angela Crow, and Larry W. Burton., 278–294. Logan: Utah State University Press.

17

COLUMBIA COLLEGE'S ENGLISH MAJOR
Writing for Print and Digital Media

Claudia Smith Brinson and Nancy Lewis Tuten

INTRODUCTION

Columbia College offers coeducational graduate and evening under-graduate programs, but at the heart of this institution is a private, residential, four-year liberal arts college for approximately 900 women. The college was founded in 1854 in Columbia, South Carolina, and is affiliated with the United Methodist Church. With a student–faculty ratio of 12:1, Columbia College ranks among the top-performing institutions in the country in the National Survey of Student Engagement (2011; NSSE). We have students from twenty-three states and twenty countries.

In 2008, the English department chair and the newly hired writing track coordinator realized that our writing program—an English major track called business and professional writing (BPW)—needed to be updated. First, the courses offered did not deal with the present—much less the future—reality for media professionals, who not only write and edit traditional texts but also publish and produce in digital formats. Second, many of the courses in the BPW track took a broad survey approach, attempting, for example, to introduce students to reporting, advertising, and public relations in a single semester-long writing course. Our program coordinator had worked in print media for thirty years, and her experiences writing for Knight Ridder's online ventures, filming digital videos to accompany print articles, and coaching new reporters convinced her that students' marketability depends on repeated practice in journalism skills as well as substantial exposure to multiple genres and platforms. In the spring of 2010, the faculty approved our revised program, which we call writing for print and digital media (WPDM). This track is one of three within the English program, the other two

DOI: 10.7330/9780874219722.c017

Department Name:	English Program, Division of Languages and Literatures
Institution Type:	Private, Master's M (awards between 100–199 Master's degrees/year)
Institution Size:	1,400 students
Residential or Commuter:	Residential
Student Body Description:	Diverse in terms of ethnicity and socio-economics; high percentage of students are first in their family to go to college; predominantly from South Carolina, but also from 23 states and 20 other countries
Year Major Began:	2010
Official Name of Degree:	Bachelor of Arts in English
Number of Majors:	In year one: 8 In year three: 26 In year five: N/A Current: 26
Number of Full-Time R/C Faculty:	1

being English education (for students planning to teach at the high school level) and literary studies.

Before making the decision to revise the writing track, we looked at course descriptions for journalism, mass communications, and new media programs nationwide, and we talked to department chairs about their programs. Few colleges or universities had updated their writing majors to reflect the new reality for media professionals. We concluded that Columbia College had an advantage: a small ship can turn quickly toward the future while others are still debating—or ignoring—the call. And we could afford to turn quickly because most of the technology we needed to update the program was affordable.

PROGRAM OVERVIEW AND RATIONALE

In the former BPW track, students sampled; in the new WPDM track, they focus. The revised program allows students to choose courses that shape a focused career path: They can concentrate their program on journalism, taking introductory and intermediate courses in reporting and feature writing. They can focus on public relations writing, taking introductory and intermediate PR writing courses. They can focus on Internet content production, taking an introductory course on writing for digital media, then adding design, business, and computer science courses. They can focus on creative writing, taking courses in short fiction, poetry, and creative nonfiction. Or they can focus on documentary film, taking introductory and intermediate courses in digital video and art.

All students in the WPDM track must take nine core courses. Seven of them are three-credit required courses: WRIT 200: Introduction to Reporting for Print and Digital Media, a gateway course that serves as a prerequisite to many upper-division writing courses; WRIT 355: Media Ethics and Law; WRIT 365: Substantive Text Editing; ENG 275: Advanced English Grammar; WRIT 330: Writing for Digital Media; ENG 205: Introduction to Mass Communication; and ENG 495: Senior Seminar (required of all English majors). Each WPDM major must also take at least one of two one-credit courses, WRIT 245 and 246: Writing for Campus Media, and at least one three-credit internship. We give our students a strong foundation in technology and writing for different media, and we prepare them to deal with the inevitable evolution of equipment and platforms. Hands-on practice through a combination of courses and internships provides students with not only an academic foundation but also the practical experience necessary to land their first jobs and to adapt as those media evolve.

We consider the required internship a major strength of the program, ensuring that graduates have had hands-on experience in a work environment. Our students work with South Carolina Educational Television network's filmmakers, with historic foundations' archivists, and at local broadcast companies. In previous semesters, students have worked with CEOs of local advertising and public relations companies, edited copy for both a local entertainment tabloid and a Methodist newspaper, and assisted nonprofits in their varied work, including promotion through social media.

We further prepare WPDM students for various career choices by encouraging them to take courses in other programs, including communication studies, business, art, and computer and information sciences. Students interested in documentary filmmaking, for example, are encouraged to consider several communication studies courses, including Rhetoric of Public Advocacy and Persuasion in Communication, and/or the art program's Introduction to Photography and Beginning Graphic Design.

IMPLEMENTATION NARRATIVE

Upon implementing our new major, we immediately had to address two main issues: first, confusion on campus—both for faculty and students—about how our program differs from the communication studies major and, second, low enrollment in program courses. We have engaged in lively debates with our colleagues in the communication studies program regarding our desire to offer courses in narrative video. Initially, the WPDM program proposal included both introductory and intermediate courses on digital narrative. Our students need to be able to tell stories through the printed word as well as other media, including film. During the WPDM design phase, we created a pilot journalism-oriented videography course that was team-taught by one of our faculty and a former newspaper videographer. The communication faculty, however, felt that our students could instead take their program's introductory video course, COMM 280, arguing that a campus as small as ours did not need a second set of video courses. Reluctantly, we removed our new video courses from the proposal. However, we continued to believe that our proposed video courses were not duplicative—ours were designed to teach students to use the medium of video in their careers as journalists, public relations specialists, web content producers, and, of course, documentary filmmakers. In the spring of 2010, when we hired a new faculty member with experience in creating narrative through video, we became increasingly dissatisfied with the idea of allowing our majors to take COMM 280 instead of a video course designed expressly for our program. Thus, in the spring of 2011, we proposed our own introductory video course, WRIT 355: Introduction to Narrative with Video. The course was approved, but not without resistance from the communication faculty.

In addition to the debate about video course offerings, we've also encountered confusion among some students about which major—communication studies or WPDM—is more appropriate for careers in public relations and journalism. Some students don't understand the differences between the two programs in general, and between each program's digital video courses in particular. At larger universities, students desiring careers in public relations often declare majors in *mass* communications programs, which offer a variety of majors in print and broadcast journalism, film production, public relations, communication studies, and marketing. Students on our campus see "communication studies" in our college bulletin and fail to realize that the program is grounded in the liberal arts with an emphasis on understanding communication theory and practice. Thus, a student wishing to pursue a career in public relations might gravitate toward the theory-centered communication studies program when, in fact, she also needs a heavy dose of writing courses and a foundation in journalism. Not infrequently, students majoring in communication studies end up deciding to minor or double-major in WPDM in order to gain an introduction to and hands-on practice in journalism or public relations writing skills. While we certainly believe that students benefit greatly from understanding communication theory, we also know they must be able to write a press release on day one of their careers in public relations.

A second area of difficulty has been low enrollment in our upper-level courses while we grow the program. We also struggled during the first two years to accommodate juniors and seniors who came in under an old bulletin and were completing BPW majors. While we encouraged them to switch to the newer bulletins that included the revised course offerings, some declined because their graduation dates would be delayed by curriculum changes affecting second majors, minors, or general education requirements. We found ourselves having to make numerous course substitutions since we no longer taught many of the courses offered in the BPW track.

We are learning that we must remain flexible while we continue to grow the program. For example, when we designed the program, we made WRIT 200: Introduction to Reporting for Print and Digital Media a prerequisite for nearly all other WRIT courses. While we still believe this course provides a necessary foundation for many courses, we do offer some courses for which WRIT 200 is not a prerequisite—in particular, our three courses in creative writing (poetry, creative nonfiction, and short fiction). Originally, WRIT 200 was a prerequisite for Media Ethics and Law, but, faced with low enrollment, we waived the prerequisite for several students so they could take that course concurrently with WRIT 200. We even allowed a few honors students to take WRIT 200 concurrently with ENG 102, our second-semester FYC course. We will, no doubt, continue to struggle with the tension between prerequisites and healthy course enrollment as we build the program. We also hope to increase enrollment in our courses by encouraging more students to minor in WPDM, as well as by encouraging faculty across campus to require—or at least suggest—a WPDM course as part of their majors or minors. Because employers consistently seek employees who can communicate clearly, quickly, and accurately, we believe a second major or a minor in WPDM could complement nearly every other major on campus. Columbia College does not require a minor, but the advantages of developing more than one area of expertise are clear.

REFLECTION AND PROSPECTION

We have learned a great deal through the process of developing, implementing, running, and revising this new program. First, we did not anticipate territorial disputes concerning new course proposals. Second, when we were designing the program and creating a number of courses more narrowly defined than those we had previously offered, we didn't anticipate the effort it would take a small private college to attract enough majors to fill those classes, particularly in a national economic downturn. Perhaps our biggest surprise, however, was the degree to which we needed to recruit new majors. The two faculty members primarily responsible for the WPDM program, along with the division head, are currently implementing these strategies:

- We are committed to having a WPDM faculty member attend every on-campus recruitment event sponsored by the college, and we are considering attending at least a few off-campus events in larger cities.
- Our division is undergoing a revision of our college website, and we are committed to making those changes first for the WPDM program. It is, of course, important for this program—perhaps more than any other on campus—to use the cutting-edge technology we teach our students to use. We hired a recent program graduate to work part-time for two semesters creating promotional materials that reflect our new-media approach. We asked her to create a two-page flyer that admissions counselors can pull up on their iPads when they are out recruiting. This document includes links to videos of our majors and minors talking about their internships, classroom experiences, and, in the case of our recent graduates, some of the exciting graduate school opportunities and careers available to WPDM majors. In her work on these recruitment projects, this former major also created a Prezi that provides a detailed description of our program for both prospective Columbia College students and current students who may be considering our program. She also shot video of our faculty and students in a variety of venues and created short video introductions of students, faculty, classes, and internships.
- We are identifying high schools across the country that have programs emphasizing new media, journalism, and video narrative so we can market directly to them.
- We asked the admissions office to send us a list of any student in its contact bank who had expressed interest in careers related to journalism, public relations, or writing of any kind. We then contact each of them directly, either through phone calls or e-mail messages.
- In the summer of 2012, we offered a week-long summer workshop for local high school students interested in creating video with Final Cut Pro. The workshop familiarized students with our program, introduced them to our faculty, and helped spread our reputation in the local community. Our hope is to eventually offer it as a residential summer camp and recruit participants from across the country and around the world.

- We continue to celebrate our students' classroom activities and academic accomplishments. Each semester, students in our creative writing classes hold a "Beatnik Coffeehouse," during which they read their work. An on-campus "Academy Awards" event was transformed into a community film festival through a partnership with an independent film society. And we are making a strong effort to expand our internship offerings to include more video and new media associations.

CONCLUSION

Despite the difficulties we've encountered, we are convinced that we have designed a program that is in the best interest of our students and their twenty-first century careers. People will continue to want news, novels, and films. What is in question is *how* they will receive this information. As of 2012, 70 percent of Americans who own a computer and over half of smartphone and tablet users use those devices to retrieve at least some of their daily news. Over one-third of all US adults access news solely on their computers (*The State of the News Media*, 2013). While print news organizations still produce most of the content we consume, online aggregators and social media have become key distributors. Writing programs must continue to teach the basics of good writing and editing, but we must also adapt to changing media. Students must learn not only how to create high-quality content, but also how to adapt that content to ever-changing platforms.

Columbia College believes that our cutting-edge WPDM program will be very attractive to both current and prospective students. And, indeed, interest is mounting—faculty in other programs on our campus, seeing the value in their students' gaining new media experience, promote WPDM as a good second major or minor to complement a primary course of study. Our admissions counselors report that high school students are enthusiastic about the opportunity to link their interest in writing to a viable twenty-first century career. Current WPDM students value their internship experiences so highly that many are opting for a second placement before graduation. While it would be premature to declare the revised program a success just a few years after it was approved by the faculty, we have every reason to believe that we are on the right track—our program provides an excellent academic and practical foundation upon which our students can build successful careers as writers in the twenty-first century.

Curricular Summary: The Writing for Print and Digital Media Major at Columbia College

The writing for print and digital media major prepares students for careers in digital media, journalism, public relations, and others requiring strong writing skills.

MAJOR REQUIREMENTS (43 CREDIT HOURS)

Core courses:

- ENG 205: Introduction to Mass Communication
- ENG 275: Advanced English Grammar
- WRIT 200: Introduction to Reporting for Print and Digital Media
- WRIT 330: Writing for Digital Media
- WRIT 355: Media Ethics and Law
- WRIT 365: Substantive Text Editing
- WRIT 245/246: Writing for Campus Media I/II
- WRIT 370/470: Internship
- ENG 495: Senior Seminar
- One three-credit course in literature, English language, or film

Writing track suggested courses (5 courses):

- WRIT 305: Writing for Business and Public Affairs
- WRIT 325: Feature Writing for Print and Digital Media
- WRIT 346: Introduction to Writing Short Fiction
- WRIT 347: Introduction to Writing Poetry
- WRIT 348: Introduction to Writing Creative Nonfiction
- WRIT 405: Intermediate Reporting and Writing for Print and Digital Media
- BUS 325: Entrepreneurship
- CIS 230: Introduction to Web Development

Public relations writing track suggested courses (5 courses):

- WRIT 235: Public Relations Writing
- WRIT 305: Writing for Business and Public Affairs
- WRIT 415: Intermediate Public Relations Writing
- ART 151: Two-Dimensional Design and Color
- ART 271: Beginning Graphic Design
- ART 285: Introduction to Photography
- ART 371: Intermediate Graphic Design
- BUS 310: eBusiness
- BUS 325: Entrepreneurship
- COMM 310: Persuasion

- COMM 330: Rhetoric of Public Advocacy
- COMM 340: Intercultural Communication
- CIS 230: Introduction to Web Development

Narrative and video track suggested courses (5 courses):

- WRIT 325: Feature Writing for Print and Digital Media
- WRIT 346: Introduction to Writing Short Fiction
- WRIT 347: Introduction to Writing Poetry
- WRIT 348: Introduction to Writing Creative Nonfiction
- WRIT 350: Introduction to Narrative with Digital Video
- WRIT 405: Intermediate Reporting and Writing for Print and Digital Media
- WRIT 425: Intermediate-Level Narrative with Digital Video
- COMM 310: Persuasion
- COMM 330: Rhetoric of Public Advocacy
- COMM 340: Intercultural Communication

Design and video track suggested courses (5 courses):

- WRIT 346: Introduction to Writing Short Fiction
- WRIT 347: Introduction to Writing Poetry
- WRIT 348: Introduction to Writing Creative Nonfiction
- WRIT 350: Introduction to Narrative with Digital Video
- WRIT 425: Intermediate-Level Narrative with Digital Video
- ART 151: Two-Dimensional Design and Color
- ART 271: Beginning Graphic Design
- ART 285: Introduction to Photography
- ART 371: Intermediate Graphic Design Internship
- CIS 230: Introduction to Web Development

Text and design in web publishing track suggested courses (5 courses):

- WRIT 305: Writing for Business and Public Affairs
- WRIT 325: Feature Writing for Print and Digital Media
- WRIT 346: Introduction to Writing Short Fiction
- WRIT 347: Introduction to Writing Poetry
- WRIT 348: Introduction to Writing Creative Nonfiction
- WRIT 405: Intermediate Reporting and Writing for Print and Digital Media
- ART 151: Two-Dimensional Design and Color
- ART 271: Beginning Graphic Design
- ART 285: Introduction to Photography
- ART 371: Intermediate Graphic Design
- BUS 310: eBusiness
- BUS 325: Entrepreneurship
- CIS 230: Introduction to Web Development

References

National Survey of Student Engagement. 2011. *Fostering Student Engagement Campuswide Annual Results 2011.* Bloomington: Indiana University Center for Postsecondary Research.

The State of the News Media. 2013. *An Annual Report on American Journalism.* The Pew Research Center's Project for Excellence in Journalism.

18

SEEKING GROWTH THROUGH INDEPENDENCE
A Professional Writing and Rhetoric Program in Transition at Elon University

Jessie L. Moore, Tim Peeples,
Rebecca Pope-Ruark, and Paula Rosinski

INTRODUCTION

In 2007, two of the coauthors of this chapter published a theoretical piece referencing the development of the professional writing and rhetoric (PWR) concentration within the English major at Elon University—a private, mid-sized (5,000 undergraduates), liberal arts university in central North Carolina—as a way to reflectively theorize program development. In this article, two sets of terms—"*chronos/kairos*" and strategy/tactic—were used as a heuristic for understanding the development of our specific program, but, more generally and significantly, the heuristic was presented as a framework for understanding the development of programs across institutional contexts. As we wrote then, "What we find most powerful about this framework is the way it emphasizes the rhetorical, productive, compositional nature of program development; we *write* and re-write our programs" (Peeples, Rosinski, and Strickland 2007, 58, emphasis original).

We start with this reference because, in order to talk about our program (and we would argue any program), we must understand that we are speaking of something dynamic. To write its history, its rationale, its implementation process, and its institutional connections, for instance, is to write of something that has been and is changing, something that does not have a stable or master history, something always being re-implemented and reconnected, and something that itself changes as it is rewritten constantly within ever changing contexts.

DOI: 10.7330/9780874219722.c018

Department Name:	English
Institution Type:	Private, Master's S (awards fewer than 100 master's degrees/year)
Institution Size:	5,400 students
Residential or Commuter:	Residential
Student Body Description:	Students come from 48 states, the District of Columbia, and 48 other nations; about 25% are from North Carolina and approximately 50% are from other states along the east coast; 87% complete internships; 72% study abroad
Year Major Began:	2000
Official Name of Degree:	Bachelor of Arts in English with concentration in Professional Writing and Rhetoric
Number of Majors:	In year one: 3 In year three: 10 In year five: 30 Current: 30
Number of Full-Time R/C Faculty:	5

In that 2007 article, we shared some moments of programmatic development that reflect both strategic and tactical action, reflect both chronological and kairotic time, and illustrate some of the ways our own program has been rewritten over time. Now, four years later, we share a follow-up snapshot that extends this initial framework by examining key moments that drove our recent transition attempts as we argued, unsuccessfully, for additional independence as a separate PWR major.

PROGRAM OVERVIEW AND RATIONALE

Currently, PWR is one of four concentration areas in the English department. All students majoring in English must complete a set of core courses in literature, writing, and language. Though the majority of their coursework is associated with their chosen concentrations, all receive one major: English. We are fortunate to have five PWR faculty members, although one has a split appointment with the Environmental Studies Department, one has administrative duties directing the university's writing center, and one now serves in a full-time administrative position as the university's associate provost, thus reducing how many PWR courses we can teach.

Our PWR concentration has undergone relatively minor revisions since being approved in 2000, growing out of a defunct and dysfunctional "writing" concentration that was formed in 1994. This earlier curriculum consisted of a small and disconnected set of interdisciplinary courses loosely focused on composition (e.g., tutoring and the development of writers). Between 1998 and 2000, the concentration was significantly reframed to reflect the wider discipline of rhetoric and writing studies and to appeal to a wider group of undergraduates. Rather than a concentration for the few who might go on to teach composition, it became a concentration for undergraduates interested in a program of study leading to effective contemporary rhetorical praxis, specifically within workplace contexts. The rationale behind the curricular development was driven, primarily, by what we had learned about undergraduate student interest at Elon and by a sense of the broader discipline of rhetoric and writing as much more than "composition." Most first- and second-year students could see themselves doing—and were attracted to the idea of doing—something related to writing in the world, but few were thinking they would go on to get a master's degree in composition and teach writing. Since both PWR faculty at that point had experience in professional and technical writing, writing across the disciplines, rhetoric and composition, and even creative writing, the disciplinary frame they brought to bear on the development of the concentration was broad.

Nevertheless, the concentration was initially designed within a significantly constrained context. At its creation and during its initial years, PWR was constrained by the reduced teaching load of only two faculty members, one of whom, at that time, directed both WAC and the writing center. The concentration was also constrained by the heavy English major core requirements that placed tremendous emphasis on literary study. PWR was further restricted by the institutional context, wherein a rapidly growing and heavily supported School of Communications attracted hundreds of majors and was very aggressive about dividing and claiming "disciplinary turf." As a result, there were still few courses in PWR and much need to draw from across disciplines, including communications, art, computer science, and business. PWR's identity also was hampered by the English department's stubborn view of PWR as a necessary evil, as a curricular option within the "true liberal art of English" that appealed to the practical and vocational.

Despite these obstacles, a coherent program was constructed, and a cadre of students began to animate the concentration. PWR had three required courses, including one introduction to rhetoric and professional writing course, one special topics class, and one capstone course with an embedded internship experience. Students completed the concentration with several electives, some of which could be outside of English, and there was a strong expectation that students would have writing internships (nearly 100% did, even without a formal require-ment). All PWR courses shared an emphasis on reflective practice, con-necting disciplinary content, rhetorical theory, and experiential learn-ing. The rationale guiding curriculum development was contemporary rhetorical praxis: we aimed at developing a curriculum that established strong disciplinary foundations, offered students ever-expanding and specialized practical and disciplinary experience, and supported the development of reflective practitioners. Though subsequent "tweaks" since 2000 have sought to ensure that PWR students get a more com-plete disciplinary foundation and more hands-on experience (through internships, for example); that courses are scaffolded and sequenced more consciously; and that course offerings reflect the strengths of a growing faculty, our commitment to contemporary rhetorical praxis still rings true as we look ahead to greater independence.

In 2011–2012, the PWR faculty at Elon formally pursued both an inde-pendent PWR major and a standalone PWR department[1] in response to (1) national trends for writing majors, (2) an opportune moment in the university's general studies curriculum revision, and (3) growing evidence that independence would attract and serve students far bet-ter than our current positioning. PWR students currently take courses in the English major core (including one 200-level and one 300-level literature course, one writing course—Creative Writing or Professional Writing and Rhetoric—and a 300-level English course outside of the concentration), courses in the PWR core (which includes Introduction to Professional Writing and Rhetoric, Understanding Rhetoric, Writing as Inquiry, Special Topics, an Internship, and the senior seminar course Researching Writing), and two PWR electives (for a description of the existing PWR concentration, see Peeples, Rosinski, and Strickland 2007). The proposed new major curriculum would allow students more opportunities for disciplinary study as well as space to explore interdis-ciplinary connections and double majors with related disciplines such as human services studies, political science, and international relations. Comparing the existing concentration curriculum and the proposed PWR major curriculum, we tried to make room for both broad and deep disciplinary study as well as create space for interdisciplinary exploration by removing the English major core requirements. This change frees eight more credit hours for PWR study and eight credit hours for inter-disciplinary study. Students would experience a more focused core of PWR courses, including a newly added colloquia course, which students would take for one credit for four semesters. Colloquia students would participate in technology and skill workshops, engage guest speakers from academia and industry, discuss research with faculty and other students, and present their own work.

This summary of our proposed major revisions highlights our primary emphasis on expanded space for disciplinary and interdisciplinary exploration. Within the current English major, PWR students' selection of courses is limited by English core requirements, a point that over half of the graduating PWR seniors have critiqued during their senior exit process. In addition to requesting a greater breadth of course choice within PWR, students regularly express a desire for a greater depth of course options within PWR, courses that would allow them to move deeper into the discipline. We have also seen that many PWR students' goals/needs are best met through interdisciplinary study, study appreciated by PWR but not well accommodated within the English major. The proposed PWR major would enhance both the breadth and depth of expertise/skill in areas of focus (e.g., advanced digital writing, grant writing, and publications management), and would enable and create stronger, more innovative interdisciplinary linkages through possible double majors with programs such as those listed above.[2]

The proposed major is disciplinary without being exclusionary, is both broad and deep, and leverages existing program strengths to meet students' needs and goals. Meeting students' needs and goals carries over to our interest in departmental status as well.

IMPLEMENTATION NARRATIVE

In so many ways, PWR already functions as a departmental unit, though it is still housed under English. It has identifiable physical space (e.g., the Center for Undergraduate Publishing and Information Design—CUPID); a healthy curriculum; a recognizable set of "majors" and minors; its own promotion and tenure (P&T) document; control over its own course scheduling; regular traditions throughout the academic year; its own policies in relation to honors and fellows programs; a developed internship history and set of practices; its own alumni communications and outreach; its own web presence; and more. PWR has even proposed and searched for its "own" faculty. Yet, creating a home for students through a developed curriculum, connections with other departments and programs, and PWR community-building has been difficult as a concentration within the English major.

Many students in other majors at Elon express not having a "real home" for their studies, that they settle for something that is fairly close to what they are looking for but not precisely what they want. A number of students have found PWR this way over the years, feeling like PWR is more of what they are seeking in an education and future career. Currently "hidden" within English (a place many of these students—and their parents—would not identify as a "home"), PWR is not visible enough to attract and subsequently meet the needs of these students. In addition, many potential students do not want to complete non-PWR English courses. We have repeatedly found that students external to English are disappointingly unaware of PWR as an option of study, or they resist selecting a major with additional English studies "baggage." As an independent major, PWR would gain the visibility needed to attract and address students whose interests can be best served by study in PWR, but who are unaware of or resistant to it as an option because of its placement *under* English.

We have long promoted PWR as an excellent "sister" area of study with other majors and minors, as rhetoric is by its very nature interdisciplinary, but our English designation and the associated baggage constrain many positive possibilities. As a concentration, we have strong connections to several interdisciplinary minors, including multimedia authoring and leadership studies, which have been productive and have informed our classes in interesting ways. We have also built tentative connections with human services studies and international studies, which have encouraged a few double majors, but many of these potential double major students resist the literature-heavy core requirements of the English major. A PWR major less directly linked to English that allows curricular space for interdisciplinary study would actively attract students who want to improve their rhetorical awareness in concert with another area of study.

While making connections across the university will help to inform our program and meet our students' educational goals, we are also very aware of the importance of continuing to foster a sense of community within PWR. One of the primary units for creating community within a university, and likely the strongest within academic affairs, is the individual, independent major. PWR students often note at the time of senior exits that they associate with PWR more strongly than do their peers in other majors, regularly referring to themselves as "PWR majors" even though they are officially English majors. In spite of the constraints on the concentration, PWR students graduate with a very strong sense of disciplinary identity. Major status would help PWR leap forward from its current positive position to create an even stronger, even more vibrant sense of community among its majors through programming, cross-campus visibility, clearer focus, enhanced professional development opportunities, increased social opportunities, etc.

While we have both anecdotal and empirical evidence supporting our rationale for both a PWR major and an independent department, as well as a general excitement about the possibilities these changes would create, we still face a series of uphill battles to achieve our goal.

Perhaps the single greatest challenge we face during our transition from concentration to major corresponds with our colleagues' conception of PWR. When we first proposed shifting to a PWR major, ideally within an independent PWR department, some of our departmental colleagues were appalled that our students already develop a PWR identity as opposed to a broader English identity. We explained that as our students work through the PWR concentration core, we continuously ask them to define—and to revisit their definitions of—*rhetoric* and *professional writing*. We also ask them to construct—from PWR core and elective course assignments, internships, and undergraduate research projects—portfolios that they eventually refine as their senior portfolio for external assessment. We are pleased that as they make connections among their courses and experiences, students develop a self-identity as professional writers and rhetors. Some students (particularly double-concentration students) also bring in connections to literature or creative writing and articulate a broader identity with a well-formed PWR piece.

While we are proud of students who develop a clearly articulated PWR identity, this professionalization runs counter to our colleagues' understanding even of faculty identities. Our colleagues have questioned our self-identification as PWR faculty, suggesting that such a definition is "fragile and questionable" (English Department Memo 2011) because English faculty, according to some of our colleagues, must be able to move among writing, language, and literature courses, as well as contribute to FYC. In essence, we continue to experience tension between specialists and generalists.

Furthermore, our colleagues do not understand our use of the term "professional" within our PWR identities. In a response to our proposal, colleagues wrote, "Hiving off as 'professional' one kind of writing and one kind of rhetoric is illogical and damages the historically rich composite definition of 'English.' Moving 'writing' and 'rhetoric' out of the English department, as the proposal advocates, suggests that they reside only in the area of 'professional' activity" (English Department Memo 2011). What our colleagues do not understand is that we prepare students to write professionally in any context, not just in professional contexts. As our students would note, PWR both studies communication practices and teaches students to knowledgeably practice effective and ethical communication in any given environment, be it a workplace, a community, or another social situation.

Thus, our students' full-fledged identity in PWR counters our colleagues' understanding of both student and faculty identities. Ironically, many faculty—if not most—view PWR as the service arm of the English department. In a response to our early proposal, colleagues noted that PWR's practical applications (e.g., in publishing; in technical, corporate, and nonprofit writing; and in writing for interactive media) appeal to many Elon students, and they expressed concern that PWR's separation would leave a void in English of these practical applications.

Another prominent challenge we face during our current transition attempt revolves around "ownership" of courses. If a course was proposed as part of a concentration in an English major, should it transform with the concentration into the new major? We have opted to track course learning outcomes and enrollments in order to answer this question on a course-by-course basis. If a course was designed primarily for the concentration and the course learning outcomes intentionally align with PWR program outcomes, we have proposed designating the course as a PWR course. At the same time, we have tracked enrollments in these courses in order to learn which students are taking them. The vast majority of the courses we have proposed moving to the new PWR major attract predominantly PWR concentration students—75% or more of the students enrolling in our core courses and most of our electives are either PWR concentration students or professional writing studies (PWS) minors. Typically, the remaining 25% of enrolled students are taking the course to satisfy a non-English major or minor with strong ties to PWR (e.g., leadership studies, multimedia authoring, arts administration, etc.). Only a few students from other English concentrations enroll in these PWR core and elective courses.

Two courses are exceptions to these enrollment trends. We developed Writing Studies Survey and Introduction to Teaching English to Speakers of Other Languages in collaboration with the English teacher licensure concentration (TLC), and these courses enroll students from both PWR and TLC. We initially proposed designating these courses as PWR courses because we worry the PWR-oriented learning outcomes will dissipate if there is not a clear reminder of the courses' PWR ties. Our English department colleagues questioned the courses' relevance to PWR, overlooking the history of how the courses were developed, who routinely teaches them (PWR faculty), and the mix of enrolled students. As our negotiations have progressed, though, we have expressed openness to leaving these courses designated as English courses, recognizing that strategic compromises are necessary in order to achieve our primary goal of an independent major.

These course enrollment tensions undoubtedly stem from the fact that our proposal distinguishes between PWR faculty and writing studies faculty who are not associated with PWR. The department made hires in recent years to develop a community of faculty around the university's FYC program. If it has been difficult for our English department colleagues to understand how faculty and students might develop their own PWR identity, it's perhaps even more difficult for them to envision developing a professional identity around FYC. If our departmental colleagues think certain "writing" and/or "rhetoric" courses are associated with and part of PWR since their initial development might appeal to our FYC colleagues, perhaps as a way to develop their careers beyond FYC, they tend to ignore the historical enrollments and learning outcomes of these courses in determining who should teach them, what their curricular function should be, etc. Therefore, we have faced formal challenges to our proposal to redesignate even PWR core courses, not to mention electives, under the argument that these are all "writing" courses that should not be part of any specific curriculum or faculty.

Of course, part of the challenge for us and for the administration is the scale of the English department and the timing of our proposal. The dean of arts and sciences risks offending the largest department in the college if she acts too quickly on a proposal for a PWR major or an independent PWR department. Meanwhile, the provost was attentive to the PWR proposals becoming public at the same time as a significant (and eventually failed) general studies review. This broad, proposed revision to the university's core curriculum raised questions about where "writing" fits, with many in English worried, unnecessarily, that PWR would try to "take over" all writing at Elon, while other faculty outside of English wished we would do just that. In the midst of these conversations, the School of Communication also raised concerns about PWR's use of "professional" in its name and non-PWR courses moving out of Arts and Sciences and into the School of Communication, a "professional" school. Finally, with other writing faculty at the institution, we also face the challenge of articulating who is part of PWR and who has expertise in writing but is not in PWR.

While we find ourselves using navigational metaphors (e.g., new paths) and familial metaphors (e.g., sister majors), the lack of clear policy about creating new majors and the strong emotional responses we have received also introduce other metaphors. According to our English colleagues, the process is akin to "divorce," we are a "breakaway" group, and we are attempting to "secede" from the department. The tone of these metaphors understandingly adds stress to our professional lives as we attempt to move our proposal forward.

In February 2012, the English department voted on our curriculum proposal and offered majority support for an independent PWR major. Unfortunately, we did not receive the requisite two-thirds majority support required by the English department's voting policy for major changes to departmental structure. Despite these many challenges, the English department's five-year plan does include an action item to propose a PWR major for implementation beginning in 2012 and a year one outcome of a clear direction for PWR—either as a separate department or with a clear plan for fostering PWR's growth within English. Therefore we remain committed to pursuing our transition from concentration to major, bolstered by the support of a simple majority of our department colleagues. While we have not been able to implement the new major in 2012–2013, we are using the academic year to regroup.

REFLECTION AND PROSPECTION

Although we are understandably disappointed that our major proposal did not pass, upon reflection we realize that our concentration, as a whole, has benefitted from this process and from other simultaneous events occurring on our campus. For example, recent discussions linked to accreditation requirements and potential general studies curricular revision have provided us with strategic opportunities as they generate a renewed, university-wide focus on the importance of excellent writing instruction and the value of writing in the disciplines. In the midst of these university-wide discussions about writing in the disciplines, PWR faculty have had the chance to explain our field, our courses and their objectives, and our curriculum's focus on developing effective rhetorical writers through hands-on experiences to colleagues across the disciplines. Such discussions have already opened the door for conversations about how PWR courses and the PWS minor could benefit students from other majors, and our professional expertise is being recognized as beneficial across campus.

This process has also helped us identify friends and supporters in the university community as well as create new and positive relationships with additional constituencies. Perhaps one of the most interesting new relationships we have developed is with the School of Communications. Despite a history of debating "disciplinary turf" and concerns about our use of the word "professional," some communications faculty have actively championed our efforts to develop a major, and they routinely advertise to their students the benefits of the PWS minor and PWR courses.

The exhaustive research we conducted to support our major proposal gave us an excellent picture of the broader discipline, its trends, and its challenges, and it introduced us to readings that reminded us we are not alone in our struggle. Our research into other programs encouraged us to dream big about the exciting curricular work that can be done either in an unconstrained, blue sky new department or within the constraints of an English major. Additionally, our attention to researching and understanding the policies within the department and the university may have contributed to recent clarifications to department policies.

In hindsight, we have several recommendations for others engaging in a similar process to develop an independent writing major or department. Foremost among our recommendations is to work with your dean to make sure there is a clear process for enacting curricular changes or creating new departments. Without a clear process, any work put into such endeavors will be, at best, fraught with complications or, at worst, looked upon by outsiders as inherently unreasonable or impossible, even in the face of similar events unfolding across the country. Further, even when tensions may run high, it is important to involve members of the department early in the process to maintain collegiality and good citizenship and to avoid factionalization.

We also recommend preparing a strong argument that integrates evidence from peer and aspirant institutions in order to convince "pure English" faculty that a PWR major is an opportunity to grow a stagnant department and foster stronger professional identities. To facilitate these efforts, we hope technical and professional writing organizations continue to develop research-based statements on the discipline and its curricular and structural roles in universities.

Finally, we have taken several steps to create a healthy and productive space for our faculty, our curriculum, and our current and prospective students. We have been constantly reminded throughout this process how well we work together, and we have recommitted to continuing our monthly reading and discussion groups, our writing support groups, and our efforts to publish and present at professional conferences. We will continue our tradition of yearly PWR retreats, during which we make academic and curricular plans for the coming year, form individual professional and personal plans, and identify ways to support one another in achieving our goals. We will continue our efforts to rejuvenate the PWR curriculum: collaborating on course design to ensure that we provide students with excellent project- and client-based learning experiences; growing our PWR speaker series; developing new study-abroad or study-away opportunities particularly geared toward PWR students; and engaging in ongoing, meaningful assessment to ensure that our courses and class projects are aligned with our learning objectives.

CONCLUSION

As we write this profile, we are still in a moment of transition, rewriting the PWR program. While we will not tell our readers that this process was easy or the initial outcome was not disappointing, we firmly believe our efforts were not in vain—we will carry on, regroup, and try again in a future kairotic moment. We look forward to our revisions leading to deeper community building within our program, stronger connections both within and beyond our program, and more opportunities to simply work with our students—both within and outside our classrooms. We accept that we will likely face new challenges as we continue to write and rewrite our program, but we also recognize that those challenges could become timely and strategic opportunities for growth.

Curricular Summary: The Professional Writing and Rhetoric Concentration in the English Major at Elon University

Rhetoric, one of the oldest liberal arts and developed in ancient Greece to prepare citizens for active participation in democratic society, has long been focused on connecting itself to "the life of the polis." The English major concentration in professional writing and rhetoric (PWR) reflects a national trend in higher education—as well as a long tradition within the discipline of rhetoric—to more clearly connect the liberal arts to worlds beyond the walls of academia. Though distinctly not a pre-professional program, PWR prepares students to be more critically reflective, civically responsible communicators in their daily lives and, primarily, their workplace contexts. All courses are four credits unless otherwise noted.

CONCENTRATION REQUIREMENTS (48 CREDIT HOURS)
English major core courses (20 credits):

- ENG 304: Understanding Rhetoric
- 200-level or above literature course

- 200-level or above writing course
- 300-level or above literature course
- 300-level or above English elective

Writing concentration core courses (24 credits):

- ENG 215: Introduction to Professional Writing and Rhetoric
- ENG 282: CUPID Studio (2 credits)
- ENG 313: Special Topics in Professional Writing and Rhetoric
- ENG 381: Internship (2 credits)
- ENG 397: Writing as Inquiry
- ENG 206: Intro to Teaching English to Speakers of Other Languages, or

  ENG 211: Style and Editing, or
  ENG 212: Multimedia Rhetorics, or
  ENG 217: Writing Technologies (2 credits), or
  ENG 219: Writing Studies Survey
- ENG 310: International Rhetorics, or

  ENG 311: Publishing, or
  ENG 312: Visual Rhetorics, or
  ENG 318: Writing Science, or
  ENG 319: Writing Center Workshop

Capstone (final requirement):

- ENG 497: Senior Seminar

Additional requirement:

- Completion of a comprehensive PWR portfolio that is assessed by an external reviewer

Notes

1. Following an eighteen-month proposal process, we believe that *kairos* necessitates achieving the major first—the focus of this chapter and our continued curriculum redesign efforts—but we will continue to pursue department status as part of our five-year plan.

2. Under the current concentration system, PWR courses can be used in the English major core, but few students in other concentrations integrate our courses into their plan of study. Therefore, we have historically pursued interdisciplinary partnerships, which—in many cases—have been more successful than partnerships with other concentrations within the major.

References

English Department Memo. 2011. Memo to authors, January 6.

Peeples, Timothy, Paula Rosinski, and Michael Strickland. 2007. "'Chronos' and 'Kairos,' Strategies and Tactics: The Case of Constructing Elon University's Professional Writing and Rhetoric Concentration." *Composition Studies* 35 (1): 57–76.

Afterword

FINDING THE BIGGER PICTURE
What Have We Learned?

Greg Giberson

Since the publication of my volume (with Tom Moriarty) *What We Are Becoming* in 2010, I have been asked the same basic question by many people looking to develop writing majors at their institutions: "What does a writing major look like?" At first glance it seems like a pretty straightforward question. Deb Balzhiser and Sue McLeod attempt to answer a similar question, among others, in their article "The Undergraduate Writing Major: What Is It? What Should It Be?" The dramatic differences among programs represented in this book provide more support for Balzhiser and McLeod's (2010, 422) analysis that "we have little consensus about what a writing major should look like." Conveniently, their analysis appears to be a pretty direct answer to the question posed to me so many times, with my question and their answer even referencing program attributes as somehow visual. Unfortunately, as far as answers go, it's a rather disappointing one for those asking the question.

Upon reflection, however, I've come to realize that the people asking "what does a major look like?" have been asking a much different question than Balzhiser and McLeod. While Balzhiser and McLeod were asking macro-level questions about the ways our discipline is or should be reflected in this emerging thing called "the writing major," those individuals posing the question to me were asking micro-level questions about how a version of the discipline could be constructed within the confines and constraints of their home institutions through the development of a unique, locally situated writing major. So, what most people have actually been asking me is "What does a writing major look like *at my institution?*"—a subtle yet important distinction. Unfortunately, I still don't have an answer to that question—at least not a direct one. The complexities inherent in developing a new program with very few

DOI: 10.7330/9780874219722.c019

precedents and a very short history are many and local, as each chapter in this volume illustrates. However, I do want to offer some suggestions for helping those who would ask the question to find their own answers.

A HEURISTIC OFFERING

While this volume cannot address the unique, local circumstances at all institutions, there seem to be some shared, important parameters that all program developers work within during the conception and implementation of their programs, whether they recognize those parameters or not. Most of the programs I am familiar with struggled through the process in a very nonlinear, haphazard way, unaware of the internal and external forces that would come into play at different stages during their development. The following is my attempt to articulate some of these general parameters in an effort to help those interested in developing programs or in the process of doing so to be more intentional and prospective in their program building. A more thoughtful approach to program building provides the best chances for local success.

However, understanding the parameters that guide our program development and impact what our programs ultimately become is important beyond the individual institutions we are designing these programs within. As Tom Moriarty and I argue in *What We Are Becoming*, "the unique, local circumstances faced by our colleagues developing and participating in individual programs and the decisions they make in regards to those local circumstances have important implications for the broader discipline" (Giberson and Moriarty 2010, 2). Indeed, the programs we create become reflections of the discipline itself. I have argued on many occasions that whether or not all members of the discipline would recognize a specific writing major as a "real" writing major, the fact that it is identified as such at that institution makes it "real" for the students who graduate with it. The version of the discipline forwarded by that program will define the discipline for its students. Those students go on to the professional world, graduate school, etc.—they will define the discipline for their employers, family, and friends. For those in graduate school, their undergraduate education will frame their graduate education, impacting how they understand the expanded discipline they will engage with in their graduate work.

There's little doubt, assuming we accept this argument, that this proliferation of often dramatically different versions of the discipline will impact the discipline itself in unpredictable and unforeseen ways. So, when we create new programs, we must be thoughtful and intentional in how we create them. With that in mind, what follows is a brief heuristic designed to provide a starting point for those considering proposing a new major. As readers will see, the questions are interconnected, recursive, and open ended, with each answer raising more questions—questions that will hopefully lead to deeper analyses of various local circumstances. The goal for the heuristic is to help readers be as thoughtful and thorough as they can be in conceiving their programs through a close examination of the limits and opportunities presented by their local circumstances.

Question 1—What support can you expect from:

> Department colleagues?
> Colleagues outside the department?
> Administration?
> Students?
> Others?

Program proposals have multiple audiences, with different concerns that need to be addressed. Because of this, it is important to identify and articulate where you will find support and, more importantly, where you might encounter roadblocks. These initial questions of support will ultimately lead to other concerns and questions: Do you fully understand the program proposal process? What committees will vet the proposal? Who will make final decisions? What are their concerns? What are the historical, political, and professional connections between the different players in the process? Which roadblocks can be addressed through the proposal and which ones cannot? How might you leverage student support? Questions such as these will help you identify administrative and faculty allies to aid you in navigating the process efficiently and successfully.

Question 2—What resources do you have at your disposal, and what resources might be available for your new program?

> Budget
> Faculty
> Technology
> Space
> Current courses
> Other

While not always clear, many—if not most—of the local circumstances discussed in each chapter are related to resources, available or not. Anyone who has developed or coordinated a program knows that what can and cannot be accomplished is often tied to the different resources available to the program. For example, a major in writing for new media would be difficult to implement in an institution that does not provide a great deal of access to new technologies or consistent, substantial technological support. Similarly, a major in technical writing in a department with no technical writing specialists (and little prospect of attaining new hires), would find it difficult to make an argument for such a program. So, fortunately or unfortunately, what our programs look like will be influenced by the resources we do or do not have. As the question suggests, however, you should certainly investigate recently approved programs to see what kinds of extra support were provided. While a few of the programs presented in this volume had to design their majors around the limited resources they already had available, most found that with a new program, new growth was possible—having a good idea of what and from where it will come is crucial.

> Question 3—What will be the focus of the program, given the resources available?
>
> Question 4—What are your goals for the program and how do they relate to the discipline?
>
> Question 5—What should students to be able to "do" upon graduating from your program?
>
> Question 6—What disciplinary values are important in your program and how will you foreground those values?

These final four questions are designed to help articulate what a program can and should be, given the parameters established through consideration of the first two questions. Too many of the stories shared in this volume and elsewhere lament or imply a lack of forethought concerning program goals, student outcomes, and how those could be realized.

Ultimately, this brief heuristic, and the additional questions it will no doubt raise, is designed to encourage program developers to think about their fledgling programs in broader terms. When going through the machinations of implementing a new program, we can easily get overly focused, even myopic at times, and forget the bigger picture. However, the programs themselves, once implemented, will exist within that bigger picture. The more thoroughly and thoughtfully conceived programs are from the outset—taking into account their unique institutional parameters and local contexts—the more likely they are to be approved, implemented, and successful.

REFLECTION AND PROSPECTION: WHERE
MIGHT WE BE HEADED?

As I am looking through the final manuscript of this volume with a beat up copy of *What We Are Becoming* sitting next to me, I can't help but be a little reflective about both projects. As Tom Moriarty and I worked on that first collection, I remember the two of us coming up with multiple versions of the book—different sections, chapter configurations, and themes we might use to make sense out of different and often disparate understandings of the writing major presented in those chapters. As with all edited collections, we had to settle on an organizational structure, but to this day there is still something unsettling and unfinished for me in the seeming randomness of the organization as it relates to the declarative statement that is the title.

During the 2013 CCCC convention in Las Vegas, I spoke with one of the original reviewers of *WWAB*, and he expressed the same exasperation with the difficulty of making organizational sense out of the chapters. While he offered praise for the book, calling it timely, interesting, and compelling, he also expressed how difficult it was to nail down thematically and organizationally. Perhaps that aspect of the book—and the evolution of the writing major itself—is meaningful.

While the title for that first collection was intended to be a placeholder, it seemed to take on a meaning that neither Tom nor I questioned, nor did we talk about it much. It just came to be the final title. Looking back at it now and considering how far we've come in terms of the field's work on the writing major (and taking into consideration all I have learned working with the chapter authors on both books), I am starting to more fully understand the significance of that title. But more on that later—back to that unsettled feeling.

The current book—with its consistent inter-chapter organizational structure—will, I hope, mitigate the lingering unsettledness remaining after the publication of *WWAB*. Indeed, the information, focus, and organization are much more consistent, which suggests that it should be much easier to make connections between programs and begin to make some broader statements about what the major is, where it is headed, and the various avenues by which it might get there. Indeed, I believe we have succeeded in bringing together discussions of specific programs in a way that allows us to paint a broad picture of the various programs out there, the types of institutions within which these programs are being developed, and the different material conditions that impact these programs. But still that unsettled feeling.

In Sue McLeod's (2010) afterword from *WWAB*, she saw potential for the collection to be a "stimulus" for a "discipline-wide discussion about the major in writing studies," and (based on the growing number of references in journals, book chapters, and reviews of the book) I think by and large she was right. Our intention for the current collection is to provide a more focused snapshot of what different majors look like and how they came into being. And I think we have accomplished that—it will be another valuable contribution to the ongoing conversation on the writing major. But still that unsettled feeling.

Throughout the editorial process, we wanted to focus on the major itself—ultimately using some strong editorial hands to eliminate historical narratives that seemed relevant yet tangential to the programs themselves, that told us more about department politics than programmatic nuance. Looking back at the chapters now, and specifically at the brief histories they include, I am beginning to understand the unsettled feeling in my gut—I am starting to believe that it is and has been a feeling of excitement and anticipation.

When we sent out the original Call for Proposals (CFP) and vetted the forty-five or so proposals, we had in mind a collection much like what we ended up with: a book with profiles of programs that were organized and structured in essentially the same way. When we sent directions to our selected authors, we provided the organizational structure we wanted for chapters. As we began receiving drafts, we realized that most chapters were not going to come to us as organized as we had hoped. It was evident that the authors wanted to tell their own stories, creating their own frameworks for contextualizing and explaining their local programs. Having been a part of developing and revising two different programs, I certainly understand the inclination to want to tell one's story in his or her own way. Program development can be a very personal thing.

As editors, we decided that we actually liked what the authors were sending in, and we decided to shelve the idea of inter-chapter organizational consistency. A common observation about differences in programs had to do with local circumstances, so we decided we were comfortable with those differences being made more apparent through the inter-chapter variances. Reviewers disagreed.

Once the reviews came back, strongly suggesting more organizational consistency among chapters, we had to go back, rethink our approach as editors, and return to our original vision. We realized we had got caught up in the interesting narratives that indeed demonstrated how local contingencies affect program development, but did not really focus on the programs themselves. We had forgotten one of the goals of the book: to be a useful tool for others who might be developing or revising a writing major.

While the book itself truly is a collection of program profiles, as we originally set out to publish, I also see it, at least in historical shadows, as something a bit more—something that portends as much as it does informs. These micro-histories, taken together, can be seen as an emerging macro-history, one that makes the title of the first collection apropos to say the least.

Readers will find, or will have found if they indeed read the afterword *afterward*, that each program seems to be in transition in many ways. Some majors—such as the programs at New Mexico Tech and West Virginia State, whose majors have been around since the early 1980s—recount the various transitions their programs have made as the discipline has grown and changed over the years. Whereas others, like Metropolitan State and Oakland, focus on the very real transitions within their programs that a new major can both initiate and be a symptom of. However, taken as a whole, it seems that each program is on a somewhat similar trajectory, though in different positions on the same continuum, and experiences the same sort of transitions. In other words, these programs and the departments and units connected to them seem to be *becoming* something different, whether intentionally or not and whether by the same means or not. But "What *are* they becoming?" is the important question.

That is not to say (and I am certainly not arguing) that the majors themselves are heading toward the type of consistency that some might wish were possible. I don't think the local is leaving anytime soon. Indeed, the chapters in this collection demonstrate how local circumstances force program developers, knowingly or not, to make important decisions (some related to the program itself, but others not) that impact what it is and what it can be. These local circumstances and material conditions are, more often than we'd probably like, the most influential determinants for what the programs are and what they can become. However, I do believe that these chapters taken collectively tell a story of a discipline that is *becoming* something, and that we are heading collectively in a particular direction, though not the direction that we as editors expected to find or even thought to consider as we were working on this volume. But it is exciting—and unsettling at times—and that is good.

References

Balzhiser, Deborah, and Susan H. McLeod. 2010. "The Undergraduate Writing Major: What Is It? What Should It Be?" *College Composition and Communication* 61 (3): 415–33.

Giberson, Greg A., and Thomas A. Moriarty. 2010. "Introduction: Forging Connections Among Undergraduate Writing Majors." In *What We Are Becoming: Developments in Undergraduate Writing Majors*, ed. Greg A. Giberson and Thomas A. Moriarty, 1–10. Logan: Utah State University Press.

McLeod, Susan H. 2010. "Afterword." In *What We are Becoming: Developments in Undergraduate Writing Majors*, ed. Greg A. Giberson and Thomas A. Moriarty, 287–9. Logan: Utah State University Press.

APPENDIX

Table of Institutional Data

DePaul University

Department Name:	Writing, Rhetoric, and Discourse
Institution Type:	Private, Catholic, Doctoral Research University (DRU)
Institution Size:	25,000 students
Residential or Commuter:	87% commuter
Student Body Description:	Diverse student body; high percentage first in their family to go to college; high school GPA average 3.55; 33% come from out of state
Year Major Began:	2010
Official Name of Degree:	Bachelor of Arts in Writing, Rhetoric, and Discourse
Number of Majors:	In year one: 8 In year three: 40 In year five: N/A Current: 40
Number of Full-Time R/C Faculty:	13
Curricular Summary:	p. 20

University of Arkansas–Little Rock

Department Name:	Rhetoric and Writing
Institution Type:	Public, Doctoral Research University (DRU)
Institution Size:	13,000 students
Residential or Commuter:	Commuter
Student Body Description:	Almost all students work; diverse in terms of ethnicity, socio-economics, age, etc.; high percentage of transfer students; high percentage first in their family to go to college; majority are women
Year Major Began:	1993
Official Name of Degree:	Bachelor of Arts in Professional and Technical Writing
Number of Majors:	In year one: N/A In year three: N/A In year five: N/A Current: 58
Number of Full-Time R/C Faculty:	19
Curricular Summary:	p. 33

DOI: 10.7330/9780874219722.c020

University of Rhode Island

Department Name:	Writing and Rhetoric
Institution Type:	Public, High Research Activity University (RU/H)
Institution Size:	16,300 students
Residential or Commuter:	44% residential
Student Body Description:	Most students work part-time, though some work full-time; lack of diversity in terms of ethnicity and age (71% white); high percentage of writing and rhetoric double majors
Year Major Began:	2007
Official Name of Degree:	Bachelor of Arts in Writing and Rhetoric
Number of Majors:	In year one: 12 In year three: 45 In year five: 90 Current: 92
Number of Full-Time R/C Faculty:	7
Curricular Summary:	p. 45

Loyola University Maryland

Department Name:	Writing
Institution Type:	Private, Master's L (awards at least 200 Master's degrees/year)
Institution Size:	6,000 students
Residential or Commuter:	Residential
Student Body Description:	The majority of undergraduate students identify as white, with less than 20% identifying with another ethnic group; most are not first-generation college students; only 18% come from Maryland, with the majority of students coming from the Mid-Atlantic and Northeast; about 60% of students participate in study abroad programs; about 84% of students graduate in six or less years
Year Major Began:	Interdisciplinary Writing (IW): 1983 Writing (W): 2006
Official Name of Degree:	Bachelor of Arts in Interdisciplinary Writing and Bachelor of Arts in Writing
Number of Majors:	In year one: 26 (IW), 2 (W) In year three: 26 (IW), 47 (W) In year five: 37 (IW), 52 (W) Current: 27 (IW), 47 (W)
Number of Full-Time R/C Faculty:	9
Curricular Summary:	p. 58

University of Central Arkansas

Department Name:	Writing
Institution Type:	Public, Master's L (awards at least 200 Master's degrees/year)
Institution Size:	11,700 students
Residential or Commuter:	Commuter
Student Body Description:	Diverse in terms of ethnicity, socio-economics, age, etc.; high percentage of full-time enrollment
Year Major Began:	1999
Official Name of Degree:	Bachelor of Arts in Writing
Number of Majors:	In year one: N/A　　In year three: 74 In year five: 87　　Current: 146
Number of Full-Time R/C Faculty:	12
Curricular Summary:	p. 71

Oakland University

Department Name:	Writing and Rhetoric
Institution Type:	Public, Doctoral Research University (DRU)
Institution Size:	18,000 students
Residential or Commuter:	Commuter
Student Body Description:	Most students work part-time or full-time; they are diverse in terms of ethnicity, socio-economics, age, etc.; high percentage transfer from a local community college; high percentage are the first in their family to go to college
Year Major Began:	2008
Official Name of Degree:	Bachelor of Arts in Writing and Rhetoric
Number of Majors:	In year one: 15　　In year three: 35 In year five: 45　　Current: 45
Number of Full-Time R/C Faculty:	9
Curricular Summary	p. 82

University of Wisconsin–Stout

Department Name:	English and Philosophy
Institution Type:	Public, Master's L (awards at least 200 Master's degrees/year)
Institution Size:	9,000 students
Residential or Commuter:	Residential
Student Body Description:	Primarily traditional (18–22-year-old) students who live on campus; includes a small group of working adult commuter students.
Year Major Began:	2000
Official Name of Degree:	Bachelor of Science in Professional Communication and Emerging Media
Number of Majors:	In year one: 40 In year three: 81 In year five: 48 Current: 103
Number of Full-Time R/C Faculty:	10
Curricular Summary	p. 95

Metropolitan State University

Department Name:	Communication, Writing, and the Arts
Institution Type:	Public, Master's M (awards between 100–199 Master's degrees/year)
Institution Size:	10,000 students
Residential or Commuter:	Commuter
Student Body Description:	Most students transfer here after collecting credits from several different schools; most students work, at minimum, part-time; diverse in terms of ethnicity, socio-economics, age, etc.; high percentage are first-generation college students
Year Major Began:	2012
Official Name of Degree:	Technical Communication and Professional Writing
Number of Majors:	In year one: 80 In year three: N/A In year five: N/A Current: 94
Number of Full-Time R/C Faculty:	9
Curricular Summary:	p. 104

New Mexico Institute of Mining and Technology

Department Name:	Communication, Liberal Arts, Social Sciences
Institution Type:	Public, Master's M (awards between 100–199 Master's degrees/year)
Institution Size:	1,800 students
Residential or Commuter:	Residential
Student Body Description:	68% male, 32% female; majority of students are in-state; New Mexico Tech is considered a Hispanic-serving institution
Year Major Began:	1983
Official Name of Degree:	Bachelor of Science in Technical Communication
Number of Majors:	In year one: N/A In year three: N/A In year five: N/A Current: 25
Number of Full-Time R/C Faculty:	5
Curricular Summary:	p. 117

York College

Department Name:	English and Humanities
Institution Type:	Private, Master's S (awards fewer than 100 master's degrees/year)
Institution Size:	5,500 students
Residential or Commuter:	Residential
Student Body Description:	Most students work, at minimum, part-time; middle class socioeconomically; high percentage first in their family to go to college; 50% from Pennsylvania and nearly all of the remaining 50% from surrounding Mid-Atlantic states
Year Major Began:	2002
Official Name of Degree:	Bachelor of Arts in Professional Writing
Number of Majors:	In year one: N/A In year three: N/A In year five: N/A Current: 78
Number of Full-Time R/C Faculty:	7
Curricular Summary:	p. 131

PART II. ENGLISH DEPARTMENTS

Texas Christian University

Department Name:	English
Institution Type:	Private, Doctoral Research University (DRU)
Institution Size:	8,900 students
Residential or Commuter:	Residential
Student Body Description:	Most students are of traditional age (18–21); roughly 60% are women, 40% are men, and 17% are minority; the most popular majors are pre-professional (business, nursing, engineering, communication); selective admissions (65% of students in the top 20% of their class)
Year Major Began:	2006
Official Name of Degree:	Bachelor of Arts in Writing
Number of Majors:	In year one: 17 In year three: 46 In year five: 52 Current: 64
Number of Full-Time R/C Faculty:	7
Curricular Summary	p. 147

West Virginia State University

Department Name:	English
Institution Type:	Public, Baccalaureate Colleges-Arts & Sciences (Bac/A&S)
Institution Size:	4,000 students
Residential or Commuter:	Commuter
Student Body Description:	Most students work a minimum of part time; established Historically Black Colleges and Universities (HBCU); fully accessible; multigenerational population of students, mostly local Appalachian background; high percentage are first in their family to go to college
Year Major Began:	1982
Official Name of Degree:	Bachelor of Arts in English with a Writing Option
Number of Majors:	In year one: N/A In year three: N/A In year five: N/A Current: 33
Number of Full-Time R/C Faculty:	10
Curricular summary	p. 160

University of Wisconsin–La Crosse

Department Name:	English
Institution Type:	Public, Master's L (Baccalaureate Colleges-Arts & Sciences)
Institution Size:	10,000 students
Residential or Commuter:	Commuter
Student Body Description:	Most students work, at minimum, part time; high number of international students; substantial percentage of first-generation college students; 58% female
Year Major Began:	2004
Official Name of Degree:	Bachelor of Arts in English, emphasis in Rhetoric and Writing
Number of Majors:	In year one: 5 In year three: 10 In year five: 40 Current: 93
Number of Full-Time R/C Faculty:	6
Curricular Summary:	p. 172

Florida State University

Department Name:	English
Institution Type:	Public, Very High Research Activity University (RU/VH)
Institution Size:	40,000 students
Residential or Commuter:	Mixed
Student Body Description:	Women account for 54.8% of enrollment; minorities total 27.2%; average age for undergraduate students is 21.1; students from all 50 states and the District of Columbia attend, and over 130 countries are represented
Year Major Began:	2009
Official Name of Degree:	Bachelor of Arts in Editing, Writing, and Media
Number of Majors:	In year one: 300 In year three: 700 In year five: N/A Current: 700
Number of Full-Time R/C Faculty:	7
Curricular Summary:	p. 188

Penn State Berks

Department Name:	English
Institution Type:	Public, Baccalaureate Colleges-Diverse Fields (Bac/Diverse)
Institution Size:	2,800 students
Residential or Commuter:	Commuter
Student Body Description:	Most students are local residents, with a high percentage of commuters; most students are enrolled full time, but work either full- or part-time; approximately 20% of students are minorities; approximately 20% are considered adult learners; and 60% are female, 40% are male
Year Major Began:	2001
Official Name of Degree:	Bachelor of Arts in Professional Writing
Number of Majors:	In year one: 10 In year three: 25 In year five: 30 Current: 30
Number of Full-Time R/C Faculty:	5
Curricular Summary:	p. 202

St. Edward's University

Department Name:	English Writing and Rhetoric
Institution Type:	Private, Master's L (awards at least 200 Master's degrees/year)
Institution Size:	5,300 students
Residential or Commuter:	Mixed
Student Body Description:	Hispanic-serving institution (31.7% Hispanic/Latino in 2012); 82% of students from Texas; 8.4% international students; many domestic students have a connection to Holy Cross Catholic heritage; special programs for first-generation college students and students whose families are migrant workers
Year Major Began:	1987
Official Name of Degree:	Bachelor of Arts in English Writing and Rhetoric
Number of Majors:	In year one: N/A In year three: 155 In year five: 144 Current: 120
Number of Full-Time R/C Faculty:	10
Curricular Summary:	p. 215

Columbia College

Department Name:	English Program, Division of Languages and Literatures
Institution Type:	Private, Master's M (awards between 100-199 Master's degrees/year)
Institution Size:	1,400 students
Residential or Commuter:	Residential
Student Body Description:	Diverse in terms of ethnicity and socio-economics; high percentage of students are first in their family to go to college; predominantly from South Carolina, but also from 26 other states and 12 other countries
Year Major Began:	2010
Official Name of Degree:	Bachelor of Arts in English
Number of Majors:	In year one: 8 In year three: 26 In year five: N/A Current: 26
Number of Full-Time R/C Faculty:	1
Curricular Summary:	p. 225

Elon University

Department Name:	English
Institution Type:	Private, Master's S (awards fewer than 100 master's degrees/year)
Institution Size:	5,400 students
Residential or Commuter:	Residential
Student Body Description:	Students come from 48 states, the District of Columbia, and 48 other nations; about 25% are from North Carolina and approximately 50% are from other states along the east coast; 87% complete internships; 72% study abroad
Year Major Began:	2000
Official Name of Degree:	Bachelor of Arts in English, emphasis in Professional Writing and Rhetoric
Number of Majors:	In year one: 3 In year three: 10 In year five: 30 Current: 30
Number of Full-Time R/C Faculty:	5
Curricular Summary:	p. 239

CONTRIBUTORS

JESSICA BARNES-PIETRUSZYNSKI earned her doctorate in English studies from Illinois State University. Currently, she is an associate professor of English at West Virginia State University. As the chair of the English Department's Composition Committee, Jessica started the writing center on campus and reintroduced much-needed basic writing classes on campus. Because of her appointment as faculty advisor for the school newspaper, The Yellowjacket, she now splits her research time between advancement of writing and journalism, as well as within her specialization, Victorian literature. In 2012 she was awarded Outstanding Teacher of the Year after being nominated by a former student and writing major.

DARSIE BOWDEN is a professor in the Department of Writing, Rhetoric, and Discourse at DePaul University, where she also directs the First-Year Writing Program. She currently serves on the executive board of the Council of Writing Program Administrators and coordinates the CWPA's Network for Media Action. She is author of two books, The Mythology of Voice and Writing for Film, as well as numerous articles and book chapters.

CLAUDIA SMITH BRINSON has won more than three dozen state and regional reporting awards, was a Pulitzer finalist, and was a two-time winner of the Knight Ridder Award of Excellence during her thirty-year career in journalism. She has provided national coaching in reporting, writing, and editing, and she wrote a nationally distributed column for Knight Ridder. Brinson has also won an O. Henry award for her short fiction, and has written for women's magazines. She is now a senior lecturer at Columbia College, where she designed and serves as director for the Writing for Print and Digital Media program.

MATT DAVIS is an assistant professor of English at the University of Massachusetts–Boston, where he teaches graduate and undergraduate courses in literacy, composition, and new media. He also directs the professional writing and tutoring programs. His research interests include literacy studies, technology and writing pedagogy, and collaborative learning and writing, and his work has appeared in *Teaching With Student Texts* (2011) and Enculturation.

DOMINIC F. DELLICARPINI is dean of academic affairs and the Naylor professor of writing studies at York College of Pennsylvania, where he also served as writing program administrator for thirteen years. DelliCarpini has published widely in the areas of WPA, undergraduate writing majors, and civic rhetoric, and he has also written and edited a number of textbooks. DelliCarpini served on the executive board of the Council of Writing Program Administrators, and he is an active member of the WPA Consultant–Evaluator Service for Writing Programs. Additionally, DelliCarpini currently holds the office of secretary on the executive board of the Conference on College Composition and Communication.

ROSÁRIO DURÃO is an assistant professor of technical communication at New Mexico Tech. She teaches courses in visual communication, international professional communication, and technical writing. Her research interests lie in international professional communication, information design and data visualization, science and technology studies, and complexity. She is the founding editor of connexions, an international professional communication journal.

KRISTIE S. FLECKENSTEIN is a professor of English at Florida State University, where she teaches graduate and undergraduate courses in rhetoric and composition. Her research interests include feminism and race, especially as they both intersect with material and visual rhetorics. She has published in a variety of venues, including College English, College Composition and Communication, Rhetoric Review, Computers and Composition, and JAC. She is the recipient of the 2005 CCCC Outstanding Book of the Year Award for *Embodied Literacies: Imageword and a Poetics of Teaching* (2003), and the 2009 W. Ross Winterowd Award for Best Book in Composition Theory for *Vision, Rhetoric, and Social Action in the Composition Classroom* (2009). Her current project explores photography as a resource for visual rhetoric in nineteenth-century debates about racial identities.

JULIE DYKE FORD, professor of technical communication at New Mexico Tech, has over fifteen years of experience teaching technical communication and writing courses. She served as director of New Mexico Tech's bachelor of science in technical communication for eight years. Her research has focused on technical communication pedagogy, engineering communication, and knowledge transfer, and she has published numerous articles on these subjects.

ANN GEORGE, professor of English at Texas Christian University, teaches courses in rhetorical theory and criticism, composition, and style. She is coauthor of Kenneth Burke in the 1930s (2007), coeditor of Women and Rhetoric between the Wars (2013), and currently working on a book manuscript, "A Critical Companion to Kenneth Burke's Permanence and Change" under contract at University of South Carolina Press. Her articles have appeared in Rhetorica and Rhetoric Society Quarterly.

GREG GIBERSON is an associate professor in the Department of Writing and Rhetoric at Oakland University in Rochester, Michigan. He is coeditor (with Thomas A. Moriarty) of the collection *What We are Becoming: Developments in Undergraduate Writing Majors* (2010) and coeditor (with Tom Giberson) of *The Knowledge Economy: Academics and the Commodification of Higher Education* (2009). His research focuses on the development of undergraduate majors and how those majors have and will affect the field of writing and rhetoric.

LAURIE GROBMAN is a professor of English and women's studies at Penn State Berks. Grobman's teaching, research, and service interests center on service learning and community-based research, bringing together students and community organizations to produce meaningful work while enriching students' learning experiences. She has published two single-authored books, *Multicultural Hybridity: Transforming American Literary Scholarship and Pedagogy* (2007) and *Teaching at the Crossroads: Cultures and Critical Perspectives in Literature by Women of Color* (2001); two coedited collections, *Undergraduate Research in English Studies* (2010) and *On Location: Theory and Practice in Classroom-Based Writing Tutoring* (2005); and more than thirty articles in peer-reviewed journals and books. A coedited collection, *Service Learning and Literary Studies in English*, is forthcoming from MLA.

CHARLOTTE HOGG is associate professor and director of composition at Texas Christian University, where she teaches writing, rhetoric, and literacy courses at the undergraduate and graduate level. She is the author of From the Garden Club: Rural Women Writing Community (University of Nebraska Press, 2006), coauthor (with Kim Donehower and Eileen E. Shell) of Rural Literacies (SIUP, 2007), and co-editor (with Donehower and Shell) of Reclaiming the Rural: Essays on Literacy, Rhetoric, and Pedagogy. Her scholarly and creative work has also appeared in Women and Literacy: Inquiries for a New Century, Great Plains Quarterly, Clackamas Literary Review, The Southeast Review, and elsewhere.

GEORGE H. JENSEN is chair of the Department of Rhetoric and Writing at the University of Arkansas–Little Rock. His research interests include personality and writing, rhetorical theory, and memoir. Recent books include *Storytelling in Alcoholics Anonymous: A Rhetorical*

Analysis (1995), *Identities Across Texts* (2002), *Post-Jungian Criticism: Theory and Practice* (2004), and *Some of the Words Are Theirs: A Memoir of an Alcoholic Family* (2009).

BRYAN KOPP is an assistant professor of English and writing programs coordinator for the Center for Advancement of Teaching and Learning at the University of Wisconsin–La Crosse. He teaches courses in rhetoric and writing, professional writing, and FYC. His current scholarly interests include cultural rhetorics, genre studies, critical theory, writing pedagogy, writing in the disciplines, professional writing, and the scholarship of teaching and learning.

BARBARA L'EPLATTENIER is a professor in the Department of Rhetoric and Writing at the University of Arkansas–Little Rock. Her research interests include historical and archival studies, writing program administration, and professional writing. She is coeditor of *Historical Studies in Writing Program Administration* (2004) and *Working in the Archives* (2010).

CARRIE LEVERENZ is associate professor of English and director of the Institute for Critical and Creative Expression at TCU, where she served as director of composition from 2000 to 2006 and as director of the New Media Writing Studio from 2006 to 2010. Her research focuses on writing program administration and computers and writing, with special attention to how cultural difference affects writing, teaching, and institutional leadership. She recently co-edited (with Amy Goodburn and Donna LeCourt) Rewriting Success in Rhetoric and Composition Careers (Parlor Press, 2012) Her current work investigates the relevance of research in design thinking for the teaching of writing.

MATTHEW LIVESY is an associate professor in the English and Philosophy Department at University of Wisconsin–Stout, where he directs the Bachelor of Science program in professional communication and emerging media. In 2007 he assumed leadership of the precursor degree, in technical communication, and oversaw its revision and expansion into its current form; enrollment in the major has tripled since the revision. He teaches both introductory and capstone courses in the major, as well as a wide range of other writing courses.

DREW M. LOEWE is an associate professor of English writing and rhetoric at St. Edward's University, where he also directs the writing center. His research and teaching interests include rhetorical theory and criticism, composition theory and pedagogy, argumentation, and legal writing. More about Drew can be found at drewloewe.net or on Twitter (@ drewloewe).

BRAD LUCAS is associate professor of English at TCU, where he teaches courses in new media writing and rhetoric. He is former editor of the journal Composition Studies, and his recent work has appeared in Working in the Archives: Practical Research Methods for Rhetoric and Composition (2009) and The Changing of Knowledge in Composition: Contemporary Perspectives (2011).

BARBARA MALLONEE, associate professor emerita, taught writing for forty years at Loyola University Maryland, where she also chaired the writing department three times and directed the Honors Program and the Alpha Program for first-year students. She codirected, with historian John Breihan, Empirical Rhetoric, a six-year, NEH-funded WAC program, which inspired many professional publications. She is a published essayist with a particular interest in nature writing, a member of the Society of Friends, and twice chair of the Friends School Baltimore Board of Trustees. She coauthored *Minute by Minute: A History of the Baltimore Monthly Meetings of Friends.*

LAURA MCCARTAN, PhD in rhetoric and professional communication from Iowa State University, is an associate professor in the Department of Communication, Writing, and the Arts at Metropolitan State University in St. Paul, Minnesota. In addition to teaching lower-division writing, she teaches in the masters of liberal studies program and co-coordinates gender studies.

LIBBY MILES is an associate professor in the department of writing and rhetoric at the University of Rhode Island, where she has variously served as department chair, director of graduate studies, writing center director, and assessment coordinator. Recipient of the URI Foundation Excellence in Teaching Award, she regularly teaches throughout the vertical curriculum, from a hybrid 100-level course to advanced tutor training and rhetorical theory for undergraduates to the histories and theories of writing instruction and assessment for graduate students. With colleagues from soil science and sociology, she coauthored *The Practice of Problem-Based Learning* (2007), and has also published in *College Composition and Communication, JAC, College English,* and *WPA: Writing Program Administration.*

MARIE E. MOELLER is an assistant professor of English at the University of Wisconsin–La Crosse, where she teaches courses in professional writing, rhetoric, and FYC. Her current research operates at multiple intersections of medical rhetoric, disability studies, bioethics, and technical communication.

LISA MONGNO began her career at the University of Central Arkansas when the writing program was formed in 1997. Since that time, she has cofounded the National Writing Project site there, and has been awarded over $500,000 in grant money for the university. She currently teaches freshman composition, senior thesis, and grant writing in the graduate program. Mongno holds a master's degree in technical and expository writing from the University of Arkansas—Little Rock and is a graduate of the Donaghey Scholars Program there.

JESSIE L. MOORE is associate director of the Center for Engaged Learning and associate professor of professional writing and rhetoric at Elon University. Her research focuses on multi-institutional research structures for studying high-impact learning practices, writing transfer, second language writing, and faculty development, particularly as it relates to the teaching and practice of writing.

JODDY MURRAY teaches writing, rhetoric, and new media at Texas Christian University in Fort Worth.

JULIANNE NEWMARK, an associate professor of English at New Mexico Tech, teaches courses in technical communication, visual rhetoric, writing, and American and Native American literature. She also serves as the editor of Xchanges, a multimodal e-journal that publishes the blind-reviewed scholarly works of undergraduate and graduate student writers in the fields of technical communication, writing, rhetoric, and WAC.

JIM NUGENT is an associate professor of writing and rhetoric at Oakland University. He holds a PhD in rhetoric and technical communication from Michigan Technological University, a master's degree in technical writing from Illinois State University, and a bachelor's degree in math and computer science from the University of Illinois at Urbana-Champaign. His research interests include neosophistic rhetorical theory, the teaching of technical writing, and certificate programs in technical communication.

PEGGY O'NEILL, professor of writing, chairs the writing department at Loyola University Maryland after serving as director of the department's composition program for over a decade. She teaches courses in composition and rhetoric, and her scholarship focuses on writing pedagogy, assessment, and program administration. Her work appears in several composition and rhetoric journals as well as edited collections, and she currently coedits the *Journal of Writing Assessment*. She has coauthored two books, *A Guide to College Writing* and *Reframing Writing Assessment to Improve Teaching and Learning*, and edited or coedited four books.

LORI OSTERGAARD is an associate professor, Chair of the Department of Writing and Rhetoric, and former director of first-year writing at Oakland University in Rochester, Michigan. Her archival research examines the history of composition and rhetoric at midwestern normal schools and high schools. She focuses primarily on the research, theories, and practices of educators working during the first three decades of the twentieth century. Her collection, *Transforming English Studies: New Voices in an Emerging Genre*, which she coedited with Jeff Ludwig and Jim Nugent, is available from Parlor Press.

KIM HENSLEY OWENS is an associate professor and FYC coordinator in the Department of Writing and Rhetoric at the University of Rhode Island. Her recent publications include articles on childbirth rhetorics in *Rhetoric Review* and *Written Communication*; articles on teaching in *Enculturation* and *Pedagogy*; coauthored articles in *Computers and Composition* and *Composition Studies*; and chapters in the edited collections *Joy, Interrupted* and *Textual Mothers/Maternal Texts*. Kim teaches a variety of courses ranging from FYC to travel writing to rhetoric to graduate seminars. She also trains writing teachers at the college level and prospective K–12 teachers.

SCOTT PAYNE earned his PhD in rhetoric and composition at the University of Louisville. His specializations include writing program administration, composition pedagogy, and teaching FYC, as well as upper-level courses in composition and rhetorical theory. He has nearly twenty years of experience serving as either a department chair or writing program coordinator. He currently chairs the Department of Writing at the University of Central Arkansas.

TIM PEEPLES, professor of English/professional writing and rhetoric, and associate provost for faculty affairs at Elon University, has taught FYC through advanced writing and rhetoric courses, including visual rhetoric, document design, style and editing, composition pedagogy, writing center tutoring, theories and histories of rhetoric, and publications development and management. In addition to ten years of mid- to senior-level administrative experience as assistant to the president, associate provost, and associate dean, he has ten years of WPA experience, serving in directorships of WAC, a writing center, and a pre-engineering writing program, as well as in assistant director positions for programs of composition, business, technical, and professional writing. Tim's research focuses, generally, on the reproduction of rhetorical space and rhetorical subjects through rhetoric, writing, pedagogies, organization(s), and management/administration.

MICHAEL PENNELL is an associate professor in the Division of Instructional Communication and Research at the University of Kentucky. Before joining the University of Kentucky, he spent eight years at the University of Rhode Island in the Department of Writing and Rhetoric. During his tenure at URI, he taught a variety of courses, including writing in electronic environments, a capstone course for majors on electronic portfolios, and a graduate course on research methods. He has published articles in journals such as *Computers and Composition, CCC, Pedagogy, Business Communication Quarterly*, and the *Community Literacy Journal.*

JOHN A. PERRON, C.S.C., is an associate professor of English at St. Edward's University. With Anne Crane, I.H.M., he cofounded, in 1975, what later became the English Writing and Rhetoric major. In addition to directing this major, he was formerly director of Freshman Studies. His research interests include what writers do when composing, how sociocultural environments and discourse communities influence composing practices, and the history of rhetoric.

JEFFREY PIETRUSZYNSKI, like his wife and coauthor, holds a doctorate in English studies from Illinois State University and is an associate professor of English at West Virginia State University. In his current position, he has also been appointed the coordinator of general education and director of the Faculty Center for Excellence in Teaching. His research interests include pedagogical investigation and the role of English studies in higher education. Although a Shakespeare scholar by specialization, he also spends time working to advance the study of writing and composition in both first-year and major-specific curriculum.

REBECCA POPE-RUARK, associate professor of English/professional writing and rhetoric at Elon University, teaches courses in rhetoric, professional communication theory, publishing, grant writing, and FYC. She coordinates Elon's professional writing interdisciplinary minor and the Center for Undergraduate Publishing and Information Design (CUPID), as well as serving as the founding and managing editor of the peer-reviewed journal Perspectives on Undergraduate Publishing and Information Design (PURM). Her recent research examines Agile project management ideology and frameworks used in software development and the opportunities to adapt those strategies to improve student collaboration and help faculty better manage research, teaching, and service activities.

MARY RIST is a professor of English writing and rhetoric at St. Edward's University. Her areas of specialty include discourse analysis and applied linguistics. A member of the St. Edward's faculty since 1994, she has served as area coordinator of the writing and rhetoric major since 2007. She has also served as associate dean of humanities, director of the university's Freshman Studies program, and director of the writing center.

PAULA ROSINSKI, associate professor of professional writing and rhetoric and the writing center director at Elon University, has taught classes in FYC, professional writing and rhetoric, multimedia rhetoric and visual design, style and editing, and writing center theory and practice. Her recent research focuses on the transfer of rhetorical knowledge and writing strategies between self-sponsored and academic texts, reframing rhetorical theories and practices in multimodal environments, and the reproduction of rhetorical subjectivity in writing and rhetoric. As one of the coauthors of Elon's Quality Enhancement Plan designed to enhance the teaching and learning of writing for all students, faculty, and staff on campus, she is also working on redesigning the physical space and consulting practices of the writing center to include multimodal consulting.

VICTORIA SADLER, PhD in rhetoric and scientific and technical communication, is an associate professor in the Department of Communication, Writing, and the Arts at Metropolitan State University in St. Paul, Minnesota. She teaches in the BA and MS programs in technical communication and professional writing, and she coordinates the undergraduate technical communication curriculum.

CAREY E. SMITHERMAN is an associate professor of writing and the director of first-year writing at the University of Central Arkansas. She also currently serves as the interim writing center director. Her research interests include FYC theory and pedagogy, writing center theory, and service learning. Carey teaches FYC, professional writing, rhetoric, and advocacy writing. She received her PhD in rhetoric and composition from the University of Louisville.

DARCI THOUNE is an assistant professor of English and coordinator of the Freshman Writing Program at the University of Wisconsin–La Crosse. She teaches FYC and undergraduate courses in rhetoric and writing. Her current scholarly interests include the scholarship of teaching and learning, writing assessment, rhetorical genre studies, and the intersections of fat and queer studies.

NANCY LEWIS TUTEN has taught writing and American literature courses at the college level since 1982. A tenured professor at Columbia College, she serves as head of the Division of Languages and Literatures and as coordinator of the WAC program.

JULIE WATTS is associate professor in the English and Philosophy Department at University of Wisconsin–Stout. She coauthored the proposal that established the MS in technical and professional communication in 2009 and has been its program director ever since. She has presented and published on various aspects of writing instruction, learning communities, and teaching and learning, most recently in Written Communication.

CHRISTIAN WEISSER is an associate professor of English at Penn State Berks, where he coordinates both the professional writing program and the WAC program. Christian is the editor of *Composition Forum*, a peer-reviewed scholarly journal in rhetoric and composition. He is the author or editor of numerous publications, including *Moving Beyond Academic Discourse, Natural Discourse* (with Sid Dobrin), and *The Locations of Composition* (with Christopher Keller). Christian teaches courses in technical writing, environmental rhetoric, and the discourse of sustainability.

KATHLEEN BLAKE YANCEY is a Kellogg W. Hunt professor of English and distinguished research professor at Florida State University. She has served as president of NCTE; chair of CCCC; president of the Council of Writing Program Administrators; and president of South Atlantic Modern Language Association (SAMLA). Editor of College Composition and Communication, she cofounded and codirects the Inter/National Coalition for Electronic Portfolio Research. Author or coauthor of over ninety articles and book chapters and author or coeditor of eleven scholarly books—including *Portfolios in the Writing Classroom; Reflection in the Writing Classroom;* and *Delivering College Composition: The Fifth Canon*—she is the recipient of both the WPA Best Book Award and the Donald Murray Prize. Her coauthored *Writing across Contexts: Transfer, Composition, and Sites of Writing* was released in 2014.

MICHAEL J. ZERBE is an associate professor of English and humanities and the writing program administrator at York College of Pennsylvania, where he coordinates both the professional writing major and the FYC program. Formerly a Health Communications Fellow at the National Cancer Institute, Zerbe's research focuses on scientific rhetoric as a cultural literacy, and his book *Composition and the Rhetoric of Science* was published in 2007 by Southern Illinois University Press. More recently, Zerbe has published on undergraduate writing majors and organized a CCCC special interest group on undergraduate research in rhetoric and composition. In 2009, Zerbe was awarded a Fulbright to teach in Bulgaria.

INDEX